The Technique
of the Picture Story

A PRACTICAL GUIDE TO THE PRODUCTION OF VISUAL ARTICLES

The Technique

of the Picture Story

BY DANIEL D. MICH, Executive Editor • EDWIN EBERMAN, Art Director

LOOK MAGAZINE

McGRAW-HILL BOOK COMPANY, INC., NEW YORK AND LONDON

1945

SACKETT & WILHELMS LITHOGRAPHING COMPANY

Foreword

IN THE FALL of 1944 the Washington Square Writing Center of New York University announced the first course ever offered in "The Technique of the Picture Story." Lectures delivered in that course, expanded, revised, and given a sharper discipline of form, helped to provide the basis for this volume. Some of the picture sequences here collected were among those to which reference was made in the lectures and class discussions.

The publication of this book will be a further corrective to those who believe that nothing important can be taught about writing, photography, or any other art form, who believe that significant judgment must spring from intuition. Although the authors of this book, who conducted the lecture course itself, would readily admit the importance of those judgments which elude precise formulation, and recognize that some persons have unusual talents in one or another area of expression, they believe no less firmly in the value of training. They know the waste that must result in a publishing house, or in any other kind of business, where knowledge gained from experience is not collected, refined, and shared with others through some method deliberately arrived at. The necessity for education was there whether or not the University had a part in it. The picture story was obviously a union of picture and text. It was not to be assumed, however, as the editors of LOOK discovered, that a good writer would know picture values, or that an experienced photographer would recognize the story "angle" or know the words which would illuminate a picture. When all allowances had been made for special talents, competence in this new pictorial method was clearly not all intuitional: there remained much that could be learned.

This volume is important, too, as another clear sign that the world of communications is One World. The days have passed when professional insularity was possible. Radio, television, books, magazines, pictures, facsimile broadcasting, wire recordings: these and other still-undiscovered techniques are merely alternative methods, one better suited than another to a particular occasion. They have but one unifying purpose: to break down the barriers of prejudice and ignorance that have so long kept us from living in peace with our fellow men throughout the world. If we can but know the events and conditions of their lives, can recognize their difficulties and understand their aspirations, we shall be better able to shape a world where their children and ours can live together in peace and harmony. Any book which can help to spread a knowledge of the techniques making possible such an understanding deserves our gratitude.

Finally, this book should be a gentle rebuke to those who, quick to recognize the immense popular appeal of picture magazines, may have been so preoccupied in their efforts to discover every outlet to the total audience and to play upon every note in the register of sensibility within each audience group that they have had no time to reflect on what they are doing and how best to do it. The editors of LOOK know that teaching is good not only for those who learn but also for those who teach: the very process of explaining a purpose, a method, a point of view, a belief is itself clarifying and illuminating to those who attempt it, and gives a surer touch and a clearer vision to him who thought himself a professional. Such a reflective and analytical approach to this new medium is heartening to those who see in the picture story an important new means of reaching men's minds and so shaping the course of future events.

It is a pleasure to acknowledge the debt of the Washington Square Writing Center to the editors of LOOK for their leadership in inaugurating this first course of its kind, and for the generous subvention which has enabled the University to offer tuition scholarships to a number of well-trained applicants each semester since the course was first announced. New York University has been glad to co-operate with the publishing profession in this experiment, sharing as it does the same belief in the value of training, and the same hope that each new technique of communication will help men in the world of tomorrow to draw up their chairs and talk together.

Paul A. McGhee
Director, Division of General Education
New York University

Acknowledgments

THE AUTHORS wish to express their gratitude to:

Harlan Logan, editor and general manager of LOOK, who goaded and guided them into the preparation of this book.

Paul A. McGhee, who made it possible for them to conduct at the Washington Square Writing Center of New York University the first classes ever given in the technique of the picture story.

Henriette Kish, who ably assisted in the supervision of instruction at New York University.

The editors of *Life* and *Coronet,* who graciously gave permission for the reproduction of picture stories from their pages, and the editors of trade papers and house organs whose work appears in Chapter 8.

D. D. M.
E. E.

Contents

Introduction

THIS VOLUME has a double significance for American readers. It is a source and reference book for the general public and free-lance writers who want to learn the goals. and methods of picture-magazine publishing; it is a practical textbook for teaching the techniques and procedures of picture-writing, the most radical and recent advance in modern journalism. In a sense, *The Technique of the Picture Story* is a *Das Kapital* in the publishing world. Not wholly that, of course. But it is a pioneer book of principles in a revolution that impresses this writer as touching some of the fundamentals of present-day publishing, from newspapers and magazines to textbooks.

Our civilization has had various revolutions and evolutions in its methods for disseminating information. It had one when Europe substituted print for the news-bearing minstrel of medieval days, when it discarded wandering bards, roaming from castle to castle and singing the prowess of their chieftains, and turned to the corantos and broadsheet ballads which recorded in print the adventures minstrels had been chanting. But when the bard gave way to the balladmonger, when oral transmission of news was superseded by type, by intellectualized symbols that only the learned could understand, often imperfectly, journalism lost a personal appeal, an emotional quality, a universality it has never recaptured. There were always those who could understand word-of-mouth communication, but not print.

Pictures were printed from wood blocks and used as a medium of communication long before the discovery of movable types. (The letters in our alphabet were once pictures.) But after the arrival of type, pictures became mere ornaments or illustrative aids to understanding printed pages. They continued in use because inked symbols of words and ideas were not adequate to convey information. Word symbols lacked the drama, the sensuous appeal, the realism, the universality that pictures possessed. But after the invention of movable types in 1476, the primary purpose of pictures was for illustration, to supplement or reinforce the printed text.

It has been only a half century since we began learning anew the power and possibilities of pictures, their values in communications. The stereopticon views of a bygone era were a plaything, largely a luxury. The cinematograph was for the diversion of children and grown-ups with juvenile minds. Educated men and women apologized when they were seen coming from motion-picture shows. Comic strips were condemned even for children.

But all these uses of pictures and drawings were conditioning factors in a progressive communications revolution. Little by little, reproduction of pictures was improved. Little by little, their mass appeal came to be recognized. So-called yellow journalism popularized the comics. Motion pictures introduced newsreels and dramatized Dickens and Thackeray. Advertisers dared cartoons and humorous sketches to overcome sales resistance. Like so many other radical movements in history, the demand for pictures was from the masses upward. Then, in journalism, came *The Mid-Week Pictorial, Photo History,* and eight years ago, *Life* and LOOK, with their purpose to glorify pictures, to make them dominate the magazine page, to have them tell the story, using explanatory text in a subordinate position.

That was the beginning of a revolution that has grown to a point where a dozen or more of the great publishing houses in the United States are experimenting with full-length visual books, volumes that tell their story or develop their thesis with a minimum of reading material instead of in print with accompanying illustration. And it is the principles and procedures of this revolution in editing and publishing that *The Technique of the Picture Story* presents.

To date, the goal in picture-writing is an integration of pictures and running commentary. An amount of explanatory text, however, is still regarded as a necessity. Pictures are not expected to replace words. Certainly they will not in most books; but they will, wholly, in many. This new language for mass readers is in its infancy. It hasn't yet learned to walk confidently without aid. Yet, actually, one of the inspirations the reader receives from *The Technique of the Picture Story* is that the new, world language of pictures will also give us a new world of picture literature. Some day there will be Tolstois, Thackerays, and Poes in picture production who will write without words; and with the sensuous appeal and power that vivid pictures always have, these writers in the visual language of the future will sway classes of people that have never been reached before in ways that have never been touched.

Paul A. McGhee's explanation of this volume in his foreword recalls early days in the colleges of law, when barristers contended that law could be learned only in the offices of practicing attorneys. It brings to mind current criticism of schools of journalism, not so insistent as in other days, that reporting and newspaper editing cannot be taught. Great lawyers and star reporters probably cannot be produced in the schools. It may be that the bar and the newspaper office are the only places where they can be developed. But the fundamentals of law and the craft of reporting and editing can be transmitted. Education has proved it can send into the attorney's office and the editorial room young men and women who have been given the rudiments of their vocations and been guided beyond many of the defeats that baffle every beginner.

The Technique of the Picture Story, a pioneer text in a pioneer field of magazine making, may need Mr. McGhee's explanation. But it must also be welcomed by everyone interested in the advance of journalism. Maybe no great picture-writers will be produced through study of this volume alone. Possibly great picture-writers, like star reporters, can be created only in the picture-magazine office—in the daily drill and dreams and drama of conveying information through the medium of visual presentation. But young men and women with ambition to become picture producers or writers can gain from this volume the practical fundamentals of the new visual language. The information essential to a successful beginning is between the covers of this book.

I have been so much stimulated from merely reading it that I wish I had the art and the craft to write this introduction in pictures unaccompanied by text—in the art that has possibilities of becoming the print-language of the nations.

M. LYLE SPENCER
Dean, School of Journalism
Syracuse University

CHAPTER 1

Four Basic Uses of Pictures

IF THIS BOOK fulfills its purpose, it will show how, in recent years, periodicals have devised a technique of blending pictures with words to create a new means of communication. The book will also analyze that technique for the benefit of those who wish to understand it and perhaps work with it.

Let us confess at the outset that the new technique is in its infancy. Only the merest beginning has been made in developing it as a conveyer of information.

That beginning, however, has been impressive. Millions of persons throughout the world are now reading the picture language which appears on most of the pages of this book—a language largely developed in the last decade.

Proper understanding of this language begins with understanding the various ways in which modern periodicals employ pictures; and by "pictures" are meant not only photographs, but also drawings, paintings, charts, graphs, cartoons and other means of visual communication. A glance at one of today's successful picture magazines will reveal that much of its editorial content is the work of crayon, pen and brush as well as camera.

Fortunately for the picture-story writer, or picture-story producer as some editors prefer to call him, he has the same important role in creating a story utilizing drawings as in creating one done with photographs. His is the responsibility for planning; for developing the story line, as the Hollywood phrase goes, or "getting the

right angle," as magazine editors often say, and for writing captions and text so that words blend with pictures into a smooth, cohesive whole.

It is not an easy kind of writing. Some expert craftsmen, dealers in words for twenty years or more, find it beyond them. Others balk at spending three fourths of their time in planning and supervising— as the picture-story producer often must do—and only one fourth at the typewriter. Yet, for the man or woman with a genuine feeling for the medium, there is a deep personal satisfaction in producing and writing picture articles.

The role of the writer will be discussed in greater detail later in this book. Our chief concern in this chapter is with modern methods of using pictures in periodicals. More or less arbitrarily, we have decided that there are four basic methods. Many other analyses are possible, but these four categories cover virtually every published picture:

1. ILLUSTRATION FOR TEXT

For years, newspapers and magazines have illustrated and decorated text articles with drawings and photographs. Emphatically, that does not transform a text article into a "picture story," as many writers erroneously assume. The illustration of text is not a primary concern of this book, but in any study of the picture-story technique it must be noted that there is a difference between using pictures as illustrations and using them to tell a story or develop a thesis.

Pictures used as illustrations do serve useful purposes: they "dress up" the printed page, make it more attractive; they add to the story's impact on the reader; they increase readership. But, so used, they are merely adjuncts to words.

2. PICTURE-TEXT COMBINATIONS

In this category lies the modern picture magazine's most important contribution to the art of communication. It is the category to which most of this book is devoted.

Obviously, any article in which text and pictures are combined is a picture-text combination in one sense. In this book, however, the words "picture-text combination" are used to describe an article in which the storytelling is done by *related* pictures, arranged in some form of continuity. The text in such an article is important, but subordinated to the pictures, and much of it is presented in the form of *related* captions.

Such an article is rarely, if ever, the work of one person. The key to success in handling the picture-story is collaboration — teamwork. A team of three is just about the irreducible minimum — writer, photographer and layout artist. In actual magazine-office practice, four, five or more persons are involved in the preparation of virtually every article.

3. PURE PICTURE STORIES

Examples of picture stories requiring no text at all are scarce indeed, but this chapter presents a few which are close enough to the ideal to be called "pure picture stories." Teamwork is as necessary in the preparation of these stories as in others. They are seldom obtained by chance; the photographer and his subjects almost always owe their fortunate relationship to the planning and arranging of a picture-story producer, or writer; and both photographer and writer owe at least part of the printed result to the collaboration of the layout department, which helps to present the pictures effectively and dramatically.

4. PICTURE STORIES WITHIN TEXT STORIES

Magazines often employ a picture-story continuity within a text story to increase readership by making the story visually appetizing. They are most likely to use the device when the story is on a serious subject. Tests among all kinds of readers demonstrate that such picture continuities enormously increase the reading time spent on these articles.

This device. of course, embodies a combination of categories 1 and 2, or, more rarely, 1 and 3.

Reader tests show that the connected picture story used as illustration often gets twice the readership given to the text it accompanies; yet the tests also reveal that the text benefits from the picture story, often getting twice the reader time it would receive if it were presented alone.

To summarize: most important here is classification No. 2, the picture-text combination, involving use of *related* pictures in some form of continuity.

The creation of such an article is usually the result of collaboration among three or more persons.

Most of the time of a picture-story producer, or writer (the term will be used interchangeably), is spent in planning the article, in arranging for photography or art work, and in supervising the work of photographer or artist. Only a fraction of his time is spent in actual writing.

That actual writing, however, may determine the success or failure of the article. For the role of the text is to help the pictures tell their story with utmost effectiveness and to blend with them into an integrated narrative containing as many facts as space permits.

On the following two pages, there is one example of each of the four categories mentioned in this chapter. Several other published samples from the four categories are on following pages, with a discussion of problems peculiar to each.

WHY YOUR CHILD NEEDS SEX EDUCATION

By ERNEST R. GROVES and GLADYS HOAGLAND GROVES

Educators, authorities on marriage and family relationships

Sex delinquency among young girls has recently doubled and trebled in some parts of America. Why?

Partly because of the many new conditions young people face when families move to great numbers. Partly because parents, especially mothers, are now away from home more than ever before. Partly because home brings a loosening of moral standards, a "live for the moment" attitude.

Yet none of these factors has to have such an effect. If every boy and girl received proper sex education at home or school, if only . . .

A young business woman brought her 14-year-old sister to see us. "We can't go to Mother; she'd be so upset. But Mary Lou is pregnant—"

America's youth: understanding of sex relationships is the birthright too few have received

---

Illustrated Text

The photograph above was posed especially to illustrate an article on sex education. Because of the nature of the subject, the picture had to possess charm and dignity.

BLOOD PLASMA
Saves American Flier

Dramatic pictures at Yank air base show how your blood keeps wounded man alive

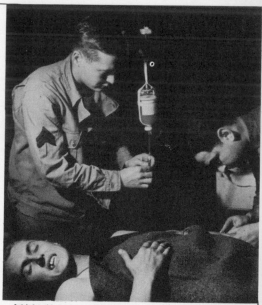

Picture-Text Combination

A pictorial chronology is blended with a text block and brief captions to tell the story of an American flier, wounded in action, whose life was saved by blood plasma.

Basic Uses of Pictures in Magazines

This is one spread of a *Life* story on modern dances. The pictures tell their own story; the one-line captions were written chiefly to provide background information.

Pure Picture Story

A picture continuity done with drawings is here used as illustration for text. With captions, the picture story is complete in itself but also adds to text readership.

Picture Story Within Text

THE TRAGEDY OF JOHN L. LEWIS

**By ROSCOE DRUMMOND
and GLEN PERRY**

Washington correspondents, respectively, for the
Christian Science Monitor and the New York Sun

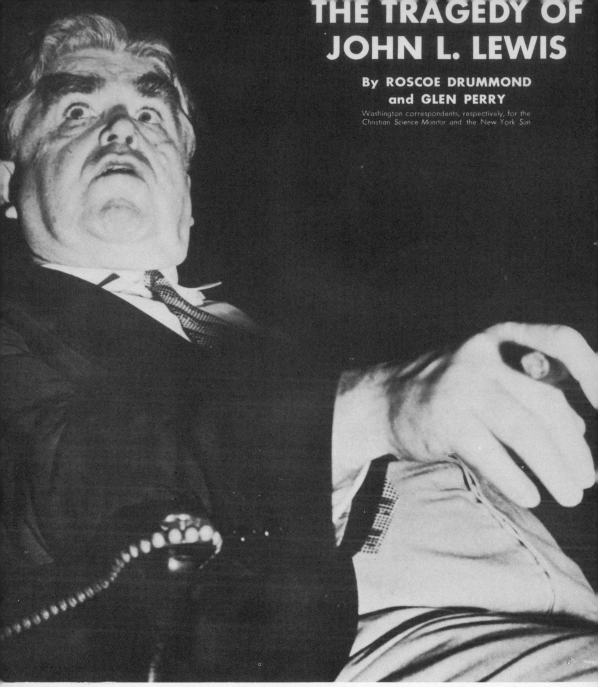

John L. Lewis at 63 . . . A sincere, able, egolatrous man . . . In 1919 he said, "We cannot fight our Government." Today he has decided that he can fight it . . . His weapons are a bedrock sense of righteousness, a full mind, a vocabulary like Shakespeare and a voice like a bull of Bashan.

ILLUSTRATED TEXT: The editors' problem in this two-page story was to illustrate a text article analyzing the actions and motives of John L. Lewis. Suggestions for the use of caricatures, cartoons and paintings were discarded in favor of photographs because Mr. Lewis is such a mobile and picturesque camera subject. The four pictures published with the article were culled from hundreds. The picture is more important to understand John L. Lewis than it is to berate him. But a full assessment of the man cannot fairly be made at this point. This, then, is an interim appraisal, an effort to explain—not a final judgment on — the motives and acts of John L. Lewis.

In preparing to write this article we have read 35,000 words of biographical material. We have discussed him with a dozen men who know him well. We have talked with his friends, his foes, his intimates. We have conferred with two historians, seven journalists, nine politicians and one psychiatrist.

And, before putting thoughts into shape or words onto paper, we spent an hour and 55 minutes with Mr. Lewis in the most candid interview we have enjoyed in 20 years.

A bogeyman with eyebrows, Mr. Lewis is charming, honest and scholarly.

He's a Great Man, But—

John L. Lewis is a man of great stature and great ability. Newsreels to the contrary — in which he chooses to look like a nightmare and act like a bogeyman—he can be charming without effort. He can be persuasive; he can be bland.

He is sincere, honest, scholarly.

He is domineering, dictatorial, egocentric.

He is, we believe, the most successful failure in American public life today. The tragedy is that John L. Lewis has at no time risen to the height of the crisis which for four dire years has towered over America.

The first reason is that John L. Lewis has remained at peace while America has gone to war. The second reason is that Mr. Lewis is moved more by his hates than by his likes. The third reason is that Mr. Lewis has an abiding disdain for those who differ with him.

Economically, he is a conservative; politically, he is ruggedly individualist. As a collective bargainer, John L. Lewis is an incomparable collective bludgeoner.

He's a Patriot, But—

Mr. Lewis is a patriot. It is not his desire nor his intention to delay or damage the war effort. He has encouraged a reduction or a cessation of the mining of coal, he does not want to lose the war; he only wants the United States to do what he asks of it. And in any argument involving anybody—including the United States of America—versus John L. Lewis, it honestly does not occur to Mr. Lewis that the party of the second part could be wrong.

Mr. Lewis doesn't want strikes, doesn't like strikes, hopes he won't have to have any strikes. "I abhor strikes," he once said. He wants always to gain his ends by peaceful methods, but gain his ends he feels he must.

Mr. Lewis knows that his name is an epithet among American boys who are fighting on the battle fronts today. We discussed it with him. He does not appear to be particularly distressed nor disturbed. He looks on it as a cross he has to bear as a cross of somebody else's making.

John L. Lewis doesn't look within himself very often or very long. He told us that he didn't go much for introspective thinking, that he didn't consider it particularly productive. We suggested that maybe he didn't do it for fear he might scare himself. He chuckled. But we weren't sure whether he was agreeing or dissenting.

We could not escape the conclusion that unconsciously Mr. Lewis looks on himself as a sort of "act of God." As he sees it, a man inherits his talents. He can claim no special virtue for them and can take no credit for his acts.

Thus it would seem to him that fate rather than selfish interest has chosen that, in the midst of the gravest hour of the Republic, he should be called on to match his strength with that of the Government of the United States.

Mr. Lewis is not awed. Indeed, he counts it almost an even battle, with the advantage only slightly on his side.

He Is a Great Labor Leader, But—

By many standards, John L. Lewis can honestly be accounted a great success. We incline to the view that singly he has done more to benefit the mass of workers in this country than any other living man or men. This is an enduring honor and reward. That which is most worthy in Mr. Lewis deserves never to be tarnished.

By other standards, John L. Lewis at this moment may honestly be accounted a great failure. Those who account him a failure, a tragic failure, will not say that he has failed John L. Lewis, but that he has failed the nation. They will say that, after rising to great heights when called on to serve labor, he failed— he seems never to have tried—to rise to greater heights when called on to serve not labor alone but all of America when America most needed men of his ability.

Mr. Lewis has succeeded because he has done so much to unite labor. He has failed because he has done even more to disunite labor.

Mr. Lewis has done much to help labor attain its rightful and respected role in a land of free enterprise, and he has done much over many years to free labor from coercive restrictions. But in the last two years he has drawn upon it national hostility, which so little of labor deserves, and he has driven Congress into passing the only coercive restrictions on labor to come out of Washington in a decade.

As a collective bargainer, John Lewis is an incomparable collective bludgeoner.

For years Mr. Lewis gave strength and vitality to the American Federation of Labor, and his Congress of Industrial Organizations gave collective strength for the first time to millions of previously unorganized mass-production workers. But he broke with the A. F. of L. and fought it, and he quit the C.I.O.

He Wants to Win the War, But—

Why has a man of such manifest ability such a divided record? How can a man of patriotism pursue a course which has the effect, whatever the intention, of imperiling the nation at a time when its very existence is threatened?

The only answer we can find to the second question is that the war does not weigh heavily with him. Of course he wants to win it, but we believe he does not passionately accept the origin, the necessity or the urgency of the war.

He said before Pearl Harbor that the President sought war in order to retain office, and he has never changed the record. He said that to get America into war was the President's "motivation and objective." He says, in effect, that it was our interference with Hitler and Hirohito, not their threat to us, that brought us into the war.

There is a strong case to be made for Mr. Lewis' United Mine Workers in their arguments with the coal mine operators' associations and with the War Labor Board. It is a case rendered stronger because the Administration has been feeble and fumbling in its efforts to check the rising cost of living. But Mr. Lewis, unlike William Green of the A. F. of L. and Philip Murray of the C.I.O., has shown no visible disposition to aid the government to control inflation.

Perhaps this is because the necessities of the war cannot seem imperative when the war itself seems unnecessary. Mr. Lewis advised against the war, and the President of the United States did not follow his advice.

In other words, Mr. Lewis does not see this war, and the Nazi-Axis thirst for world domination that brought it on, in the terms in which most Americans see it. It is only by understanding this difference between him and the nation that one can understand Mr. Lewis.

He Hates Roosevelt—and No "Buts"

Furthermore, Mr. Lewis hates Franklin D. Roosevelt. He says bluntly that the President is an English country squire type with the social conscience to want to see a contented peasantry. Mr. Lewis wants to humble President Roosevelt. That is a battle he cannot adjourn until the peace, and if—in trying to humble the President —he creates difficulties for labor and for a nation at war, it is incidental.

Mr. Lewis is more anti than pro, has more dislikes than likes. He is anti-Roosevelt, anti-war, anti-British, anti-international co-operation. His divided record can be somewhat understood through the things and persons he is against.

A List of Lewis Hates

He is against the President because he says Roosevelt has failed to solve a single social or economic problem in the last eight years.

He is against Wendell Willkie because he considers him not very bright and a foil for the President. Willkie, he says, is a Pudd'nhead Wilson. In this case Mr. Lewis' literary foot appears to have slipped—something that rarely happens. For Pudd'nhead Wilson, in Mark Twain's story, turned out to be the smartest man in town.

It is significant that Mr. Lewis has been—
For and against President Roosevelt.
For and against Wendell Willkie.
For and against William Green.
For and against Philip Murray.
For and against the A. F. of L.
For and against the C.I.O.
For and against Messrs. Hutcheson, Woll, Hillman and other labor leaders.
For and against the Republican Party.
For and against the Democratic Party.

Mr. Lewis tilted with President Wilson even as he has tilted with President Roosevelt, but in the no more than mildly critical year of 1919 he bowed to a court injunction with a patriot's remark: "We cannot fight our Government."

Today, in the grimmest hour of the grimmest war in human history, Mr. Lewis has decided that he can fight his Government. The tragedy of John L. Lewis is the tragedy of that decision. For Mr. Lewis is a great man who has fallen short of one of the greatest moments in the life of his country.

The tragedy of Lewis is that he has chosen to set his will against all America.

---

at the left was "blown" to full-page size to create dramatic impact—to startle and stop the reader, then lead him into the text. Fiction magazines use arresting paintings with short stories and serials in the same way for the same purpose. The photographer who took the large picture shot from the floor, concentrated on Lewis' face, emphasized his huge girth, bushy eyebrows and heavy jowls.

The Maoris of New Zealand rub noses, Mrs. Roosevelt breaks conventions...So this happened when she greeted her Maori guide.

ILLUSTRATED TEXT: This famous picture of Mrs. Eleanor Roosevelt rubbing noses with a Maori Indian in New Zealand was first used as the lead illustration for a text article. It has been reprinted by magazines and hundreds of newspapers and was named the best picture of the year by editors of the 1944 *Encyclopedia Britannica*. This photograph has elements continually sought but seldom found by picture-

ELEANOR ROOSEVELT
The woman nobody understands

By MARY HORNADAY
Veteran Washington reporter, correspondent for the Christian Science Monitor

Eleanor Roosevelt has lived 11 widely publicized years in the White House. Yet few Americans understand her. At times Mrs. Roosevelt has not fully understood herself. But this she does know: she would rather be wrong than miss a chance to help someone.

To understand Mrs. Roosevelt, one must keep in mind an orphaned childhood, a self-conscious girlhood, a beloved father with a weakness for alcohol, and a marriage dominated for years by a mother-in-law.

In her writings, Mrs. Roosevelt has been candid about her girlhood. Her first memories are of a mother ashamed of her little girl who had not inherited the Hall family beauty. The child writhed with embarrassment while her mother apologized to friends, "She is such a funny child, so old-fashioned."

Eleanor loved her father, whose drinking led to his death and made her an orphan at 10. Afterward, she was reared by a grandmother who nourished her awkwardness by making her wear skirts above her knees when other young ladies wore theirs halfway down their legs. Rather than hear her grandmother say "no" so many times, she pretended not to want things she really desired intensely.

Even marriage to her distant cousin—handsome, popular Franklin — did not bring fullness of life to Eleanor. Her mother-in-law was always in the offing. Mrs. Roosevelt is frank to admit that for years she suffered from having to share the planning of family activities with strong-minded Sara Delano Roosevelt, who had a house beside hers at Campobello Island, the summer home; another in New York City, the town home, and who was complete mistress in the Roosevelt family home at Hyde Park in upstate New York.

In an attempt to free herself from the danger of too much matriarchal domination, Eleanor Roosevelt eventually built her own cottage at Hyde Park.

Out of this long chain of frustrations developed three character traits: (1) her desire to defy tradition; (2) her sympathy for those who are humanly or economically frail; (3) her tendency to underestimate herself.

Rebel in the White House

Seldom do those who marvel at Mrs. Roosevelt's actions relate them to past restraints. The White House, which she reached about the time the last of her children was grown, gave her the first real chance to soar.

She flung tradition out the window, refused secret service escorts, insisted on running the White House elevator. She conducted press conferences and began to take an active part in national affairs.

Toward the end of her life, the elder Mrs. Roosevelt used to visit her daughter-in-law's press conferences and listen with an expression of incredulity.

That Eleanor Roosevelt should be the first First Lady to revolt is in a way surprising. In some respects, the Roosevelts are more tradition-respecting than most families. Christenings are still elaborate ceremonies; Dickens' *Christmas Carol* is faithfully read each Christmas Eve; and when her mother-in-law died, Mrs. Roosevelt wore deep mourning for months.

Her desire to help the weak has practically blinded Mrs. Roosevelt to the question of propriety involved in earning large sums of money as First Lady.

It has made her extremely unpopular among Southern whites who think of her first as champion of the Negro.

It led to her being flatly told to stay away from Detroit because race rioting there was laid to her efforts to help Negroes achieve economic equality.

But she does help the weak. And the unemployed West Virginia coal miners, for whom she promoted the Arthurdale Subsistence Homestead project, hailed her with tears in their eyes as "sent by Jehovah."

Mrs. Roosevelt does what she can to check the worthiness of a case before she sends money, but a few persons take advantage of her good will. One woman wrote asking for a cow to give her baby fresh milk, and when Mrs. Roosevelt sent a check, wrote back for an electric refrigerator to keep the milk cold.

She Doesn't Mind Criticism—If It's Personal

Some persons think Mrs. Roosevelt's great generosity and unselfishness are such assets in this world of hate and woe that they approve almost anything she does. Others feel that often she is not wise in the way she uses these virtues, doing in the end more harm than good for those she wants to help.

Does criticism worry Mrs. Roosevelt? Yes and no. She never worries long over personal attacks—the kind that come from people who want her not to fight for a cause, or to stay home more, or who object to her serving hot dogs to the British King and Queen. But criticism really gets under her skin when it interferes with her intense desire to do something for somebody.

She was definitely upset when Marines in the Pacific gave her the cold shoulder because they had heard she was for keeping them out there six months after the war's end. Their attitude hurt, not because it was untrue, but because it lessened her chances to cheer them.

She Belittles Her Influence

Scarcely had the Roosevelts settled down in the executive mansion when Republican Congresswoman Edith Nourse Rogers was seen emerging from the front door one day. With a sheepish look, she hastened to explain:

"I've been to see Mrs. Roosevelt. I had something I wanted done, and it's going to be done!"

Since then, hundreds of government officials and private citizens have learned the secret of getting things accomplished with the help of the President's wife. In most government departments a note from Mrs. R. gets attention second only to a message from the President.

During a decade, hundreds of Mrs. Roosevelt's suggestions have borne fruit, yet it is almost impossible to get her to admit outright that she is responsible. A humility born of her childhood still keeps her from giving herself credit for her influence on government. Over and over she insists that she exerts no influence. "I don't think it's influence to take an interest in something," she said once. When, at one press conference,

---

---

story writers and photographers—a famous personality completely off guard in a most unusual situation. Achieving this off-guard, "natural" quality in posed photographs is one of the most difficult problems of the picture-story writer, because most people tend to "freeze" before the camera. The writer must learn to put his subjects at ease, get them relaxed in the presence of the camera.

Ingrid Bergman's great charm is her naturalness. She is a natural blonde. Her high, Nordic coloring is natural. Her modesty is real —she acts because she loves to, not for fame. Often she finds herself referring to Ingrid Bergman, the glamorous star, as "she."

PICTURE-TEXT COMBINATION: This is an excellent example of the planned and "staged" picture personality article, stand-by of the modern picture magazine. Among the ingredients contributing to its success are: a widely known, glamorous, highly photogenic subject blessed with naturalness as well as beauty; the picturesque background of Minnesota farm country; a supporting cast of people with flavor and

INGRID BERGMAN
Visits a Minnesota farm

**And finds the "land of sky-blue water"
appealingly like her native Sweden**

In 1853, the first Swede came up the Mississippi to discover the rolling beauty of Minnesota. Ninety years later, another Nordic, Ingrid Bergman, rediscovered the land so poetically named by the Indians—"Minne" for water, "sota" for sky-blue.

When she went there to make a movie of Swedish-Americans for distribution in Sweden by our Office of War Information, a LOOK editor and cameraman joined the trek. Snow piled in seven-foot drifts; sleighs were faster than cars; the thermometer slid from zero to 30 below. But Ingrid, mittened and ski-booted, snuggled down in Minnesota. She lived on the 320-acre farm of the Charles Swensons in Chisago County; shoveled snow; fed calves; pitched ice-frosted hay; chattered Swedish to her hosts; went to church, Ladies Aid. It was no grand tour, but the kind of living Ingrid likes best. Because—although Sam Wood, who directed her in Paramount's "For Whom the Bell Tolls," says she will be Hollywood's top actress by next year—she is simple and completely unaffected. Her career is acting; her personal life her own. She only works in Hollywood; her home is in Rochester, New York, where her husband, Dr. Peter Lindstrom, is studying medicine. Their four-year-old daughter, Pia, doesn't even know her mother is a movie star.

An accomplished sportswoman, Miss Bergman chose skis instead of snowshoes for a cross-country call with the doctor son of the Swenson family. Like many of her countrymen, she is strong and durable. Minnesota seemed to her, as it did to early Swedish settlers, a rich and wonderful extension of the Scandinavian homeland.

She got up at five, in snow-punctuated darkness, to watch Henry, one of the six Swenson sons, do morning milking. Afterward she ate a real farm breakfast. Although she looks willowy and frail in pictures like "Casablanca," she weighs a tough 130 pounds, is 5 feet 7½ inches tall.

Her farm favorites were the brown Duroc pigs—she learned to snatch them up expertly by one leg. She was born in Stockholm and is city-educated, but her husband's people had a farm in Sweden where she vacationed. "Every actor has a dream role," she says. "Gary Cooper wants to play a cowboy. I want to do a farm girl part."

character. Yet all these favorable factors would have been insufficient if the writer had not planned well, arranged a comprehensive "shooting script" and set up the right situations for the photographer; if both writer and photographer had not "learned" Ingrid Bergman and their story line before starting out to take a picture. (Remainder of this article is on the two pages following.)

At the Ladies Aid, she met members of the Swedish Elim Lutheran Church of Scandia. Left, is the Rev. A. B. Walfrid, the pastor; Miss Bergman's 73-year-old host, Charles Swenson, stands behind her.

Ingrid, in her middle twenties, looks even younger because she is so free from artifice. When David Selznick brought her to America for "Intermezzo," she came determined she would not crimp her hair,

pluck her eyebrows or otherwise pour herself into a Hollywood mold. She never uses make-up, not even a touch of lipstick, because she feels that cosmetics mask her expressions before the camera.

Swenson family prayers were in Swedish, in Miss Bergman's honor. Despite her fervid study of English during her three years in America, she still has a faint accent, untraceable to any country. Mr. Swenson, American-born, speaks Swedish fluently. But his wife, children and grandchildren prefer English.

Her hair was cropped two inches from her head for the role of María in "For Whom the Bell Tolls." Ingrid found the short cut so convenient that vacationing in Rochester, N. Y., she kept it clipped with manicure scissors. For her new role in Edna Ferber's "Saratoga Trunk" she will wear a wig.

The great photograph at the right was taken because the writer observed that Miss Bergman was particularly charming with old people, and had the imagination to visualize a picture contrasting the actress' fresh youth with the sweet, lined face of the old lady at the spinning wheel. This picture was not in the original shooting script from which the photographer worked. That is often the case with the best ones.

On a spinning wheel from Sweden, Ingrid Bergman had her first spinning lesson. (She has a warm respect for homely accomplishments. Orphaned at 13, she became an actress despite the objections of relatives, struggled for recognition. She is one of the hardest workers in Hollywood, seldom goes to parties and hates "rests" between pictures. Yet she is not success-proud, nor self-infatuated.) When 86-year-old Mrs. Abraham Johnson (above), unaware of her pupil's identity, asked "What is your name?" Miss Bergman said "Ingrid," and took the old woman in her arms and kissed her.

Scripts are important, but they should not be followed so rigidly that they become strait jackets; writers and photographers must be left free to shoot an unplanned picture when they see an opportunity. The photography on this article required four days, three of them beginning at 5 a.m., lasting until night. Twenty-five situations were planned, 210 photographs taken, eight used.

The Battle of the North Atlantic

LOOK Photographer Frank Bauman Records the Drama of a North Atlantic Crossing

FRANK BAUMAN

The captain of a weather-beaten U. S. Coast Guard cutter stood on the bridge as the rolling swells of the North Atlantic lifted his vessel, outward bound from an "unnamed" Eastern port.

"The Battle of Britain may have been more exciting," he said, "and people are talking of the North African campaign and the Second Front. But in the last analysis, *this* is the battlefield: the stretch of sea between here and Britain. For if we lose here—we lose all. Here we simply *cannot* lose."

There is little glamour, and less glory, on the North Atlantic run. All is ordered, scheduled, planned. At rendezvous hour, engine room signals in the bowels of a score of deep-laden merchantmen ring "slow ahead," and from then until the sanctuary of a British port brings "finished with engines" the convoy moves inexorably eastward.

Despite the unceasing vigilance of its escorts—rugged, hard-hitting Coast Guard cutters, slim Canadian corvettes, destroyers manned by British, French and Polish sailors—the skulking subs still kill. Suddenly, a burning tanker lights the stormy midnight with a sickening glow. The convoy must not stop. Men die; their precious cargoes slip to the bottom of the sea. But other men grip wheels tighter, stare harder through gunsights. The ships plow on—stubbornly.

On these pages, LOOK Photographer Frank Bauman pictures such a voyage.

An officer sends messages with an Aldis lamp from the bridge wing of a U. S. Coast Guard cu

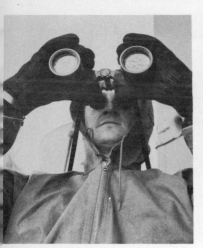

2 Binoculars are on the watch day and night. They can pick up a periscope wake in the dark. Lookouts work in shifts, four hours on, eight off.

3 Earphones listen every second. A submerged submarine engine is a dead give-away to the experts manning the secret sound-detection devices.

4 Gun crews drill every day, working to get split-second timing and speed. Every man has a battle station—a cook may also be a gunner.

PICTURE TEXT COMBINATION: The Nazis wrote the script for this picture story when the German submarine menace was at its height in the North Atlantic. Frank Bauman, the photographer, was put aboard a Coast Guard vessel escorting a large convoy, with instructions to shoot everything that happened on board his own ship and everything he could get on other ships in the convoy. His writer was a

up an outbound convoy. Radio silence is the rule at sea. Code names for escort vessels are nicknames—Slim, Charlie, Horace—freighters are numbered.

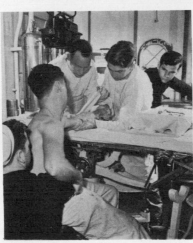

5 In mid-Atlantic a Canadian corvette comes alongside a U. S. Coast Guard cutter for secret orders, which are hauled across by a line.

6 Minor casualty: a sailor's arm is broken by a fall during a rough sea. While a surgeon holds the bones in place an orderly applies the cast.

7 General alarm! And the off-duty watches spring from their bunks. The alarm, a furious clanging, means a submarine has been spotted.

Coast Guard officer who had been a reporter and who made notes from which the text block and captions were written. In this instance, of course, the big burden was on the photographer. Success or failure depended not only on his technical ability, but also on his courage and agility, on his being able to focus on fast action almost without notice. (Remainder of article appears on next four pages.)

8 Men race to battle stations, tying life jackets on the run. This alarm came from sound detectors, but any man may give the alarm in an emergen

Action on deck was photographed whenever it happened during the convoy's long voyage, and the cameraman had to utilize any space he could find for his operations. He had no help from studio lights or professional actors, no time to arrange settings. As finally edited, his story was told in a picture sequence made up of 16 photographs selected from a total of more than 300. If this seems wasteful, it should be remembered

Ranging far beyond the limits of the convoy it guards, the cutter seeks out by sound the hiding spot of the U-boat. The chances are this is not a lone enemy, as submarines often hunt in packs of six or more.

10 The sea boils where the cutter drops depth charges in a pattern to cover the area where the U-boat may be lurking. Set to explode at the level of the sub, a charge will destroy a sub if detonated near enough to its hull.

Night battle: One U-boat at least has escaped the depth charges and, under cover of the dark, rises and fires a torpedo into the swollen belly of an Allied tanker. The flash here is from the muzzle of a three-inch gun as the cutter fires star shells to light up the sea around the torpedoed ship (out of sight at right). At night, U-boats frequently surface to fire torpedoes, almost invariably do so when seas are rough.

that even the best photographic technician needs to backstop against mistakes; that, to make sure, he should shoot the same situation several times if he gets the chance; that it is easy enough to discard unneeded pictures, almost always impossible to go back and get the missing one. "Overshooting" can be carried to extremes, but is encouraged on this kind of assignment.

12 Her cargo—4½ million gallons of high octane gasoline, afire—and her decks awash, by morning the tanker is given up for lost. The convoy has gone on without pause but a Canadian corvette remains behind to rescue survivors. By a minor miracle, some of this tanker's crew were saved. Men carrying high octane gasoline high explosives do not expect to escape if th ship is hit. The vessel, often, simply explod

13 The corvette closes in on the stricken tanker to deliver a death blow with depth charges. Detonated close to the still-sound plates on the opposite side from the torpedo wound, the charges will open the ship's seams and send her down. The sea beyond the tanker is still afire with precious gasoline as the ship wallows l on the torpedoed side. The corvette has mane vered into fire-free water to finish her c

Fast thinking enabled the writer and photographer to add the two exciting pictures above to their convoy story. When they arrived in the British Isles, they learned that submarines had sunk seven ships in the convoy, including two oil tankers. From their own deck, they had seen one of the stricken ships, but had not been close enough to get pictures. On shore, they hunted for crews of escort vessels which had been closer

4 Survivors crowd the decks of the Canadian corvette as a U. S. cutter comes alongside. Vessels of these types—smaller than destroyers— bear the brunt of merchant convoy on the Atlantic. Fair game for U-boats, their life rafts are ready for instant launching (right in picture) with containers of water and food lashed secure. The dark stains on the corvette's side are mementoes of a quick dash through the oil-flaming seas.

Burned tankermen watch stoically as a Coast Guard ship's doctor es for them what can be done at sea. This seaman's hands are not merely stained—they have been burned black from finger-nails to wrist.

16 Barely discernible in the sunburst, a thin, dark streak marks a British Isle—not the most dramatic but the most satisfying of LOOK's convoy pictures. A few more miles and another convoy will be safely home in port.

to the tragedies, finally tracked down a corvette seaman who had snapped pictures of a blazing tanker before his own vessel had sent it to the bottom with depth charges. They purchased his film, on which were pictures 12 and 13. In picture-story reporting, as in any other kind, there is no substitute for ingenuity and the perseverance to follow up every possible lead.

SPEAKING OF PICTURES...

. . . LIKE THE CAT, A SOLDIER MUST ATTACK STEALTHILY

LIKE A CAT . . .

BE QUICK

PURE PICTURE STORY: A great idea and great photography were combined by Gjon Mili to produce this picture story for *Life*. Asked by the Army to illustrate a manual instructing soldiers on jungle warfare, Mili conceived the idea of comparing a jungle soldier's problems with those of a cat attacking a mouse. He shot both cat and soldier against a plain background, using stroboscopic lights to "stop" the

craftiest enemies ever fought by the U.S. were American Indians. They used every trick in — the stealthy approach, the scouting, the sud- tal kill. Not unlike this oldtime Indian fight- day's war in the South Pacific. There the Japs rts at jungle warfare. To beat them the Amer-

icans must become even more skillful than the Japs.

Through a series of manuals, the Army is teaching its soldiers how to be expert killers. For one of these manuals Photographer Gjon Mili was asked to do a series of pictures illustrating the maxims, "Be Alert," "Be Quick," "Be Quiet," and "Be a Killer." Mili came

through with the pictures here, comparing the soldier attacking his enemy with a cat attacking a mouse. Like the cat, soldier must act stealthily and cruelly. On the next page are three methods for killing.

To make the pictures Mili was forced to acquire a black cat. Now he does not know what to do with her.

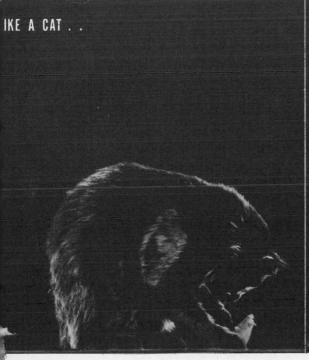

action. The result is a picture story actually requiring no text except a headline and brief labels on the photographs. This was almost entirely a photographer's triumph, but the rare writers who can think and plan in such visual terms are in demand. Most writers, even on picture magazines, cannot seem to avoid conceiving story ideas in terms of text, with pictures an afterthought.

Photographer's luck: a roving cameraman rec

Rarely does man's dormant animal passion break forth at the precise moment when someone is nearby with a camera, but it happened one day in St. Louis. Two men, nerves frazzled by midsummer heat, got into a trifling argument in a restaurant. Words led to blows. The com-

batants moved out into the street for freer action (incidentally tying traffic). Soon the original grievance was forgotten in the savage rel of physical violence. Just then, photographer Mario Cavagnaro of the Louis *Star-Times* happened by, recorded the fight in all its fury.

PURE PICTURE STORY: This amazing camera record of a savage battle on a St. Louis street was obtained by accident, as the text block states. Many notable news pictures owe their existence to this kind of photographer's luck. These are the picture opportunities which no writer or photographer can plan, or even anticipate. They occur infrequently, and the producers of picture stories for publication cannot place

ama in a street battle between two angry men

ictures show the sequence. In (1) wild punches are being exchanged; 2) the bigger man has found a more lethal weapon; (3) he also holds a arpenter's hammer. But the little fellow has acquired, in addition to his at, a length of iron pipe, and a moment later he literally bends it over his opponent's head. The resultant struggle for the pipe appears in (4), (5) and (6). In (7) a peacemaker steps in, but neither battler will let go. Finally, (8) portrays the end common to disturbers of the peace: arrest, followed by a trip to the hospital and, ultimately, to the lockup.

much trust in luck. They have to plan; they have to be ingenious enough to get a high degree of interest and impact into pictures for which they, and not Fate, pick the subjects and arrange the situations. Picking the right subject is a primary responsibility of the writer. It often takes a long time, but when the proper subject is found, the story is halfway to success.

Mickey Mouse is on the screen
and a movie fan is born

PURE PICTURE STORY: The little girl featured in this story is described in the text as "uninhibited." Most 2-year-olds are, and for that reason they are much better photographic subjects than adults, who almost invariably tend to stiffen and strike a pose for the camera. Yet almost any subject can be persuaded to be natural by a writer or photographer who has patience and a knowledge of the subject's chief interests.

BABY'S FIRST FLICKER

Barbara Ann, two years old and uninhibited, witnesses
her first movie with varied emotions, mimics the moods
and mannerisms of Walt Disney's animated cartoons

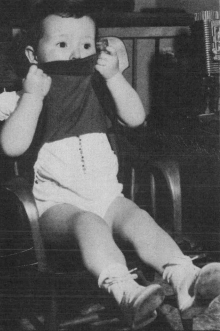

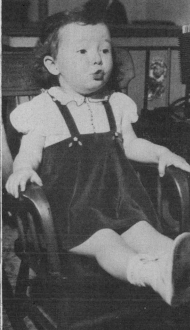

Mouse'll get his feet wet if he's not careful.

Ohmygoodness! Mickey fell in. He's calling for help.

Keep paddling, Mickey. Keep your whiskers dry.

ng way down—there are bubbles coming up.

Donald Duck is coming to the rescue. Will he make it?

Whassa matter with the movie? "Too short!"

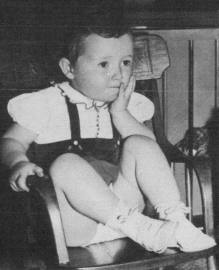

Baby's First Flicker was shot by the child's father, a professional photographer who
simply stayed out of her way and took pictures as she reacted to the antics of Mickey
Mouse. The article really requires no text, and a mistake was made in presenting it in
the picture-caption technique. Captions add nothing to this charming story told
completely and simply by pictures.

37

1

Convoys: they showed America could move a decisive force to any battle area.

3

Deterioration: German air strength was whittled down to near-impotence

2

Co-operation: French soldiers ignored Vichy, eagerly joined the Allied cause.

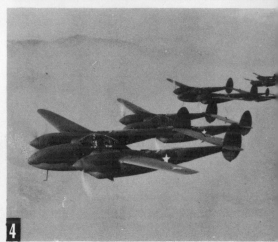

4

Air control: the Allies won it through superior planes and real teamwork

HOW HITLER LOST...The tide was turned in North Africa
continued

had for weeks been promised evacuation to Europe. Von Arnim's fresher force had been assured a mild campaign in Tunisia as a "rest" from other labors. Most of the German aviators also thought they were in for a "rest." Throughout, the Nazi radio dinned into German ears that Tunisia was a "side issue."

Thus the Nazis lacked the clarity and intensity of purpose under which troops will "fight to the last man." The Allies were so strong that extermination or surrender was the only alternative. The Germans caved in, at a time when they still had plenty to fight with, because they saw no reason to go on—and because the horror of Stalingrad was still fresh in their minds.

There was a German officer in the Armistice Commission in Morocco before we arrived there. He had been at Stalingrad until September, and had been taken out after some slight wounds and sent to Africa for a more "restful" task. French officers who dealt with him daily said later that he was completely obsessed by Stalingrad. If you remarked that it was a nice day, he

replied, "Yes, but not at Stalingrad." If you said the street was crowded, he said, "At Stalingrad the streets are crowded with the dead."

That officer was like many we faced, and overcame, in Tunisia. The fact that they were there at all is one more tribute to Hitler's pigheadedness in the face of an impossible situation.

The Importance of Tunisia

All these things hang together. It was not alone at the English Channel, Stalingrad or the Sicilian Straits that Hitler lost the war. It was also in Czechoslovakia and Yugoslavia, where two kinds of fierce opposition—sabotage and guerrilla warfare—have never ceased.

It was in all these places and many others, including the hearts of every man, woman and child in Europe who refused to "collaborate" with Nazi Germany's "New Order."

Most of all, no doubt, it was on the vast Russian front, where the infantry masses face each other. But, having been through six months in North Africa, I believe America's effort in that theater

was decisive in turning the tide. My reasons a not merely statements of events past; each or contains the future in embryo:

1 The safe arrival of our first colossal convoy laden with troops, weapons and equipmen served notice on all Germans and Italians tha the U-boat is not the invincible weapon German has always proclaimed.

This fact had a profoundly depressing effect o every Italian and even on most Germans I talke to. They had been told for years that no large scale American participation in the war was pos sible because the "deadly wolf packs of the Nor Atlantic" would prevent it.

2 The adherence of all French factions to ou cause—at first gradual, then very swift—prove that "collaboration," the only permanent hope the "New Order," was a farce.

This means danger to the Nazis in France i self. Some sources say the Germans have a pla for quick evacuation of France in the face of in vasion, deeming it too hard to hold amid the vie lent civil disorder which is certain to start th moment liberation seems at hand.

PICTURE STORY WITHIN TEXT: Here, in essence, is a combination of categories 1 and 2—a sequence-picture story used to illustrate a text article. Tests of reader habits have shown repeatedly that this kind of illustration will greatly increase the readership of a text story; they indicate that the sequence-picture story attracts more readers than the text story but that it also attracts readers to the text story. The two

S. bombing: its deadly aim wrecked even Nazi ammunition trains (above).

Prisoners: the great Allied "bag" seriously hurt Hitler's reserve strength.

mbat lessons: U. S. forces met, and passed, their first full-scale test

Conviction: cheering civilians realized that the Allies are fighting to win.

The deterioration of German bombardment ation since its supreme days in the summer of 40 was glaringly shown.

This condition can hardly be remedied, inas- ich as the Do 217—promised improvement for ich all captured Nazi fliers yearn—has so far t shown its face.

The Northwest African Air Force, formed bruary 17 out of our 12th Air Force and some its of the RAF, seized and held mastery of the over the German and Italian forces.

Since Tunisia, the NAAF has proved a mighty eapon for attack from the south upon the "soft derbelly" of Europe.

American bombardment came into its own, aying a decisive role in almost every step of e Allied advance.

Coupled with the showing of the USAAF based the British Isles, this is a milestone on Hitler's ad to defeat.

Our Army and Air Forces learned lessons hich could have been gained only in the heat d sweat of all-out battle.

This means many thousands of hardened U. S. veterans for the mighty job of invading Europe.

7 The Axis lost some 250,000 men and a great quantity of materiel.

This hits Hitler hardest in that the loss is vir- tually irreplaceable.

8 Doubters and waverers in Europe can no longer question the determination of Britain and Amer- ica to fight the war—and win it.

We Cannot Fail Now

No estimate of the war's progress is worth making unless it reiterates, at every turn, the primary importance of the Russian front. This became true in June, 1941; it remains true in the summer of 1943.

Yet the whole temperature and complexion of the war elsewhere have changed. We can tell it by the behavior of friends, enemies and neutrals —by the tone of the German press and radio— by the much altered behavior of Spain—by the new regard shown for Allied opinion in Sweden —by indications that come from Budapest, Lis- bon, the Vatican, Ankara, Berne, Helsinki.

Everyone knows that we mean business, that we have formidable weapons, that we are mov- ing as fast as conditions permit—and that Russia *is not alone.* Tunisia, following close on Stalin- grad, showed the world that the combination of Russia, Britain and the United States cannot fail if all three are determined.

Whatever we do this summer must draw some of Hitler's remaining strength from Russia; what- ever Russia does must weaken the forces Hitler can put against us. We have at last reached the point which in 1940 seemed so inconceivably re- mote—the point at which the anti-Nazi powers can work together with the knowledge that whatever we decide to do, if it is intelligently planned and firmly executed, must win.

In this our situation differs altogether from that which hypnotized a large part of the world when Hitler was at his high point in 1940. Europe was at his feet—but any move he might try there- after was almost bound to get him into diffi- culties. Today it is hard to imagine any attack or combination of attacks the Allies might make which would not lead to further weakening of the Axis and victory for us.

That is why Hitler has lost.

pages, or spread, above are from an article by Vincent Sheean entitled *How Hitler Lost the War*. The problem faced here by the editors was to create a sequence of eight photographs which would corroborate, visually, eight points made textually by the author. In this type of story, when the right photographs are unavailable, drawings can be used instead with good effect.

1 How to keep his plan for the conquest of France from the Allies? Hitler decides to tell the truth.

2 A young Nazi courier, unsuspecting his part in the plot, is sent off with the plans. His pilot . . .

3 . . . deliberately misdirected, puts down in Allied territory. They try to burn the plans, are captured.

4 Allied Intelligence decides the plans are phony. Their superiors agree that Hitler won't follow them.

5 But he does, to the letter. He surrounds and captures whole armies, cuts the rest to bloody ribbons.

How Hitler Keeps His Secrets

And how you can keep yours from him—by following two simple rules

By WALLACE R. DEUEL

Most Americans realize by now how dangerous loose talk is. Mouths are being buttoned up, sewn up, taped up and battened down. Mr. Blabbermouth is learning to keep still, and the walls that have ears hear much less than they used to.

But there's more to keeping secrets than just refraining from loose talk. That's the first lesson to be learned, but not the only one.

Hitler's first rule for keeping secrets—and it's a good rule for us—is this: Make it hard for people to find out anything and everything, including matters that aren't important at all.

Grandfather's Tintype Is a Military Secret

There are three main reasons for this rule.

The first is that you can never be sure just what is information of military significance.

The second is that the less enemy intelligence can learn without effort, the more men it must use, the more time and money it must spend, the more risk it must run of being apprehended.

The third reason for keeping everything possible secret is that even facts of no military importance may be used for military purposes.

The pictures on the walls of your living room and your brother's favorite kind of pie may seem scarcely interesting to an enemy agent, but the Nazis used just such information in attacks on the morale of the French in the summer of 1940, and they may use it against us, too.

This is how they did it—and may do it again: A spy gains access to your living room, as a door-to-door salesman, for example. He carefully notes what pictures you have on your walls and other details of the room. Later, he writes a letter to your brother in the Army.

In his letter the agent pretends to be a neighbor or a friend of the family, and he writes something calculated to upset your brother.

He may say that your mother—although she won't admit it—is suffering from an incurable disease. Or he may write that a British or Canadian — or American — officer is trying to seduce your brother's girl, and it looks as if he may succeed.

For a final touch of plausibility, the agent will mention casually that he dropped in on the family the other day and that "the picture of your grandfather over the piano looked as natural as ever."

Or take another trick: An enemy agent in the town nearest the camp where your brother is stationed learns that his favorite pie is lemon cream. Then he writes you, pretending to be a soldier friend of your brother. He makes up something about your brother calculated to demoralize *you*.

He says that your brother himself is dangerously ill, or that he is drinking heavily, or any

This Is the Nazi Trick That Broke French Morale

one of a number of other lies likely to upset you. And to give his story a final touch of plausibility, he speaks casually of your brother's passion for lemon cream pie.

Tricks like these are usually found out after time. But, if the lie keeps you or your brother worried for any considerable length of time, it may interfere with your ability to work or his ability to become a better soldier.

If these deceptions are successful at a crucial time, such as during an attack or some other crisis, they may make an appreciable difference. This sort of thing helped panic the people of France at the time of the big offensive.

It's hard to prevent the enemy from finding out seemingly unimportant details like these if he is willing to devote enough time and energy to learning them. It's hardly worth while to try to prevent him from learning some of them. People can't maintain utter silence all the time about everything. Furthermore, the chances are against every door-to-door salesman's being an Axis spy.

But being forewarned you can be on your guard against tricks like these, and you can practice being reasonably discreet. What the enemy doesn't know won't hurt you—or your brother.

PICTURE STORY WITHIN TEXT: Because of the obvious impossibility of getting photographs to illustrate the text piece, *How Hitler Keeps His Secrets*, a segment of it was converted into a sequence-picture story done with drawings. The picture story is complete enough in itself so that the reader will get an important part of the author's message even though he reads none of the main text.

7:30

1 Admission—After an uncomfortable night, Mrs. William Gelbach, 32, of Upper Darby, Pa., nervously enters the Philadelphia Lying-in Hospital to have her first baby. Her husband, an Army officer, is stationed in Hawaii.

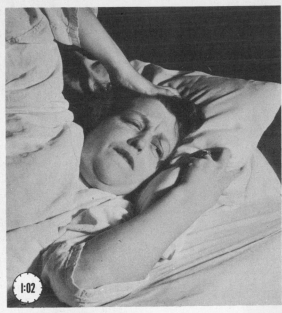

1:02

2 Active labor begins—Patient goes through preliminary, unavoidable stage of distress as doctor determines whether she is definitely in progressive labor before injecting the analgesia. Pain killer must not be used too soon.

Painless Childbirth

A new technique, continuous caudal analgesia, promises merciful relief

By THEODORE IRWIN
LOOK's science editor

Has the Biblical curse of womankind—"In sorrow thou shalt bring forth children"—at last been lifted?

Medical science, meeting the long-standing challenge of Hippocrates—"Divine is the work to subdue pain"—has now apparently triumphed over the torment of childbirth.

On these and following pages, LOOK presents a remarkable pictorial sequence of a mother giving birth to her child with virtually none of the traditional agony of travail. Depicting the step-by-step administration of a new pain-killing technique, continuous caudal analgesia, these photographs are the first of their kind to be published anywhere.

Still in a stage of development, target of controversy within the medical profession, the new method is unquestionably a far-reaching stride toward an age-old goal.

As used in childbirth, continuous caudal analgesia consists of drug injections around the nerves at the base of the spine which block pain in the birth canal and womb, yet do not affect the muscles needed for voluntary delivery. An unbreakable, two-inch needle is inserted into the sacral hiatus, a small opening in the triangular bone situated in the caudal (tail) region. The analgesia, a drug which abolishes only pain sensations and permits the patient to retain all her faculties, is usually metycaine, a coal-tar product.

Results thus far have been striking. Among 36,000 mothers who were given caudal analgesia in the past two years, complete relief from suffering was achieved for about 81 per cent and partial relief for 12 per cent. Failures were due largely to inexperience of doctors. Infant deaths in caudal deliveries were reduced to a low of one in 63 cases—about two fifths of the infant mortality rate throughout the nation. Maternal deaths, 12 among the 36,000—seven of them probably preventable—were about one seventh the average U. S. mortality rate in childbirth.

Use of the Method Is Limited

Eager prospective mothers, however, should pause before clamoring for the new procedure. They must realize that:

Continuous caudal analgesia can be used only in hospitals, and not one in ten U. S. hospitals is ready for it today.

It is not suitable for all women.

Only specially trained doctors should attempt the technique. Less than 1,000 U. S. doctors have enough experience with it.

The method is not infallible and there are certain potential hazards.

Because of these factors, and considering that about a third of American babies are born outside hospitals, probably not one mother in a hundred will benefit by caudal analgesia in the next five years.

It is not surprising that doctors are slow to adopt the revolutionary method, for it has been in use only a little over two years. The originators are two brilliant young U. S. Public Health Service surgeons, Drs. Robert A. Hingson and Waldo B. Edwards. As recently as 1940 Hingson, a serious-minded Alabamian, was stationed on a Coast Guard cutter engaged in rescuing diplomats from Europe and survivors of ships sunk in the North Sea. Edwards, an affable Missourian, was treating Eskimos at Dutch Harbor. A year later, they found themselves assigned to the Staten Island (N. Y.) Marine Hospital of the U. S. Public Health Service.

Here, when the shrieking of Coast Guardsmen's wives in labor disturbed some male patients, Drs. Hingson and Edwards (who was appointed obstetrician) were ordered to remain with the mothers and quiet them, if possible. Thus, they witnessed a great deal of agony.

Although at least five relatively safe methods of analgesia are in use, none has been developed to perfection. Common practices are likely to alter normal labor, affect heart and lungs, starve mother and child of vital oxygen, or fail to abolish pain completely. The two doctors decided to explore pain-control through a new anatomical approach.

Dr. Hingson, who had previously worked in anesthesia at the Mayo Clinic, recalled that he had used sacral-block analgesia (first attempted in 1901) for a cancer operation. So the team tried a single injection on a mother, but she had pain relief for only 40 minutes and they had to

PICTURE STORY WITHIN TEXT: One of the most satisfactory examples of a photographic picture story successfully blended with text is *Painless Childbirth,* beginning above and continuing on four following pages. It is the story of caudal analgesia, in which a drug injected at the base of the spine kills pain in childbirth —a difficult, delicate but important subject for a national magazine audience.

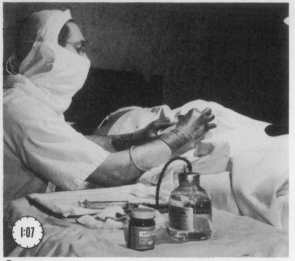

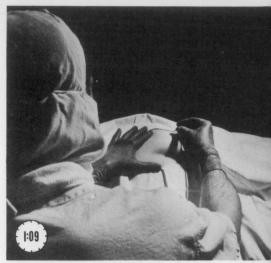

3 First injection—After needle is inserted in sacral canal at base of spine and initial metycaine dose (10 cc.) injected, Dr. Robert Hingson, the anesthetist, connects continuous-flow tube from drug bottle to needle collar.

4 Testing—To make certain that needle is situated accurately and dr taking proper effect, Dr. Hingson tests patient's sensations over the s area. Injected needle, unbreakable, remains in place until after baby is

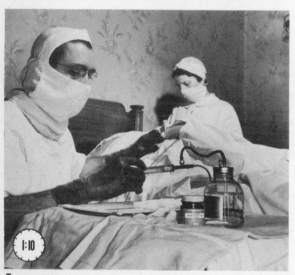

5 Second injection—As Nurse Mary Degler checks mother's blood pressure, second dose—20 cc., equal to 1½ tablespoonfuls—is administered. When properly used, drug itself has no harmful effects on either mother or baby.

6 Taking it easy—Now the muscles in birth canal are relaxed. Ho report reads: "Subjective relief in 10 minutes." Usually pain is blocke 5–20 minutes. Her perceptions keen, mother can carry out doctor's direct

The pain-killing procedure has drawbacks as well as merits

re-inject. The next logical step was to leave the needle in place and continue the doses as long as needed. Experiments with procedure and various drugs followed; an unbreakable needle was developed. And, starting at the Jefferson Medical College in Philadelphia, they studied 22,000 human sacra collected in American medical schools. Other doctors later modified the technique.

Dr. Hingson's own son was the 17th "caudal baby"; Dr. Edwards' youngest child, the 38th.

Today, Dr. Hingson is teaching the method to doctors from all parts of the country at Philadelphia Lying-in, a unit of the Pennsylvania Hospital (oldest in the U. S.), where LOOK photographer Robert Sandberg took these pictures. Dr. Edwards continues his work at Staten Island. Thus far, the team has demonstrated the technique before 11,000 doctors at 56 medical institutions. This month, at the American Medical Association's annual meeting in Chicago, an entire session will be devoted to caudal anal-

gesia, and its merits appraised.

Some of the major drawbacks of method, besides its restriction to hospital specially trained doctors, are these:

    1. The needle's nearness to the spina umn means danger of improper injection.

    2. Since the injected region is hard to ilize, there is some risk of infection.

    3. The method may not be used for tw of five women—those who are anemic, obese, too tense, inclined to hysteria or sen

One woman's experience in having a baby was the simple, obvious and correct focus for the picture story on caudal analgesia. The text had to be broad and general, partially historical, somewhat statistical. But picture stories with these characteristics are seldom if ever successful. The focus must be as narrow as possible if the article is to make the average reader feel and understand the information being offered. The

Tea for two—Dr. John C. Ullery, her obstetrician, joins Mrs. Gelbach for snack. Without pain, fear or emotional upset, she can safely have nourishment. Under caudal method, patients knit, listen to radio, sleep, play cards.

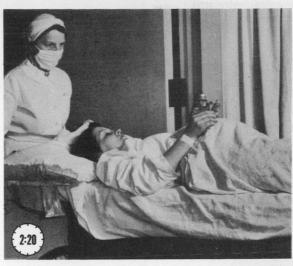

8 Ready for delivery—Obstetrician carefully watches progress of labor, and finally patient transfers to stretcher on her own power—"I didn't feel my knees," she said. Holding analgesia apparatus, mother is rolled to delivery room.

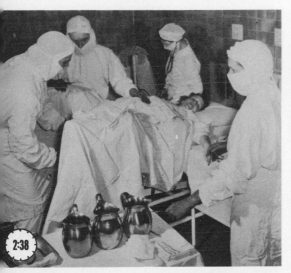

Two minutes to go—At 2:30, patient has third metycaine dose. Now, Dr. Ullery examines position of baby's head while his assistant holds hand on mother's abdomen to identify uterine contractions, which she doesn't feel.

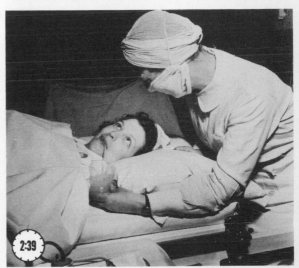

10 One more minute—"I was very thirsty, so a nurse gave me fruit juice. I didn't feel a thing while the baby was being born, wasn't even asked to bear down." Report reads: "No nausea, no vomiting, no headache, no dizziness."

the drug; nor are women with skin infections, philis, an abnormal sacrum or certain obstetrical complications suitable.

4. Under some circumstances, it is undesirable for the mother to be conscious at birth.

5. A trained doctor must be in attendance throughout the procedure, and many obstetricians are too busy to give that much time.

Advocates of the method, however, contend that it is harmless—if surrounded by proper safeguards and competently supervised.

The chief benefits are:

1. All but early pains are eliminated.
2. Labor is often shortened, facilitated.

3. Less blood is lost, thus saving the mother's vitality. Well-nourished during labor, she is not exhausted after birth; recovery is quicker, breast feeding is not delayed.

4. The method is a godsend in cases of premature or prolonged labor, heart and lung trouble, whenever strain is inadvisable.

5. Complications arising during delivery are fewer, more easily handled. Headaches, nausea and vomiting are minimized.

6. Birth injuries and shock are reduced and the baby's chances of survival greater.

7. The drug has no narcotic effect on the infant. It is born vigorous rather than limp and presents no resuscitation problem.

Dread of pain has been an important factor in childless marriages and one-child families. To date, Drs. Hingson and Edwards have received 4,000 letters from women who said that fear of the torment had restrained them from having a child. More than 200 babies were planned for, and are alive today, because of caudal analgesia. One pregnant woman even wanted to fly up from Brazil to have her baby in comfort.

The miracle of birth has apparently been streamlined. Thanks to medical science, the rack of travail is no longer inevitable.

sequence used in presenting this story is just as obvious, and just as right, as the one-person focus. It enables the reader to follow, step by step, the mother's progress from entrance into the hospital to painless delivery of her child. Dramatic interest was added to the layout of this story by a simple visual device recording time of each step on the photographs.

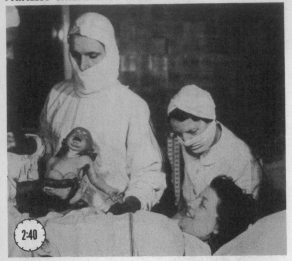

2:40

11 Five seconds after—"I could hardly believe it was over." Infant cried at once, "seemed to come out talking." As in most caudal cases, baby is not blue and oxygen-starved, needn't be spanked nor treated with a resuscitator.

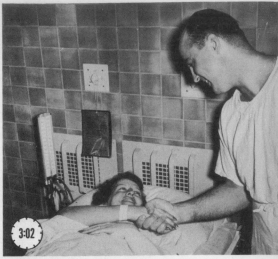

3:02

12 Congratulations!—"How soon can I have my *next* baby?" Mrs. Gelbach asks her obstetrician. With other methods, immediate reaction is often "Never again!" This mother doesn't feel at all exhausted, will recover rapidly.

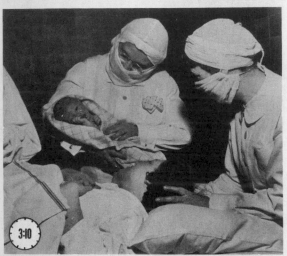

3:10

13 Off for the nursery—Alert and gnawing on thumb, oiled and wrapped in warmed blanket, baby is taken to nursery. Weight: 7 pounds, 11 ounces. She'll be named Diane Marie. Doctor is now removing patient's legs from stirrups.

3:30

14 "It was amazing!"—Back in her room, zestfully eating meal, patient describes experience to her mother, Mrs. H. J. Paffenbach: "Feel fine . . . had no sensation whatever . . . just numb . . . it was easy, almost like watching a movie."

An appraisal by a leading medical authority

Originators—Drs. Waldo Edwards (left) and Robert Hingson initiated new method.

Measures to alleviate the pains of labor have come and gone. One after another they were hailed as the *sine qua non* of proper delivery care, but the continued search for new methods must be accepted as evidence that ultimate success is still to be achieved. It would be unwise and unjust to decry the efforts of those who desire to provide relief to women in labor. But it seems equally unwise and unjust to prospective mothers to make them believe that each new procedure is generally applicable, or that it is absolutely safe. Thus, there is still need for a more definite evaluation of caudal analgesia, which should be regarded as a major surgical procedure.

This measure is not entirely free from risk. It must be carried out by specially trained personnel and is only to be employed by an adequately staffed and supervised hospital service with cooperation between anesthetist and obstetrician. It is not to be accepted as a routine procedure nor as a mere salvation from pain.

GEORGE W. KOSMAK, M.D.
Editor, American Journal of Obstetrics and Gynecology

Planning and patience in unusual degree went into the production of this article. Six months elapsed between the day it was originated and the day it was constructed. The writer who handled it became an expert on caudal analgesia. The doctors who invented it were helpful in securing permission for the pictures to be taken at Philadelphia Lying-In Hospital. So was the U. S. Public Health Service. But after all

4:55

HAPPY MOTHER, HEALTHY CHILD
In placid repose, neither shows any sign
of the traditional ordeal of childbirth

arrangements were made, writer and photographer spent three weeks at the hospital
awaiting a patient who could meet story specifications and who would sign releases
for publication of photographs. The result was worth all the effort; it is a picture story
with impact and substance, simple, cohesive and complete in itself, but given added
significance and substance by the text.

CHAPTER 2

What Is a Good Picture?

WE HAVE SEEN that the picture-text combination article, backbone of the modern picture magazine, is constructed by arranging *related* pictures in some form of continuity, and by writing text so that it will blend with pictures into a cohesive story. But no arrangement of pictures and no writing, however skillful, can transform a set of poor pictures into a good article.

So, although the picture-story writer need not have much technical knowledge of photography, he must have an understanding of picture values and picture effects. This is true whether the pictures are photographs or drawings, though in this chapter we are concerned only with photographs; the special problems involved in doing picture stories with drawings are discussed in Chapter 6.

The question "What is a good picture?" will produce as many answers as you care to seek. The salon photographer, interested in making an "artistic" impression, is likely to scorn the action shots of the news photographer. The latter reciprocates the feeling. The portrait specialist probably has little in common with the cameraman who delights in sweeping industrial panoramas. And so on, until the layman becomes giddy.

The experienced producer of picture articles can utilize all kinds of photography. The beginner is advised to be guided by two general rules:

1. Concentrate on pictures of people doing things that they normally would do,

in places where the action normally would take place.

2. Narrow the focus—to one person, if possible.

Like all rules, these are made to be broken in exceptional circumstances. However, it is invariably true that the producer or writer who departs from them is reducing his chances of success.

In the light of that fact, the question we are trying to answer becomes something like this: What is a good picture for our specific purpose—the creation of a picture-text combination article?

There is still no answer applicable to every picture. Human judgments differ on photographs, as they do on paintings and politicians. However, definite qualities to be sought in individual pictures, aside from their relation to the whole story, are:

1. STORYTELLING QUALITY
2. PHOTOGRAPHIC QUALITY
3. IMPACT
4. SIMPLICITY
5. BEAUTY

Examples of pictures which have such qualities are to be found in this chapter. As the reader can observe, it is an exceptional picture which has all five, yet in most instances a picture must have a minimum of three to be classified as "good."

Storytelling quality is virtually always an essential, because each picture must move the story along in relation to the picture preceding or following. It can be argued that any legible picture tells a story of some kind, but ours has to do double duty; the closer it comes to telling a story which reaches into the reader's life, or with which he can vicariously identify himself, the better.

Photographic quality is the photographer's technical concern, but also the producer's responsibility. A writer working with photographers must learn tricks of lighting, timing and distance, must assist in making arrangements for the photographer which are likely to produce the best results—his picture story can be made or broken by the quality of the photographic "copy." Nothing that he can do in this regard, however, is so important as the skill and experience of the photographer.

Impact is the quality in a picture which arouses an emotion—makes the reader cry or laugh, or yearn or hunger, or boil with rage or scorn or, perhaps, just feel pleased. It is really the sum total of all the other qualities the picture possesses.

Forceful impact is difficult to achieve in a posed picture. It is more often found in the chance news shot, snapped by a photographer on the scene of exciting action. Yet, the picture-story producer fails in his job if he does not continually strive for the same kind of off-guard effect in his planned pictures.

Simplicity should be the rule in the composition of 99 pictures out of 100. In the hundredth case, the rule may be so completely smashed that the effect will run to chaos and confusion; but this is permissible only if the confusion itself is the essence of the story the picture is supposed to tell: e.g., the clutter of gadgets on the late President Roosevelt's desk. For the most part, the writer should steer the photographer away from complicated backgrounds, mottled patterns, confusing shadows and overcrowded rooms.

Beauty, of all the qualities listed here, is most difficult to define and probably most difficult to achieve in a picture. Yet there are many ways of achieving it. A good writer-photographer team will catch the beauty in a rugged old face, or a bright young one; in the pattern of teen-age youngsters pitching hay against a fleecy sky; in skiers flying down a snow-covered slope, in a child playing with a puppy. They will not resort to such clichés as photographing a sunset or rain on cobblestones to get beauty into their stories. Such inanimate favorites of the salon artists are too likely to get in the way of the stories they have to tell—stories of normal people doing things normally.

Revolution in Germany is the story told by this remarkable photograph taken in 1919 and rediscovered for American publication in 1944. Snapped during a bloody battle between German soldiers and civilian rebels, it shows hand-to-hand struggles,

prostrate casualties in the street, wounded soldiers reclining in pain beside the curb. A picture like this, packed with dramatic storytelling quality, deserves prolonged examination and will have new appeal each time it is seen.

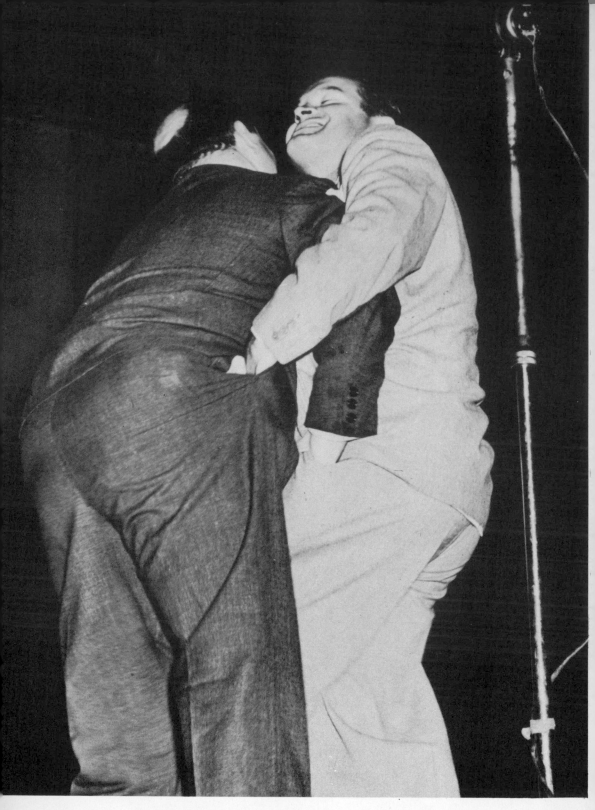

To make this picture tell its story properly, the photographer had to find an angle from which he could catch Bob Hope and his "stooge," Jack Pepper, picking each other's pocket. To do this, he shot up from below the platform on which they were standing. Only for such a storytelling purpose are angle shots really justified, but most photographers keep trying them, hoping for unusual effect.

Wash day on Guadalcanal, published in *Life,* is one of the great human-interest photographs of World War II. It satisfies some of the enormous home-front curiosity about living problems of men on fighting fronts. Without knowing, one is inclined to suspect that the photographer "arranged" the picture, at least to the extent of making sure enough men were on hand and grouped as he wanted them.

The story of a boy and girl in love is still the most appealing that can be told, pictorially or otherwise. This shot of an Army nurse and her partner, an Air Forces pilot, both lieutenants, was made at a dance in the South Pacific. The photographer picked his subjects well, and wisely allowed no background to intrude on the tale of fervor and happiness related by eyes, smiles, attitude.

The smiling gentleman is Frank Sinatra trying to push his way through a mob of autograph collectors at the Los Angeles railroad station. The harried man with the high forehead is a radio press agent assigned to protect Frankie from his admirers. This picture was shot from above and, in spite of the obvious confusion of the scene, brings out such minute details as pencils, notebooks, rings.

"Puppy love" could be the title of this charming picture taken for an article on a youth conference which revealed that modern teen-agers keenly feel a lack of, and need for, better sex education. The photograph, of course, was posed. It owes its genuineness and appeal to the fact that the writer selected subjects with care and posed them in a natural setting against an unobtrusive background.

An English kitchen in wartime is revealed in all its cramped shabbiness by this photograph, one of several hundred made for an article entitled *Hometown England*. It tells an expressive story of the spirit of English resistance; for, despite the cracks in the walls and the crowded conditions indicated by ragged clothes above the kitchen stove, mother and child seem genuinely fond of living.

Anybody who has ever eaten corn on the cob knows well that this tousled youngster is having trouble with kernels in his teeth. The picture has universal human appeal, but the inclusion of the background in the upper right-hand corner was a mistake. Cover this portion of the picture with your hand or a piece of paper and notice how much more sharply the features of the boy stand out.

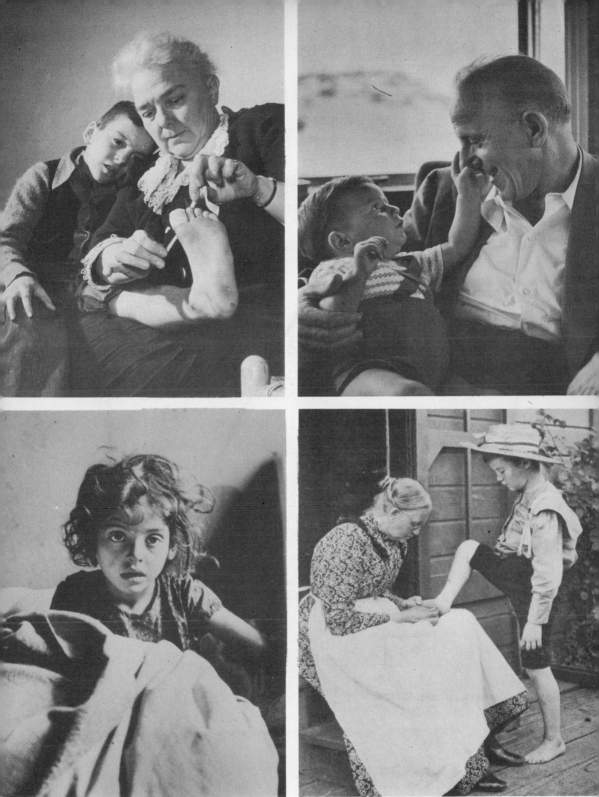

Each of these pictures strikes directly at human sympathy and understanding, and demonstrates the appeal of children as picture subjects. With the exception of the starving child (lower left) each situation recalls a moment in the memory of all of us, child or adult. And poignant appeal in the eyes of the little Polish refugee definitely places this picture in an editor's "good" category.

Virtually every picture in this chapter has photographic quality, but the shots on this and the opposite page are presented to show that photographic quality is more than mere technical excellence. This picture of boys idling on a dim street corner because they have nowhere else to go establishes a definite mood and points up the tragedy of neglected youth everywhere in wartime America.

You can learn a great deal about Henry Kaiser from this *Life* portrait of the great industrialist having lunch at his desk. It has photographic quality in all senses of the term: interesting composition, good lighting, extreme sharpness of detail, and, for a posed picture, a high degree of naturalness. Even so, it could have been improved by eliminating the framed photograph in background.

The nature of the impact you get from this unusual picture of Westbrook Pegler may depend some on your feelings about the subject, but it is undeniably the best photograph ever made of the cynical columnist. After Mr. Pegler was persuaded to get into the driver's seat of the tractor, the successful trick was to keep him talking so that the photographer could snap him with his mouth open.

Three dead Americans on a beach at Buna, New Guinea, were photographed by a *Life* photographer against a background of their wrecked landing craft. As have many of the best war photographs, this picture has the impact of horror. In any attempt to outlaw war, peacemakers could do worse than employ as an educational force the shockingly realistic combat photographs taken during World War II.

A wounded flier is·lifted from his torpedo plane after an attack on the Japs at Rabaul.
This is one of hundreds of excellent combat pictures made by the United States Navy's
photographic section under Commander Edward Steichen, a famous photographer.
The expression on the hurt boy's face and the tenderness of his comrades speak more
eloquently of the human tragedy in war than a volume of words.

A tough fighter is Billy Arnold, and *Life's* straight-on shot of the Philadelphia welter-weight shows it. Without asking the subject to do anything except square his shoulders and look directly into the camera, the photographer achieved an effect of real ring ferocity, heightened by front lighting which cast a heavy shadow on the wall behind. The bandaged hands also contribute to the effect.

The impact of this picture is unquestionable. It is the age-old impact of sex, made both violent and attractive by Ingrid Bergman and Gary Cooper in Warner Brothers' *Saratoga Trunk*. No successful modern magazine ignores the reader appeal in sex, but the responsible ones avoid dealing with it objectionably and try to contribute their share of reliable, scientific and much-needed sex information.

A bomb hit London just before this picture was taken. It wrecked the bus in background and injured the woman shown on stretcher. Both the rescue squad and the photographer were on the job before the dust had settled. Under the circumstances, the man with the camera achieved a notable result. With only a flash bulb to combat poor visibility, he produced a picture filled with action and detail.

A macabre sense of humor prompted somebody to prop the skull of a Japanese soldier against a wrecked tank for this picture, which appeared in *Life*. According to the caption in the magazine, composition was arranged by American troops, but it would not be surprising if a writer or photographer thought of it first. In any case, the picture is what editors call a "stopper." You can't ignore it.

Human reactions to violence are the stock in trade of the photographer who took this picture at a scene of a street murder in Brooklyn. He is Arthur Fellig, a New York free-lancer who calls himself "Weegee." At all hours, day and night, he responds to police emergency calls, focuses his cameras on scenes attendant upon a big city's fires, murders, suicides, riots. "Impact" is his middle name.

67

As will be seen on subsequent pages, beauty in photography is not always dependent on a beautiful girl, but if a beautiful girl is the subject, it certainly does no harm. The girl in this *Life* close-up is movie actress Veronica Lake, photographed with light concentrated on one side of her honey-blond hair, her face in shadow. This type of photography is considered "arty," should be used sparingly.

The English countryside, a long-time favorite of poets and painters, provided background for this beautiful photograph, taken by a LOOK photographer. The straw stack, gnarled old tree and twelfth-century church in the background all helped to frame the rugged horse being led to work. This kind of atmospheric shot, however beautiful, belongs in a story only if it does not impede action.

The natural beauty of Deanna Durbin is presented charmingly in this picture of her trying on hats in her bedroom. Her round, plumpish face is properly framed with a big bonnet; dark vertical lines on her light housecoat add length to her figure; uplifted arms and gaze into the mirror provide just enough action to keep the photograph from becoming a stilted, stylized, deadly fashion shot.

There can be beauty as well as horror in a war action picture, as this official United States Navy photograph proves. In the foreground is a slice of the deck of the American aircraft carrier on which the photographer was stationed. The stricken plane trailing smoke is a Japanese bomber hit by American gunfire and diving through a long arc into the sea back of the carrier in the distance.

Underwater ballet was the title of the article which contained this photograph of Esther Williams performing in MGM's *Ziegfeld Follies*. The photographer had to shoot through glass at Miss Williams, who worked 10 feet under water in a tank containing 300,000 gallons. The star could stay submerged only seconds at a time; as a result, she had to work 18 days to finish a three-minute dance.

Scenic beauty, an element not found in every picture story but an asset whenever it can be worked in naturally is the backdrop in this photograph of skiers moving down a mountain. The foreground action is made more exciting by shadows stretching in front of the figures, as well as by the snow-covered peaks and pines in the background. Sports action often provides chances for photographic beauty.

Simplicity is essential to the success of a very high percentage of photographs used in picture articles. This example, taken in Pishan, China, for an article entitled *Hometown China*, is simplicity itself. The picture shows a young Chinese scholar studying by the light of an oil lamp. The light in the photograph is concentrated in the lamp, on the scholar's fine face, his lesson, his hands.

74

An unknown Marine hero lies beneath the wooden grave marker in this gripping, starkly simple picture from *Life*. The photographer stood below the slight incline on which the grave was built and shot it against an empty background, thus enabling his picture to tell its story with direct and tragic force. It was used with an article by Robert Sherrod on the bloody American conquest of Saipan.

This picture is dramatic chiefly because it is so simple. It was one of several used in a picture story entitled *War Is Mud,* and photographs piled up evidence from all theaters of war to substantiate the theme. Cutting off the top of the soldier and the mired truck beside which he was walking served to focus attention where it was wanted. (Cutting a picture in this way is called "cropping.")

The charm in this photograph of *Mother's Little Helper* is enhanced by the utter simplicity of the background, the concentration on the earnest young lady and her activity. The milk bottles add a touch of authenticity without cluttering things up. The lesson seems obvious enough, but it is surprising indeed how few picture-story writers learn it except by the wasteful trial-and-error method.

CHAPTER 3

Picture Continuities

WEBSTER DEFINES the word *continuity* in two ways:

"1. Quality or state of being continuous.

"2. Something that has or gives continuousness or sequence; specifically, a scenario for a motion picture."

For our purposes, the second definition is the more important, and the example of a motion-picture scenario is apt: many of the problems involved in constructing picture articles are similar to those involved in making movies.

Once the subject of the article has been decided, the biggest problems facing the writer are focus and cohesion, the one bearing on the other.

It has already been suggested that the broader the focus, the greater the difficulties, and that the ideal picture-story focus is one person. In actual practice, however, so narrow a focus is not always possible and various other devices besides concentrating on one person must be used in building an article into a cohesive, continuous whole.

Analysis of successful picture articles to learn what holds them together reveals that there are seven commonly used types of continuities. Published examples of them will be found on subsequent pages of this chapter. They may somewhat arbitrarily be labeled:

1. SIMPLE CHRONOLOGY
2. NARRATIVE CHRONOLOGY
3. REPEATED IDENTITY
4. HOW TO
5. PARALLEL OR CONTRAST
6. LAYOUT
7. DEVELOPMENT OF A THEME

For the picture-story writer, the first five types of continuities are most important, but this chapter will attempt to define all seven and demonstrate how they are used.

A *simple chronology* virtually defines itself. It is an unrelieved time sequence requiring no particular starting point or conclusion. Its pictures and captions are held together only by their common subject matter. Your mother's album depicting your youthful years is an excellent example of a simple picture chronology, and the album device has become a favorite with writers and editors handling picture stories of important personalities. (For examples of the *simple chronology* type of continuity, see *Midas in Moscow* on pages 80-81, *A Baby's Afternoon* on pages 82-83, *Women Warriors* on pages 84-85.)

A *narrative chronology* is also a time sequence, but a more complicated one. It has elements to be found in a good piece of fiction—definite beginning, suspense, a climactic conclusion. This type of article is easy to do with drawings, difficult with photographs. However, it has been successfully handled both ways. (See *Take Her Down* on pages 86-87, *Sinatra's Kiss* on pages 88-89.)

Repeated identity is the most important of the continuity devices, and most frequently used. Every picture personality article is a repeated identity continuity—the identity of the personality is repeated in picture after picture. But in other stories the repeated identity may be an object, a mood, a family or a situation rather than a person. (See *Invasion Heroine* on pages 90-91, *Night Clothes on Broadway* on pages 92-93.)

The *how-to* continuity in its simplest form is a time sequence of pictures showing the reader, step by step, how some task or feat is accomplished. This device is often used in sports articles and in articles on popular science, cooking, homemaking and so on. (See *Booby Traps* on pages 94-95, and *Sam Snead* on pages 96-97.)

The *parallel or contrast* type of continuity can be highly useful in an instructive article because, effectively employed, it will put over editorial points simply, speedily and vividly. It usually takes the form of "right and wrong" or "do and don't" pictures placed side by side. "Before and after" pictures juxtaposed in a technique long used by advertisers also belong in this category. (See *Gaslight* on pages 98-99, *Let the Baby Be the Boss* on pages 100-101.)

Layout continuity is not often a direct concern of a picture-story writer, inasmuch as it usually is achieved in the art department, but the writer should know as much about it as possible. This continuity is simply a matter of design—a layout artist's arrangement of borders, boxes, panels or typography to give visual cohesion to an article which may or may not possess it otherwise. (See examples on pages 102-103.)

The *development of a theme* continuity is really the presentation of an idea or argument with the aid of photographs or drawings arranged in logical relation to one another. Advertising agencies frequently use this type of continuity to sell their clients' products, and editors are beginning to use it to sell political, social or economic ideas. (See *Donald Duck Dodges Depression* on pages 104-105.)

Obviously there is overlapping among the continuities; two or more of the seven types can frequently be found in the same article. In fact, most successful picture stories result from combinations of several continuities.

For example, consider a simple idea of never-ending interest: *How to Bathe a Baby*. It is plainly a *how-to* continuity; it may use several other kinds of continuity also. As one means of achieving cohesion, all the pictures may focus on the same mother and baby; then it becomes a *repeated identity* continuity. To add interest, it may be planned as a story with beginning, suspense and climax; then it becomes a *narrative chronology*. To drive a lesson home, it may have pictures showing common errors to avoid in bathing baby; then, it is also a *parallel or contrast* continuity. Finally, a layout artist may design it so that it will follow certain visual and typographical patterns throughout; it is then a *layout* continuity, and winds up as an article held together five ways instead of one.

The average reader will not be aware of the fact that these continuity devices have been employed to lead him into and through each picture story. But by using them in the planning and the execution of his stories, the writer will assure himself of readership.

Midas in Moscow

W. Averell Harriman, U. S. Ambassador to Russia, is a mass-minded millionaire

By PATRICIA COFFIN
LOOK staff writer

Although William Averell Harriman can count Roosevelt, Churchill, Stalin among his personal friends, he is little known to the general public. Yet, endowed with good looks, great wealth, blue blood and the No. 1 diplomatic post of the decade, Harriman has fiction beaten with fact. At ease in Teheran or at "21", he is one of the country's foremost financiers: chairman of the board of the Union Pacific, partner of Brown Brothers Harriman & Co., on leave of absence from the boards of numerous major corporations.

As a liberal capitalist, Harriman is eminently fitted to handle the job of U. S. ambassador to the Soviet Union, a post involving the delicate balance of understanding between Communism and democracy. True, he inherited the Union Pacific from his father, is said to have made $100,000,000 on his own. On the other hand, he supposedly gave John L. Lewis $100,000 on an unsecured note when Lewis was organizing the United Mine Workers of America. "And there is more where that came from," Harriman is alleged to have told him. Yet friends who accuse him of being a "damned crusader" voice the suspicion that Harriman yearns to become as great a business power as was his famous father.

A Tycoon in His Twenties

When the elder Harriman died in 1909, Averell inherited his father's far-flung business enterprises. Guardians took care of his interests until he was graduated from Yale in 1913. Although he idolized his father, stocky, dynamic E. H. Harriman, of whom it was said "he fears neither God nor Morgan," tall, deliberate Averell also had great respect for his mother. Mrs. Harriman, left $71,000,000 in her husband's 99-word will, daily went to his 5th Avenue office to attend to her affairs. She died in 1932, "the richest woman in America."

Harriman, early in his career, built minesweepers during World War I, introduced the first partially prefabricated ships, by 1920 owned a merchant fleet of his own. During this period he went to Russia on manganese deals, to Germany for zinc, to Poland and Silesia for trade.

During the roaring 20's he was a busy *bon vivant*, buying horses, making big business deals. An outstanding figure in racing, he became interested in polo, achieved an eight-goal rating and in 1928 played in the international matches between the U. S. and Argentina.

Disposing of his steamship holdings in the late 20's, Harriman returned to his first interest —railroads; which did not stop him from buying, in 1929, a controlling interest in the newly formed Fairchild Aviation Corp. or, the next year, from entering into what was called the largest merger of private banking houses ever consummated— the consolidation of Averell Harriman & Co. with Brown Brothers & Co.

It took daring to put $5,000,000 into the Union Pacific Railroad during the depression when other roads were retrenching and passenger traffic falling off. But Harriman gambled, as he likes to at poker and croquet, for high stakes. He gave the public streamlined, Diesel-driven travel, and ocean-liner service at bargain prices. He built Sun Valley—a St. Moritz in America. Cus-

Labeled one of America's 10 handsomest men by Madeleine Carroll, envoy Harriman can't live it down.

Simple Chronology

The most elementary of the continuity devices often takes the form shown above—a picture "album" integrated with a personality article. These are two pages from a LOOK piece on Averell Harriman. Compiling such an album is an arduous editorial task, involving painstaking research

Harriman No. 1, mother of his daughters, Mary (Shirley W. Fisk) and Kathleen, divorced him in 1929.

...een, ex-*Newsweek* reporter, current Embassy hostess—one of her father's most able (unofficial) assistants.

...velt's envoy and adviser since 1932, Harriman (in Moscow) is close to Churchill, a friend of Stalin.

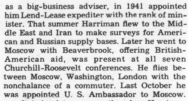

Unmistakably American, with keen eyes, a contagious grin, our man-about-Moscow is as unobtrusive in a crowd as Gary Cooper. Russia likes Harriman's interest in labor, his unrugged individualism.

Harriman, an advertiser's dream of a diplomat, likes horses and dogs, Scotch and soda, the sparkling expanse of his pet project, Sun Valley. He has let his 150-room house in Harriman, N. Y., fall into aristocratic dilapidation. The Harrimans' New York duplex has no dining room, and although their Sands Point, L. I., estate is magnificently comfortable, it is unostentatious. Harriman's private New York office is almost austere except for a special desk which resembles a disemboweled spinet. He travels in a C-47 instead of his Rolls—mark of the change of pace in his life.

As soon as Roosevelt set up the National Recovery Administration he called Harriman in as a big-business adviser, in 1941 appointed him Lend-Lease expediter with the rank of minister. That summer Harriman flew to the Middle East and Iran to make surveys for American and Russian supply bases. Later he went to Moscow with Beaverbrook, offering British-American aid, was present at all seven Churchill-Roosevelt conferences. He flies between Moscow, Washington, London with the nonchalance of a commuter. Last October he was appointed U. S. Ambassador to Moscow.

It is hard to say exactly when Harriman changed from the bon *vivant* into an intellectual Samaritan. Not that he eschews all frivolity—he dropped into the Stork Club during a recent visit to New York, was not recognized and was barred. He hugely enjoyed the joke. But he has acquired, in the past 10 years, the manner of a man with a mission. Perhaps Mr. Roosevelt's reliance on him as a business adviser and emissary forces him to take himself more seriously than he did in the days when he was making business history.

Harriman wants world peace as well as peace between Capital and Labor. In keeping with his personal philosophy, he is working for what he wants with what he's got. As he puts it: "It is as indefensible for a man with money not to use it for the benefit of his country, as it is for a laborer to refuse to work."

in the files of picture agencies and final selection of a dozen or two photographs to be used out of the hundreds that are usually available on any well-known personality. If the subject has a real family album to which the editor can gain access, it often solves the problem of picturing early years and supplies pictures of parents, wives and children not readily obtainable elsewhere.

SPEAKING OF PICTURES . .

. . . THESE FOLLOW A BABY'S AFTERNOON FROM BATH TO BATH

① IN A CRISP, CLEAN PINAFORE DANA STARTS FOR THE PARK

② TRIP OVER IS MADE WITH HER MOTHER AND DOG, COLONEL

③ DANA DOESN'T LIKE CARRIAGES, SOON CRAWLS O

⑦ STILL MODERATELY CLEAN, SHE RENEWS AN ACQUAINTANCE

⑧ SOON BORED WITH FRIEND, SHE TESTS WATER FOUNTAIN

⑨ ON CLOSE INSPECTION WATER DOESN'T SPLASH ENOU

⑬ IMPORTANT FIND IS THIS RAW MATERIAL FOR MUD PIES

⑭ AN OLD HAND AT IT, DANA EXPERTLY MOLDS A SMALL PIE

⑮ ONE PIE MADE, SHE RINSES HER HANDS IN THE WAT

This simple chronology from *Life* is a series of scenes from the afternoon of an endlessly curious young lady. It could have covered the child's whole day or week, or have been confined to an hour. This kind of picture story is usually planned and executed jointly by a writer and a photographer. Before deciding on their procedure, both would need to be well acquainted with the subject, familiar with her routine.

Experienced parents have found that no matter what ingenious playthings they purchase for their children there is no substitute for mud. This fact is true even in Manhattan, which may not have any of the rabbits and chickens that delight country children but always seems to have plenty of dirt and enough water to make the dirt interesting. The pictures which appear on these pages of Dana Glen's adventure in Washington Square illustrate this natural affinity.

Dana, who lives with her mother and father a few blocks from Washington Square, has her mother's smile and her father's curiosity. She also has a 16-month old mind of her own, dislikes baby carriages and much prefers spending a quiet afternoon exploring the park. A few months of this sort of investigation have convinced her that although she especially likes park's water fountains and some of the other children, her happiest moments are when she is making big, oozy mud pies.

ONLY WAY TO LURE HER BACK IN IS WITH ICE CREAM

5 OUT OF THE CARRIAGE AGAIN, SHE IS OFF OVER THE FENCE

6 MAKING FIRST MUD PIE OF AFTERNOON SHE SEES FRIEND

PRESSURE OF FINGER SEEMS TO GIVE DESIRED EFFECT

11 FOUNTAIN MAKES PUDDLE THAT HAS TO BE INVESTIGATED

12 WATER IS STILL CLEAR ENOUGH FOR SUITABLE REFLECTION

WELL SMEARED WITH MUD, DANA GETS TO HER FEET

17 WIPING HANDS CAREFULLY ON DRESS, SHE EYES A SUNDAE

18 ABOUT AS COOL AS ICE CREAM IS STRIPPING TO THE SKIN

As a preliminary to actual picture-taking, the writer usually prepares a shooting script, or scenario, in which are listed all the anticipated situations and poses. The script may also suggest camera angles, ranges and so on. It is seldom followed to the letter; inevitably situations develop and opportunities for pictures arise which no writer, editor or photographer can foresee.

PALLAS ATHENE OR MINERVA WAS GODDESS OF DEFENSIVE WAR

QUEEN PENTHESILEIA LED OTHER AMAZONS IN LEGENDARY BATTLES

VALKYRIES WERE FABLED SUPERWOM

BOADICEA RULED OVER WHAT IS NOW NORFOLK, ENGLAND, DEFENDED HER DOMINION AGAINST EMPEROR NERO IN 61 A.D.

ZENOBIA, QUEEN OF PALMYRA, LOST WAR WITH ROMA

MOTHER ROSS FOUGHT WITH ENGLISH AGAINST FRENCH

DOUGHTY HANNAH SNELL ENLISTED IN ENGLISH ARMY IN 1745

MAID OF SARAGOSSA OPERATED CANNON DURING SIEG

A loose simple chronology device helps to hold together this *Life* compilation of pictures dealing with women warriors through history. The story was suggested by the adoption of Pallas Athene as corps insigne for the WACs. Consequently, the story begins with a print of Athene. Given another angle, it could have started with a picture of Joan of Arc or Molly Pitcher. Likewise, it could have ended with a

When the WAACs, first enrolled women soldiers serving with the U. S. Army, adopted a brass head of Athene as corps insignia, they acknowledged historical precedent for their military mien. Mythological Athene was the original woman warrior. But ever since man began to clutter up the earth with his needs and greeds, woman has been at his side, enthusiastically assisting in the ensuing battles.

Below are some fighting women of earlier times when wars were unscientific, informal affairs often without benefit of uniform. Though prejudice sometimes impelled these ladies to dress in trousers and false beards, their efficiency was remarkable. Indeed, some appear ferocious enough to jusify Kipling's contention that the female is more deadly than the male.

MILLS, ENGLISH SEAMAN, FOUGHT HARSHLY

RUSSIA'S CATHERINE THE GREAT RULED WITH HER SWORD

MADAME SANS-GENE ATTACKED AUSTRIANS DURING TOULON SIEGE

PITCHER TOOK HUSBAND'S PLACE AT CANNON AT BATTLE OF MONMOUTH

MARY ANN TALBOT SERVED IN ENGLISH ARMY

JOAN OF ARC IS MOST FAMOUS WOMAN WARRIOR

HEAD WAS PIRATEER UNDER CALICO JACK IN 1715

DEBORAH SAMPSON, RIGHT, WAS WITH CONTINENTAL ARMY

CLARA BARTON WAS FIGHTER, FOUNDER OF RED CROSS

picture of a heroine of the American Civil War or of a modern Russian guerrilla, depending on the editorial objective. A simple chronology, which is not dependent on a specific time span or specific series of actions, develops no suspense and reaches no real climax. In all these respects it differs from the narrative chronology, examples of which are shown on the following pages.

"Take Her Down"—Most Gallant Order of the War

Commander Howard Gilmore gives his life to save his submarine after a battle with a Japanese ship

AMERICAN HEROES

Two immortal Navy phrases have come out of this war. The first, "Sighted sub, sank same," was radioed by Ensign Don Mason from his plane off our Atlantic Coast (LOOK, July 14, 1942). The second, "Take her down!" was the order Comm. Howard Gilmore called out in the Pacific night from his bullet-swept submarine bridge. Gilmore, native of Selma, Ala., graduate of Annapolis (1926), in eight months—around the Aleutians, off Japan, in the South and Southwest Pacific—damaged 1 destroyer, 1 transport; probably sank a merchantman, sank 2 destroyers, a tanker, 4 merchantmen.

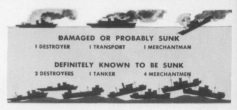

DAMAGED OR PROBABLY SUNK
1 DESTROYER   1 TRANSPORT   1 MERCHANTMAN

DEFINITELY KNOWN TO BE SUNK
2 DESTROYERS   1 TANKER   4 MERCHANTMEN

STORY BY DON WHARTON—DRAWINGS BY GLEN THOMAS—TWENTY-NINTH IN LOOK'S AMERICAN HERO SERIES

1 As his sub plows the dark surface toward her base after a mission off Rabaul, Gilmore, bunking in the conning tower to be near the bridge, gets a hurry call.

2 On the bridge, Commander Gilmore finds Lt. "Jeff" Davis has spotted an unrecognized Japanese ship a mile to starboard, turns his submarine to stalk the [...]

3 Darkness hides the enemy's identity. Distance and angle are too great for accurate shots. The sub holds her fire and continues maneuvering for better position.

4 In the blackness, the Jap ship also turns, suddenly comes out of the murk, bears down on the sub — trying to ram her. Expertly, Gilmore alters his course a[...]

5 In a desperate battle of navigation, Gilmore changes speed. He gives his craft a couple of zigs, outwits the Jap skipper — and rams crashing into his quarry.

6 The force of the blow sends the sub swerving alongside the ripped merchant[...] The Jap ship lists heavily, instantly opens fire with a .50-caliber machine [...]

Narrative Chronology

The vital elements of a good fiction story are found in the picture article based on a narrative chronology: definite beginning, heightened suspense as the narrative develops, and a climactic ending. This example, from LOOK's series on American heroes, was done with draw-

ear the bridge," Gilmore shouts. "Stand by to dive!" Davis scrambles down the
ch, Signalman McCabe following. A second burst tears into the six others.

8 Davis hurries to his post in the control room. McCabe turns, raises his head through
the hatch, sees Lookout Wade wounded on the bullet-raked deck, helps him in.

ring Jap bullets, McCabe leans out again, gropes around, touches Lookout
ley, whose right leg has been shot away. McCabe gets Baxley through the hatch.

10 Gilmore, Ensign Williams and Lookout Kelly are still missing. McCabe peers out
again. By him stands Lt. Comm. Arnie Schade, the submarine's executive officer.

t of the dark comes Gilmore's voice. "They got
, Arnie," he says to Schade—and issues his last

order. Schade hesitates, calls out: "Close the hatch!"
The diving horn sounds. Then — water washing over

the deck where her helpless skipper lies—the sub responds to his final, heroic command: "Take her down!"

---

ings. Fictional treatment of a factual narrative requires extremely careful research
on the part of the writer, who must be the artist's guide on minute details of the
action. Readers react violently if details are drawn inaccurately. The picture situations and captions in this article were culled from a 3,000-word script prepared
by the author after several weeks of investigating the story from all angles.

1 **A touch of perfection** is given to Frankie by make-up man Jack Byron while Farrar Matthews, Sinatra's personal man, puts The Voice into a coat.

3 **Frank is fussy** about tie angles. Perhaps no other person ha affected the cravat styles of a nation more significantly than has S

2 **Hair stylist Fritzy La Bar** whips Gloria DeHaven's blondeness into shining, kissable glory—while papa Carter DeHaven, also nervous, looks on.

4 **Lips are inspected** with purely professional interest by bot taking parties. Gloria's lip line must be voluptuous; Frankie's firm

Here is a photographic narrative chronology with a climax which spoofs the whole thing—Frank Sinatra's first movie kiss, from preparation in the make-up department to the "gag" swoon in picture 8. The two-line captions in this piece are noteworthy for flip gayety and for emphasis on details—the time it took to prepare for the kiss, the exact hour and minutes of its delivery, its duration, the approval of the Hays

last-minute instructions: "Millions of girls will sit in darkened theaters all over America waiting for just this moment. Make it special."

7 **The Kiss**—at exactly 5:56, after two hours and 26 minutes of preparation. It lasted 30 seconds, received a nod of approval from the Hays office.

demonstration by director Tim Whelan: "The stage kiss should hint, fulfill. It should be tender, a promise, thrilling in its warm restraint."

8 **The Swoon**—as Gloria conformed to Swoonatra tradition. Studio cynics said she didn't faint, that Frankie had enough trouble holding *himself* up.

office, the director's instructions to Sinatra. Such trivia help enormously to increase reader interest in articles on professional entertainment. In fact, intimate personal data in text block and captions add interest to personality articles in any field. A primary requisite in a picture-story writer is an ability to pack dozens of such facts into comparatively small space.

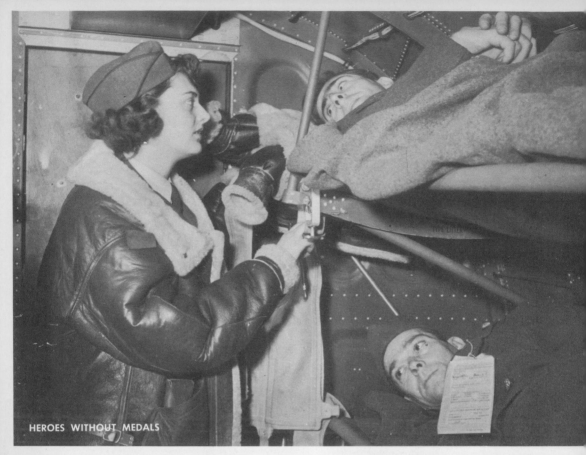

HEROES WITHOUT MEDALS

Lt. Jean Tolen, 24, of Minneapolis, typifies the American girls, trained nurses in civilian life, who have volunteered for one of the war's most dangerous jobs. Because evacuation planes carry military personnel and materiel on outgoing

trips, nurses like Jean are exposed to enemy fire until the second half mission, when, carrying wounded, the planes bear the Red Cross e Here Jean tends stretcher patients en route from an A.E.F. base to E

Invasion Heroine: the flying nurse
She evacuates wounded from battle zone to base hospital, across the Atlantic and home

1 **At home base** in England, Jean plays bridge with fellow members of a Medical Air Evacuation Transport Squadron before taking off on her flight.

2 **Each nurse teams** with a surgical technician on all flights. Here J teammate Sgt. Fay Funkhauser of Lafayette, Ind., set up litters in th

Repeated Identity

This is the form of continuity most frequently used in picture articles; probably the most useful, and certainly the surest guarantee of a cohesive result. The repeated identity may be that of an individual, a family, an object, or a situation. The best possible focus is one individual,

t the advanced base, Jean supervises loading of stretcher patients. vacuation planes—usually heavy C-47s—have 10 minutes in which to nd, load patients, and take off. Occasionally wounded are flown to the U. S.

4 Flying over water, wounded wear "Mae Wests"—G.I. for chesty life preservers. Here Jean chats with a soldier well enough to sit up. Plane has room for 18 litter patients or 24 sitting patients, usually carries some of both.

ack in England, Jean sees her charges transferred to waiting ambulances. er duties in the air include the giving of intravenous medication and lood plasma, and emergency treatment to combat the effects of altitude.

6 Her responsibility ends as she checks the passenger list with Sergeant Funkhauser. Thanks to girls like Jean, medical risk in air evacuation is slight. In 1943, there were 160,000 evacuations, only 11 deaths in flight.

as in the article above on a flying Army nurse. As an individual, the nurse is not as important to writer and photographer as the subject would be in a personality piece on a celebrity. But she is extremely important as an active human being through whom the whole story of air evacuation of the wounded can be told. Without such a specific focus, a picture story tends to become confusing.

NIGHT CLOTHES ON BROADWAY

Broadway is clean this season. None of the shows is really nude. But by a curious coincidence, such intimate feminine apparel as nightgowns, housecoats, pajamas and lingerie is worn in 14 of the 29 attractions now on Broadway. In *The Voice of the Turtle* Margaret Sullavan (*below*) wears a pair of boy's pajamas. In *The Doughgirls* Arleen Whelan is swathed in yards of fluff (*see p. 58*). In *Over 21* Ruth Gordon wears a pair of short pajamas. Whether there is any significance in this preoccupation with boudoir attire is extremely doubtful. In most instances the exigencies of the plot demand it. In *The Two Mrs. Carrolls* Elisabeth Bergner rises from a sick bed. In *Over 21* a fine bit of comedy stems from the fact that Miss Gordon is locked out of her bungalow in her pajamas. In *Othello* Desdemona is strangled in bed. In vesting their heroines in shifts, Broadway producers are following a classic precept. Will Shakespeare, no slouch when it came to playing to the balcony, allowed such ladies as Ophelia, Juliet, Lady Macbeth to appear in sleeping attire, with great stage effect.

IN "THE VOICE OF THE TURTLE" MARGARET SULLAVAN WEARS BOY'S WHITE BROADCLOTH PAJAMAS. WITH NO LITTLE DIFFICULTY SHE LOCATED THESE FOR $3.50 AT WALLACH'S

In this article from *Life,* the repeated identity is that of night clothes worn in Broadway plays. The individuals and the plays are all different, but the night-clothes theme holds them together—not so well as a one-person focus might but well enough so that the story is something more than a collection of miscellaneous photographs of actresses in various stages of undress. This is palpably a manufactured "angle" for a

In "The Doughgirls" Arleen Whelan wears *mousseline de soie* negligee which lends itself to business of striding angrily about whipping her skirts around her. She has tried unsuccessfully to reach her sweetheart on the phone, is furious at her failure.

In "Doctors Disagree" Barbara O'Neil relaxes in a silk jersey housecoat designed by Valentina. Evening before this scene takes place she had performed a difficult brain operation on a small boy and saved his life. *Doctors Disagree* closed Jan. 15.

In "Over 21" Author-Star Ruth Gordon wears Mainbocher's short pajamas. About to go to sleep on living-room couch of rented bungalow, she realizes light is still on, that switch is on the porch. When she steps outside, door slams, locking her out.

In "Life With Father" Dorothy Stickney wears a $60 reproduction of a nightgown shown in *Godey's Lady's Book*. Mother, having been dosed unwittingly by her sons, comes weakly downstairs and extracts promise from Father that he will be baptized.

picture story, but so are most approaches used by magazine editors and writers. A natural story line, so obvious that it requires little thought or development, rarely occurs. Even when he has a message that he wants very much to deliver, a writer will not produce an effective story unless he can find the right device to get it easily and forcefully before the reader.

The American soldier lying in the foreground was blasted by a booby trap beside a Fascist monument in a little Italian town. His arms are up, but he is dead, the rubble of the explosion around him. At right, men of an engineering unit search for other mines, using a pancake-shaped electrical detector which produces a buzzing sound in the operator's earphones passed over metal. Such an instrument is ineffe however, for detecting mines incased in p

---

How To

The foundation of this type of picture-story continuity is the time-tested formula of showing the reader how to do something, or how something is done, or both. In its simplest form it is a sequence of instructional pictures and captions. The example above is comparatively com-

BOOBY TRAPS

With the enemy gone, death in a thousand disguises waits for the unwary

[Th]e booby trap, as wicked a weapon as this war has produced, is in [e]ssence a peculiarly fiendish type of mine; and mines are almost [o]ld as gunpowder. They came into their own, however, during the [tre]nch warfare of 1914-18 when engineers dug, or mined, their way [und]er enemy positions, placed explosives, detonated them from a [dist]ance. The Germans developed small mines to be buried in the [ene]my's path and set off by electricity. The advent of the tank [bro]ught the necessity for an automatic mine, one that would oblig[ingl]y explode under enemy armor, and today all armies have half a [doze]n types of mine that will blow the tread off a 60-ton tank the [insta]nt they are touched off. It was an easy and obvious step to the [sma]ll anti-personnel mine or booby trap.

On these pages LOOK explains the workings of the simple but [dead]ly booby trap. The photographs were made at the Army Air [Bas]e in Richmond, Va., where the 939th Aviation Engineers Camou[flag]e Battalion has established a school for the study of booby traps [and] mines. The equations below draw an analogy with fire to show [the] basic elements of a booby trap.

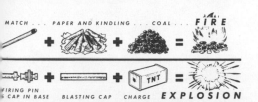

MATCH . . . PAPER AND KINDLING . . . COAL . . . **F I R E**

[F]IRING PIN & CAP IN BASE + BLASTING CAP + CHARGE = **E X P L O S I O N**

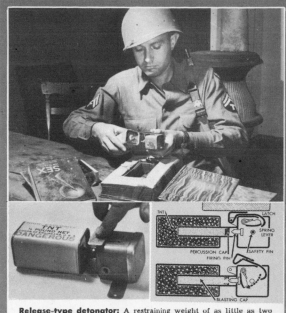

Release-type detonator: A restraining weight of as little as two pounds on the trigger latch of this detonator holds it down, prevents firing; when weight is removed, firing pin strikes. Sometimes hidden in a hollowed-out book, this trap might also be placed under a large anti-tank mine, to go off if the mine, found by enemy sappers, were lifted.

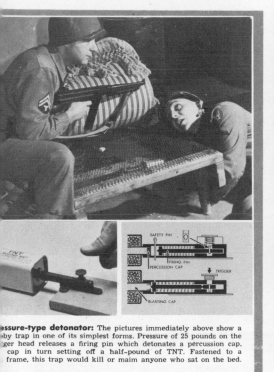

[Pre]ssure-type detonator: The pictures immediately above show a [boo]by trap in one of its simplest forms. Pressure of 25 pounds on the [trig]ger head releases a firing pin which detonates a percussion cap, [the] cap in turn setting off a half-pound of TNT. Fastened to a [bed] frame, this trap would kill or maim anyone who sat on the bed.

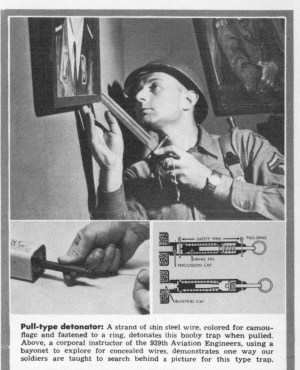

Pull-type detonator: A strand of thin steel wire, colored for camouflage and fastened to a ring, detonates this booby trap when pulled. Above, a corporal instructor of the 939th Aviation Engineers, using a bayonet to explore for concealed wires, demonstrates one way our soldiers are taught to search behind a picture for this type trap.

plicated. The article shows how several kinds of booby traps are constructed; how they are exploded; and, finally, wrong and right ways of dealing with them in a variety of situations. Diagrammatic drawings have been combined with photographs to add information on workings of these deadly contraptions. Almost any photographic how-to story can be made more informative by addition of drawings.

Snead's mighty drives are perfect blends of power and timing

On the tee, Sam uses standard over-lap grip, 15-ounce club with stiff shaft. He (1) lines up ball opposite *left* heel, (2) holds body parallel to line of flight, (3) begins shifting his weight to right leg while still in early stages of backswing.

While raising club head in near-perfect arc (4), Snead keeps his chin straight at ball. He twists body gradually (5) with full backward turn and shoulders. As backswing ends (6), left knee is unlocked, power tur

By unwinding body during downswing (7), Sam increases power. Speed of club is so great at split second before impact (8) that even magic-eye camera records only a blur. His chin is still pointed at tee (9) even *after* the ball is in flight.

The ball is away, but the drive is *not* finished. With weight back on left Sam follows through (11) until club head completely circles his be His extra-punch drive enables him to out-hit most rivals by 25 to 3

Sam demonstrates an explosion shot — the "duffer's nightmare"

To pry ball from trap, Sam recommends: anchor your feet *deep* in the sand (1) *before* swinging. He uses over-lap grip on No. 9 iron, takes stance close to ball (2), begins backswing (3) in much shorter arc than that used for driving.

Other important rules: swing, *don't scoop*; take plenty of sand if ball Snead uses sharper backswing (4) on this stroke than others, but twists body (5), unlocks knee (6), again keeps chin in line with

Precision is more valuable than power here; Sam's swing (7) is designed to lift rather than smash. Body unwinds (8) comparatively slowly, but hands are *ahead* of ball at impact, only an inch behind (9) as ball spins towards green.

Club head moves faster than ball for fraction of second after impac Sam keeps *his* head down (11) until end of short follow-through. Com tion of club head at finish of explosion with that at finish of drive

---

The how-to treatment is more frequently employed in the participant-sports field than in any other. Millions of books and pamphlets show young America how to play shortstop, how to stroke a tennis ball, and so on. Whole advertising campaigns have been based on the same picture technique. In the story above, four magic-eye camera sequences detail every move of Sam Snead, golf champion, as he drives, hits

Snead's iron strokes — like his drives — are clean and crisp

on technique is strikingly similar to that which Snead uses for woods. ifferences: Sam places the ball (1) opposite *center* of stance—slightly his hands (2). Backswing (3) begins with almost exactly same details.

Snead's backswing is shorter than for the driver, but longer than he uses for the sand iron. Compare pictures **4, 5** and **6** above with the same numbers in the tee-shot sequence on page 63; the stance, stroke and body twist are virtually identical.

considerable body turn into downswing (7, 8). For maximum distance ages 150-175 yards with a No. 5), club head should swing only low o pass under ball. Note how club shaft bends (9) as camera records im-

pact. Golf's cardinal rule—*keep your head down*—is emphasized again (10) as Sam sweeps into his follow-through (11). Not until the stroke is completed (12) does he look up to follow ball's flight and begin thinking out his approach shot.

On the green, Sam's advice is simple: think before you putt

is personal—Snead says style is meaningless, that each golfer should he fashion that best *relaxes* him. Sam himself uses a reverse over-lap takes his position slowly (2) and rests weight (3) solidly on *both* feet.

Sam putts off left side of stance (4), although some crack pros prefer center or right balance. Length of backswing (5) depends on distance. As Snead's club meets the ball (6), his knees are bent, his body loose—*never tight or tense.*

trokes with his wrists (some golfers use their arms). This 10-footer ly a brief follow-through (7) as ball rolls toward cup (8). To com-or sloping green, Sam aims to left of cup, propels ball in a curve (9).

End of a perfect round—a bull's-eye. His head is down even as ball nears cup (10-11) and plops in (12). Although he can't remember shooting over 85, Sam offers comfort to duffers—"If you can just break 100, the rest will come easy."

an explosion shot out of a sand trap, approaches a green, and sinks a putt. Arrows and dotted lines help the photograph tell the reader how Snead achieves golfing greatness. The article is deceptively simple, just as a golf shot is simple for Snead; but it had to be carefully planned and executed to get the right camera angles. More than 400 pictures were taken in order to produce these 48.

Charles Boyer and Ingrid Bergman play Gregory Anton and his wife Paula in movie. At this point she is unaware he is plotting her mental breakdown. In *Angel Street's* original company, these roles were played by Judith Evelyn and Vincent Price (*in*

picture at right) whose stage name was Manningham. In contrast to blooming, apple-cheeked Miss Bergman, Miss Evelyn is frail, pallid. Because of Boyer's accent M-G-M made Manningham a foreigner. Price wears a Vandyke and Boyer only his usual toupee.

MOVIE OF THE WEEK:

Gaslight

Bergman and Boyer are the stars of a taut psychological chiller

Last week, in the darkness of motion picture houses throughout the U.S., audiences gasped with fright as gaslight flickered over the moody Victorian household on the screen. They knew that violence was afoot and that any minute blood might splotch the neat antimacassars. The movie was *Gaslight*, a handsome M-G-M period piece about a man who sets out to drive his bride insane in order to complete some unfinished business in connection with the untimely death of another woman. Directed by George Cukor, it is a taut psychological chiller. But besides its scariness *Gaslight* has the fine, disciplined performances of Charles Boyer and Ingrid Bergman in the lea roles to recommend it.

Like *Angel Street*, the most durable mystery in current Broadway history, the movie is an ad tion of *Gaslight*, Patrick Hamilton's London pl 1938. On the idea that the screen will never re the stage, *Angel Street* devotees may carp at th G-M version. For one thing, the film lacks the of *Angel Street's* single set. For another, M converted the play's shuffling, meditative dete into a dashing young blade. Comparative scenes the movie and the play are shown on these p

Anton's carefully planned campaign is calculated to drive his wife insane, have her confined and thus make himself heir to house and cached jewels. He begins by trying to prove her memory is failing. He hides trinkets, then accuses her of having lost them.

Here he has just accused her of removing a picture from the wall. When she protests her innocence, he summons the servants, humiliates her by asking them to swear they didn't remove the picture. At the left housekeeper kisses Bible, at right the maid does same.

Parallel or Contrast

An ancient English poet once wrote that "comparisons are odious," and people have been repeating it for centuries. The fact is, however, that comparisons are sometimes decidedly useful in planning and construction of picture stories. Above, from *Life,* is an article with two

MOVIE

A Scotland Yard detective (Joseph Cotten) visits Paula on an evening when her husband is away. He suspects him of an old, unsolved murder, begs her to assist in establishing Anton's guilt. Leo G. Carroll enacts this role in *Angel Street*

PLAY

(right). In the movie the detective's first appearance on the scene occurs early in the story, is accomplished with considerably less suspense than in the play. In *Angel Street*, Manningham does not see him until almost the end of the play.

MOVIE

At first reluctant to believe that her husband is a murderer, Paula Anton is finally persuaded to listen to the grisly facts about his past history. Cotten's performance as the detective is romantically superficial; Carroll's a masterpiece of

PLAY

sharp characterization. Tensest moment in *Angel Street* comes when the detective is about to leave the room without his hat. Just as he reaches door he remembers it, causing audiences to sigh with relief. This business is not in the movie.

MOVIE

Proof that her husband is guilty comes when the detective shows Paula that Anton's handwriting is identical with that of man whom he suspects killed her aunt in an attempted jewel theft. Unsuccessful in the robbery. Anton married

PLAY

Paula. He believes the jewels are hidden in house she inherited from slain aunt. Scene in *Angel Street* where detective painstakingly jimmies Manningham's desk in order to secure evidence against him is far superior to that of movie.

series of photographs showing how scenes in the motion picture *Gaslight* resembled or differed from those in the stage play *Angel Street,* on which the movie was based. The parallel or contrast technique lifted this ingenious picture story considerably above the ordinary movie review. *Life* has used the same device effectively in other stories, for example in one on movie stars and their stand-ins.

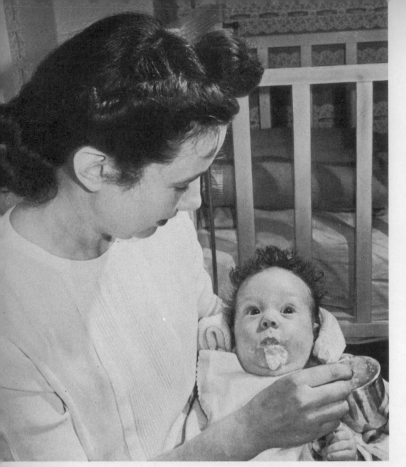

This startled baby is not ready for solid food. Her mother should wait a week or so, then try again.

Let the Baby Be the Boss

By DR. MARTHA ELIOT
Associate Chief, Children's Bureau, U. S. Department of Lab

Babies need no longer be the victims of st timetables and rigid rules prescribed for *average* baby. And firm but worrying parents r no longer pace the floor, listen to Junior's l wails and wonder whether they dare give him 2 a. m. bottle at 1:39. Instead, babies can be tre as human beings, encouraged to satisfy their in vidual desires about what, when and how m they want to eat.

This revolution in infant feeding came a when doctors' offices began to fill up with ba who were not flourishing under the clock-and- system. It was found that each baby had his rhythm of hunger—perhaps morning feed spaced three hours apart, and afternoon and ning feedings at four-hour intervals. It was found that as a baby's stomach grew, he we taper himself off into fewer, larger meals. An there developed today's emphasis on sched tailored to fit individual babies.

Leading pediatricians have discovered, too, each baby knows when he is full, when h ready for his first solid food, when he is wil to give up the bottle for the more sophistica silver cup. No baby can enjoy cereal until swallowing apparatus is able to handle it. I babies want to drink out of a cup when they ar young that their chief pleasure comes from su ing. Any baby will protest violently, and jus ably, if he isn't fed enough—he's hungry and stomach hurts!

Human nature, even in the diaper stage, n be considered. A baby who wants cereal morning at 6:30 won't like waiting until 7 for r formula. Why not let him be the boss?

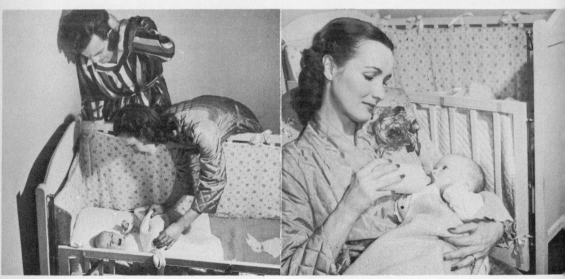

DON'T **keep a crying baby waiting** for his feeding because you have arbitrarily substituted a textbook schedule for one based on his natural hunger cycle. Babies' food demands vary.

DO **feed a hungry baby** when he wants food. Baby can't sleep wher stomach is empty because it contracts and hurts. Parents can't sleep, ei because of crying. After mother feeds her baby, both will go back to

"How to train your child" is the theme of the picture story shown here. Contrast is the continuity device used in presenting it. The "don't and do" method is time-honored, as are its close relatives, "wrong and right," and "before and after." All are frequently employed in editorial and advertising presentations, because they give the reader an immediate feeling of identification with what is happening in

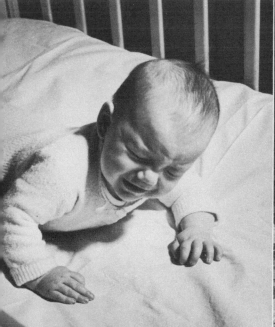

DON'T be afraid that you'll "spoil" your baby if you pick him up and play with him before the clock says feeding time. This lonesome, hungry baby is being left alone to cry till then.

DO play with your baby before feeding him if he wants a little social life. This is the best time to give him the love and attention which he needs—and then he won't mind waiting a few minutes to get his food.

DON'T try to hurry your baby into grown-up feeding habits. This year-old boy pushes his cup away, will go without his milk, because that is the only way he can explain he still needs his bottle.

DO introduce the cup habit gradually. Begin at breakfast or lunch. If your baby is not ready to give up his bottle altogether, let him finish his evening feeding this way. It is relaxing to take bottle on mother's lap.

the pictures and provide specific, quickly grasped points of information and instruction. The writer of this article planned it and helped the photographer execute it after consultation with the authority whose by-line appears above the text block. Every picture situation used was first plotted in a shooting script. After that the job was mostly a matter of being patient with the infants.

2. Elizabeth Janeway, who wrote "The Walsh Girls"

If dark, eager Elizabeth Janeway had spent a year—even two—writing *The Walsh Girls* (Doubleday, Doran), her first effort might have been another stock slick-paper magazine novelette. Instead, she used up seven. Meanwhile, married to Eliot Janeway, special writer for Time, Inc., living in the two-story East River New York apartment formerly occupied by Clare Luce, she has traveled, christened ships, borne two boys, shone on radio's *Information Please. The Walsh Girls* has been called one of the most amazing "female" novels of our era. Reason: it is livid with hate.

But her novel is in no way autobiographical. Its first form was a short story, tale of a young girl in love with a doctor who has an insane wife. It ended as a dark, unhappy novel of two sisters in love with the same man, under the same roof, with one married to him, bearing his child.

Mrs. Janeway, born about 30 years ago in Brooklyn, has lived all her life in the city, not the small town she writes about. She attended Barnard, wrote basement advertising copy for a Brooklyn department store, loves her sister.

Said one lady reviewer: "*The Walsh Girls* makes you ashamed of women." Said The New York Times: "No man who wishes to make even a fumble at understanding the other sex can miss it." Says Mrs. Janeway: "I'm the happiest girl in the world. Two boy babies, a grand husband, a book."

3. Betty Smith, author of "A Tree Grows in Brooklyn

Over 900,000 copies of *A Tree Grows in Brooklyn* (Harper's) have been sold; 50,000 copies distributed to our armed forces. It has been printed in Spanish, Swiss-German, Swedish; will be in Portuguese and French; and the movies (20th Century-Fox) bought it for $55,000.

The heroine of all this is a girl who also grew in Brooklyn, and the book is autobiographical enough to have provoked Betty's cousin into filing a $250,000 libel suit. Betty married at 17, had two children before she was 19. Divorced, she supported her girls, yet managed to attend the University of Michigan and Yale drama school.

Later, she was a feature writer on a Detroit newspaper, wrote and edited plays in Chapel Hill, N. C., where *The Tree* grew. There she married, with what *The New Yorker* called "her passion for anonymity," a soldier named Joe Jones.

She spent a year writing *The Tree*, working an hour a day, from 6 a.m. to 7. Says she: "Sometimes I didn't feel like writing, but my best stuff was done when I felt bad. I'd also scribble down ideas while I waited for pots to boil."

Now 40 and famous, she still drops her "g's" where they fall, is amused when her mother objects to Betty's washing dishes because "it might spoil your hands for 'typing'" and loves to tell about the North Carolina nurseryman who wrote: "Where can I stock the tree that grows in Brooklyn?"

4. John Hersey, the author of "A Bell for Adano"

At 30, John Hersey is a young man ticketed for fame. With two books already to his credit, *Men on Bataan* and *Into the Valley*, he came back last September from a *Life* Magazine assignment in the Mediterranean theater and, in three weeks, set down on paper his first novel, *A Bell for Adano* (Knopf). Tale of the American occupation of an Italian town, it derived advance impetus because of a deafening whispering campaign that the villain might be General Patton. Upon publication, in February, the book surged ahead on its own feet, has sold over 70,000 copies to date. Literary men were overwhelmed. Said J. Donald Adams, in the New York Times: "The most promising writer since Steinbeck; everything needed for a first-rate novelist."

Born in China, child of missionaries, Mr. Hersey attended Yale, then went on to Clare College, Cambridge, England. After a summer at private secretary to Sinclair Lewis, he began his career as a correspondent. Although *Men on Bataan* was compiled from clippings, he spent two weeks under fire on Guadalcanal gathering material for *Into the Valley*, was commended for his action in aiding wounded. On four occasions he has survived airplane crashes, two in the Pacific, two in the Mediterranean. Now paused in an intelligent apartment in New York's East Sixties, he is married, has two small sons. Future plans: books, short fiction, no Hollywood.

5. Lillian Smith, whose best-seller is "Strange Fruit

High on best-seller lists today is Florida-born Lillian Smith's first novel, *Strange Fruit* (Reynal & Hitchcock), dealing with the relations of "whites and blacks." Taking its title from the song—"Southern trees bear a strange fruit, blood on the leaves and blood at the root, black bodies swinging in the Southern breeze, strange fruit hanging from the poplar trees"—Miss Smith's tale is a shocker.

Granddaughter of an important slave owner, sixth in a family of eight children, Lillian was trained to be a concert pianist. But in her early twenties, she visited China as music teacher in a Methodist mission, there tasted her first hot anger over race prejudice. Returning home, she took over with one hand the fashionable girls' camp her father had started in Clayton, Ga.; with the other, she helped her friend, Paula Snelling, found an anti-prejudice quarterly, *South Today*. But a relentless inner compulsion drove her to dramatize her cause in a novel.

Strange Fruit, banned in Boston because Miss Smith twice used a four-letter Anglo-Saxon word, is now in its eleventh printing, sells about 15,000 copies each week. It has been compared to *Uncle Tom's Cabin*, translated into Swedish and Spanish. But, like all these five first novelists, the question of whether Lillian Smith will be called a great writer rests on one factor: her next book.

Layout

Every successful picture story has layout continuity to some degree—which simply means that it is presented in a visual or typographical pattern carried through from one page to another. In some cases, however, the need for a stylized layout pattern is extreme because of the

REPUBLICANS HAVE AN ABLE CONGRESSWOMAN

Ohio's best political traditions are well represented in Washington by Mrs. Chester C. Bolton, who is the state's first and only woman representative. Mrs. Bolton, who was elected in 1939 from a conservative Republican district in suburban Cleveland, is probably the richest member of Congress. Her husband, whom she succeeded after his death, was the son of Mark Hanna's business partner. But Mrs. Bolton has been no party hack in Congress. She voted against the Smith-Connally bill to outlaw strikes and voted for the Administration's soldier-vote bill (she has two sons in service). She voted to sustain the President's tax bill veto. Once vaguely classed with the Congressional isolationists, she rose in 1944 to speak in favor of UNRRA. Having made a good record by voting in accordance with her own convictions, she is certain of re-election in November. Here she stands in doorway of Perry House, her family's mansion on famous Euclid Avenue, which was built in 1844 and is now used as a nursing center.

LABOR TAKES A STRONG HAND IN ELECTIONS

This year the Republicans and Democrats, strong and usually equally matched in Ohio, have to reckon with a third potent voting force. These are the political action committees of organized labor, which do not nominate their own candidates, but work skilfully to elect labor's friends and defeat labor's foes in any party. In Cleveland the CIO, AFL, Railroad Brotherhoods and independent Telephone Workers' Union have a Joint Committee for Political Action which is credited with registering almost all the county's 28,000 new voters this year. The committee worked as soon to get out a big primary vote; the older parties pretty to keep it tight. When gray-haired CIO President Phil Murray (at head of table, above) was in Cleveland last month the J. C. P. A. threw a lunch for him at the Hollenden Hotel and promised more action in the fall election. They are already selling Roosevelt buttons and raising $100,000. And with CIO's Political Action Committee, they are now working to organize all of Cleveland on a ward-to-ward basis for Term IV.

CINCINNATI'S TAFTS ARE A PROUD DYNASTY

The intellectual leader of the Republican Party in Ohio is Senator Robert A. Taft, 55, who was first in his class at Yale, first in his class at Harvard Law School, and a member of the great Ohio family which dominates Republican Cincinnati. This photograph shows Bob Taft in front of a wall decoration in the presidential suite of the Carter Hotel in Cleveland, just before he held a veterans' meeting that there must be a new league of nations after this war. The great danger to such a league, he declared, would not be from U. S. isolationists, but "from the demands of England or Russia and failures in our . . . foreign policy." Bob Taft's grandfather was in the Grant cabinet and later minister to Russia, and Bob has been close to the presidency during much of his life; he played in the White House as a boy during Teddy Roosevelt's terms; his own father was President from 1909 to 1913. He himself was Ohio's "favorite son" for the presidency in 1940. This year he stepped aside in favor of Governor Bricker. But in a deadlock he would be very available.

MOST VOTERS LIVE IN TOWNS OR BIG CITIES

In Ohio town and city people outnumber farm dwellers by at least two to one. Nearly a quarter of Ohio's voters lives in the two big cities—Cleveland, which is usually Democratic, and Cincinnati, which is regularly Republican. Another quarter is divided among smaller manufacturing centers like Youngstown and Mansfield and Akron and Toledo. The rest lives on farms and in quiet American towns like New Richmond (above), where Front Street, with its old brick business blocks and new neon signs, runs alongside the Ohio River. Ohio is a good practical barometer state because its voting population is a good cross-section of the U. S. Downstate Ohio, which was settled earlier than the rest, is the center of Republican strength. The Democratic strongholds are Cleveland, with an enormous foreign-born population, and Youngstown-Warren, the second largest steelmaking district in the nation. Ohio has voted three times for Franklin Roosevelt, but it has a Republican governor, two Republican senators, and 20 (out of 23) Republican representatives.

---

weakness or absence of other unifying elements. Two examples of articles held together largely by layout treatment are shown above. On the left are four pages from a LOOK article on five writers whose first novels were best-sellers. On the right are four pages from *Life's* article entitled *Political Ohio*. In each case, the picture area and the area given to type are the same on every page.

Donald Duck Dodges Depression

—and Walt Disney shows
one way movies could help
rouse America to its peril

© Walt Disney Productions

1 If Hollywood joined the anti-depression fight, Walt Disney would the front line. Here he shows how Donald Duck might explain inf to millions. . . . Fade-in: Farmer Donald is reading "Help Wanted"

2 Essential war work at big pay—that's for Donald. Forgetting the farm, he quickly lands a good job. . . . Other studios might treat inflation or depression in cartoons, short subjects, newsreels or even feature pictures.

3 Here's Donald on his first payday, loaded to the ears with quick Like millions of others, he is now earning more than ever before millions, he rushes off to spend it on whatever the stores have t

I'LL TAKE TWELVE OF THESE, IF THAT'S ALL YOU HAVE!

4 But the situation has gone to his head. He doesn't need 12 suits—and, my, prices have certainly gone up. Still, who cares? It's his money, isn't it? And there's plenty more where that came from, isn't there?

WAR BONDS

ONE TEN CENT WAR STAMP, PLEASE

5 Not that Donald isn't patriotic. He wants to win the war. He kno Government needs money, so every now and then he lends it a l his loose change. And yet—somehow that gesture isn't quite e

Development of a Theme

When the picture-story writer tackles the problem of putting over a point of view in addition to providing information, his task becomes complicated. On the spread above, an attempt was made to persuade readers to save wartime earnings and buy War Bonds instead of luxuries.

the demands of war have put things out of balance. American indus-
is producing acres of war material (which is why Donald has such a
-pay job in the first place)—but mighty little for civilian consumption.

7 This means that the money paid war workers (and their employers) far
outweighs the value of available civilian goods. Every three dollars of
spending money bids for two dollars' worth of goods. And prices rise.

I WONDER HOW
MUCH A FRESH
LOAF WOULD COST!

ess it is checked, the inflationary spiral will eventually make Don-
 and everyone else bid fantastic sums for life's barest necessities.
e day money will be wholly worthless. Then—into depression we go.

9 Right here Donald sees the light. By putting every cent he can into War
Bonds or his savings account, he can help balance the amount of money
in circulation with the supply of goods. That helps hold prices down.

ut even more: he's investing in his own future. After the war, civilian
oods will be plentiful and cheap—for those who can buy. Life itself
ill be wonderful — for those who have money. *Donald will have it.*

11 Then he'll leave the job in the grimy city, build himself a modern new
farm, enjoy life to the full. And as he buys the things *he* wants, he'll
be helping to make *America* prosperous. Why don't *you* try Donald's way?

Several of the continuity devices previously discussed in this chapter were employed
in developing the editorial theme. For example, it is presented in a narrative chronology, with the repeated identity of a known personality (Donald Duck) and
layout devices (panels and numbers) helping to hold it together. Almost always, a
combination of continuities is more effective than a single one.

CHAPTER 4

Ideas for Picture Stories

IT IS AXIOMATIC in magazine offices that an article can be no better than the idea behind it, a conviction as true of picture articles as of text articles. Poor execution can spoil a good story idea, it is true; but even brilliant execution cannot rescue a bad one.

There are now dozens of publications using picture stories of one kind or another with varying frequency. It is impossible to set up rules to guide the selection of ideas for all publications, since each has its own audience and its own peculiarities. We have to deal in generalities and attempt to provide standards which will apply to most of the large-circulation media using picture-story ideas more or less regularly.

Discussion of these standards centers around answers to two questions:

A. By what criteria should picture-story ideas be judged?

B. What are the best sources of such ideas?

The first question may be answered by listing five qualities which are essential to good picture stories:

1. An interest that transcends spot news; a vitality that cannot be sapped by news developments.

2. Picture impact.

3. Sharp focus.

4. Focus on people, as opposed to things.

5. Universal interest.

The first of these qualities is apparently difficult for many writers to understand, especially those with newspaper experience. They point to *Life* as an example of a magazine which publishes news-picture stories. They are right; *Life* does publish some, although a great many of its true picture stories are not dependent on a current news "peg." But no other large-circulation magazine uses picture stories in the news field. One reason is this: most picture articles require considerable planning, and their preparation is generally a time-consuming process. An idea for a picture story which will be "dated" in a few weeks, or even months, is therefore of little value.

Of no greater value is an idea which does not provide the kind of picture interest and picture impact which have been discussed in previous chapters. This criterion provides another difficulty for most writers who are accustomed to thinking in terms of words. To succeed as creators of picture-story ideas, and of the stories themselves, they must stop thinking solely in terms of word images and begin thinking in terms of visual images as well. Once a writer has learned to visualize a story, his battle is half won.

The third desirable quality, sharp focus, has already been stressed repeatedly. It cannot be stressed too often; nothing so handicaps successful execution of a picture story as planning it with too broad a scope. A single picture story on a small town would be possible, but difficult; on one block in a town it would be less difficult; on a family, comparatively simple;

on one member of a family, easy.

This brings us to the fourth point, the desirability of focusing on people. Whatever the story, chances are it can be made most interesting if it is told in terms of people doing things. It is possible, of course, to focus on an inanimate object: e.g., a house. But any readership test ever made will demonstrate that the article will have more readers, and more interested readers, if there are people in the house.

The fifth quality essential to most good picture stories is universal interest. For mass-circulation magazines it is indispensable. A bane of every editor's life is the writer who consistently submits ideas for stories which fascinate him and his friends but would not appeal to the other eight or ten million persons who read the magazine. Pictures are a universal language, but picture stories can be universal only if they are based on ideas which dip into and reflect the lives and feelings of great masses of people.

The second question asked is: "What are the best sources of picture-story ideas?" These are, in the order of their importance:

1. Newspapers and news magazines.
2. Technical and trade magazines.
3. Books.
4. Your own experience.

To indicate newspapers and news magazines as the best sources of picture-story ideas is not to contradict previous advice to avoid spot-news angles. A newspaper item is hardly ever sufficient basis in itself for a picture article, but it often can be the springboard for one. For example, a brief feature in a New York newspaper noted the birth of a tiger cub at the Bronx zoo. It was accompanied by pictures. From them, a picture-magazine editor developed the idea of photographing the cub each week until it was full grown. The result—a picture story of the life of a tiger

from birth to maturity—took 24 months, but editors and readers agreed that it was worth the time and effort.

The next best sources of picture-story ideas are technical and trade magazines. From these, as from news publications, the intelligent picture-story writer can spot trends worth watching and pursuing, and frequently he can find material which has not yet been presented to a mass audience. Of course, research and planning are required to translate this material into picture language for a mass audience.

Books, especially technical books designed for specialized readership, are also an excellent source of ideas. The sale of such works is limited, but they sometimes contain information that would interest millions if presented in popularized form. Usually, it is necessary to secure the publisher's permission to use material appearing in a book, but most authors and publishers are happy to have their works mentioned in a mass-circulation publication. Here again, the picture-story writer and editor are confronted with the job of translating the raw material into visual form.

One's own experience, the fourth important source of ideas, is of first importance for some kinds of writing. In visual, factual reporting for a mass audience, however, it does not rank that importantly. Yet all experience is valuable to the picture-story worker insofar as he applies it to the creation of picture language appealing to the minds and feelings of others.

There is almost limitless opportunity for intelligent, creative writers who can learn to think in visual terms. The freelance market for the sale of picture-story ideas is limited; but there is a definitely expanding market for the talents of staff members who can plan and produce picture stories and articles possessing the qualities discussed in this chapter.

1. Panic rode on the heels of the Black Plague which swept over Europe during the Middle Ages. Crowds raced blindly from city to city attempting to escape the pestilence. Their flight only served to spread the disease faster.

3. It was started by a cow—Mrs. O'Leary's. Terrified Chicagoans sought escape from the fire of 1871 via the Randolph Street Bridge. Reason could have saved the scores of persons who were trampled to death.

2. Man is like a moth. When New York's Bowery Theatre burst into flames in 1845, the house was empty. But scores of persons attracted by the fire narrowly missed injury in the mob excitement of the spectators.

4. Two Irishmen got in an argument on July 12, 1871. New York's 84th Regiment was called out to settle the political "Orange Riot" that resulted. A needless volley from the guns of excited soldiers took the lives of several Eighth Avenue spectators.

5. "Fire!" The cry is often more dangerous than fire itself. In 1876, a blaze broke out in the Brooklyn Theatre. There was ample time for the audience to escape, but hysteria which followed the cry of "Fire!" brought disaster.

6. Killed by unmeaning murderers. When the boat General Slocum caught fire in New York harbor in 1904, frantic passengers and crew battled each other instead of the flames. Some were drowned, more died in the battle to escape via jammed gangways.

7. They wanted to be first across Manhattan's new Brooklyn Bridge in 1883. Sudden hysteria brought death and injury to the struggling mob.

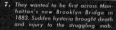

8. Chicago's Iroquois Theatre (1903) was a death trap for 575 patrons.

A newspaper publishes a story of panic spreading death and destruction through an American city. An editor on the staff of *Coronet* reads it and has an idea. Result: an exciting, shocking picture story on panic through the ages, eight pages of which are shown here. This is an example of a "compiled" picture story—the combination of a good idea and painstaking search for photographs and drawings that vividly and

9. Death took the Holiday. Jammed with picnickers, the steamer Eastland waited at its landing in the Chicago River. Slowly it began to capsize, catapulting terrified passengers into the water.

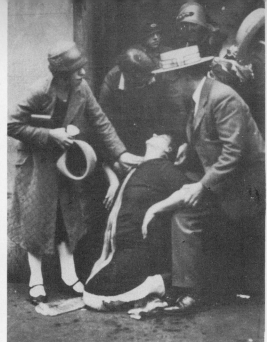

11. Hero worship was the reason. Ten thousand film fans milled before Campbell's Funeral Church, New York, in 1926, to get a view of Rudolph Valentino's coffin. Mounted policemen broke up the mob, but not before a hundred-odd women were injured by the hysterical throng.

10. Escape for those boxed in between decks became impossible when the grand staircase collapsed under the weight of hundreds battling for their lives. Thus, only a few yards from land, nearly a thousand victims, such as the woman shown above, were sacrificed to panic.

19. Panic, not bombs. On June 5, 1941, Chinese leaving Chungking's largest air raid shelter after a Jap foray suddenly heard another alarm. Those outside attempted to get back inside against the tide exiting. Bodies piled up ___, the air inlets were blocked. An estimated 4,000 lost their lives.

20. Race hatred is man-made animalism. We are still hearing repercussions of the Detroit riot started in March, 1942, by white pickets who opposed Negroes moving into a defense housing project.

dramatically support the central theme. The putting together of such an article requires patience in high degree and a thorough knowledge of picture sources. Important picture magazines have picture-research specialists who spend all their working hours in such searches. Other publications depend more heavily on the advice and assistance of numerous commercial picture agents.

109

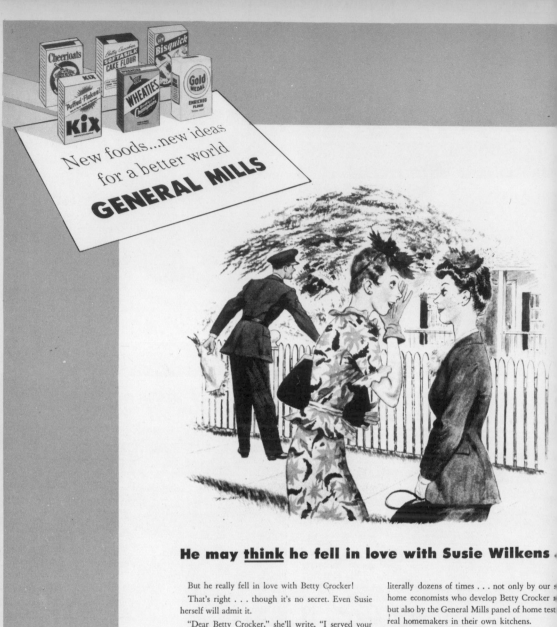

The article beginning on the opposite page ran through seven pages in LOOK in the days when America's Army training program was going full blast in all parts of the country. It is presented here, just as it appeared in the magazine, with the first page facing a General Mills advertisement. Although many of them hate to admit it, editors have a responsibility to advertisers as well as readers—not to permit

Night and day, the Leesville Hotel is bombarded by incoming Army wives. Turned away, Dorothy Dennis (center) asks her husband, "what next?"

Don't Visit Your Husband in an Army Town

Congested and hectic, it's generally no place for a soldier's family. The wise wife stays at home

On train, plane and bus they come—sleepy-eyed, grimy, slumped in seats—the vast, unrecruited legion of servicemen's wives. Invading communities near our more than 1,200 military camps, each is determined to snatch a few hours, weeks, months if possible, with her soldier.

In most camp towns, the problem of accommodating visitors has become critical. Rooming houses and hotels, if any, are bursting; civilian homes are overflowing. Army wives have had to sleep in railroad stations, sit up in all-night cafes, even live in remodeled chicken coops. Food prices and rents have skyrocketed. Sanitation fa-

cilities are overtaxed. Wives who left friends, parents and comfortable homes behind find such towns no romantic garden spots, but dull, dusty, grim.

This is the documentary story of one Army wife and a representative camp town. Dorothy Dennis, wife of Sgt. James Wiley Dennis, of Lewisburg, Tenn., arrived in Leesville, La., eight miles from Camp Polk, a month after he was transferred there. Her experiences, paralleling those of thousands of other Army wives, are pictured in the following pages.

Like every other camp town, Leesville is harassed but booming. Since January,

1941, when the Army started to build Camp Polk, Leesville's population has jumped almost sixfold—from 3,200 to 18,000. Until then, the town—in an area of cutover timberland—struggled along. In recent months, the community has expanded its water supply and sewerage systems, paved streets, cooperated in building 475 housing units (chiefly for officers).

Despite such valiant and zealous efforts to meet "the invasion," Leesville is a flat disappointment to the young bride of a soldier. To Dot Dennis—and to virtually every other migrant wife—"back home" soon became "God's country."

advertising domination of editorial content, but to plan a magazine so that advertising copy with direct appeal to women will run, if possible, with editorial matter having the same appeal, and so on. The article above, interesting to both men and women, originated with an idea obtained from a newspaper story describing the Army's difficulties in dealing with camp-following wives.

DOT ARRIVES IN LEESVILLE...
After her 490-mile trip from home, seeing
Jim is momentary heaven. But the battle
to stay in this Army town has only begun.

In judging the suggestion for an article on wives visiting husbands in Army camps, the editors decided: (A) that it had a potential interest transcending "spot" news; (B) that it would not produce startlingly exciting pictures but should develop many of real human interest; (C) that the story could be executed with a sharp focus, i.e., on one army wife; (D) that it automatically focused on people doing things; (E) that it

. . AND SEARCHES FOR A PLACE TO LIVE

Almost anything with four walls becomes home to an Army family.

"**. . . o Vacant Rooms"** faced Mrs. Dennis at both of ...sville's two small hotels. After consulting the ...O and local Red Cross office, she was lucky to be put up for three days (maximum) at Camp Polk's Guest House, generally reserved for relatives of ill soldiers. During that time. Dot explored the coun- tryside. At Sandy Hill, two miles from camp, she found eight Army families living in the settlement shown above; one privy for "Ladies," one for "Gents."

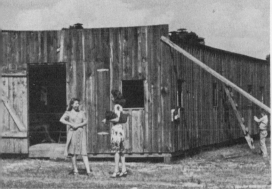

. . . o local girls, a waitress and a laundress, share this habitation with Mrs. ...lter Joyner, of North Carolina, and her soldier-husband, who pays $15 a ...nth for their space. "Homes" like this were abandoned by laborers who built ...mp Polk. The Army declared many unsanitary shacks "off limits" for soldiers.

Property owner: Pfc. C. J. Rollo, of Montgomery, Ala., paid $35 for this "bunga- low" to house his wife and 9-month-old child (above). Soldiers had built it for a previous tenant. Four out of five residents of Leesville have taken in roomers or boarders; in Mayor Oscar Morris' home there are now four families of Army men.

. . . st of the Army wives in this 12-room boarding house at New Llano, four ...es from Camp Polk, work in a laundry or cleaning plant. Not all the housing ...nd around Leesville is ramshackle. A number of tourist cabins are comfort- ...e, but rent as high as $4.50 a night. Neat cottages are already occupied.

"It's like camping out," is the philosophical attitude of Mrs. John Lawrence (standing), of Scranton, Ia. This is the best home she and her husband could find—three miles from Leesville, only $3 a week. Cows and turkeys wander about the place. Some Army couples live in trailers, some in converted railroad cars.

DOT FINDS A ROOM CONTINUED ON NEXT PAGE

would be of interest to many millions of Americans. Thus, it met the requirements we have set up for picture-story ideas and was assigned to a writer and photographer. Two of the writer's primary tasks were to find the right locale and a genuine Army wife who would photograph well. Pages 2 and 3 of his story, shown above, indicate that he succeeded with both problems.

Army couples occupy three of the five rooms here.

After combing the area, Sgt. and Mrs. Dennis pounced on this 10 x 12 room in James Laurent's home, over a mile from Leesville, nine miles from North Camp Polk. Rental is $9 a week. Eight adults, five children, are cramped in the cot- tage, compete for one bathroom. A few yards from the window, a garbage d attracts swarms of flies. Odors from an overflow of sewage are almost unbear: Dot deplores the heat, the lack of privacy, optimistically hopes to move s

DOT FINDS A ROOM AND LEARNS IT'S NOT "HOME, SWEET HOME"

Household chores are made difficult by inadequate facilities. Although sociable, Dot has made no friends, spends much of her time in her room reading. Many wives sit around USO or the camp Service Club.

Icebox in yard is used by all four families. Once a day, Dot takes the 20-minute walk to Leesville for her shopping. Big event to her is Jim's homecoming in the evening—sometimes 'as late as 11 o'clock.

Walking on Sunday—virtually their only re tion. On week ends, Dot and Jim go to a movie other evenings they stay at home. Leesville is busy with housing to tackle amusement probl

Because no picture in this article could be counted on for terrific impact, the writer had to prepare a shooting script which would provide the impact of "human interest" through the cumulative effect of many related pictures. He prepared this script, or picture outline, after visiting the camp and the nearby town, Leesville, La., and observing the daily activities of the sergeant's wife who had consented to be the

Shopping in a town outside an Army camp is frequently a scramble. Food prices in Leesville are at least 10 per cent above those in the nearest city, Alexandria.

heroine of the piece. Her own surroundings provided the picture situations, and her monotonous routine was the obvious chronology to use. Picture-story writers are frequently asked: "Don't you have a lot of trouble getting people to pose?" The answer is: usually not. Most human beings, even the richest and most important ones, seem to delight in having their pictures taken.

Besides the 37 bars in and near Leesville, the town offers little more than some trinket shops, half a dozen restaurants, a shooting gallery, a few grocers, makeshift stores, a courthouse and jail. Rooming houses dot the side streets. There are no parks, play grounds or libraries. Streets are cleaned irregularl

Sipping a "coke" is one way to kill time until Daddy is through soldiering for the day. One in five wives brings along a child or two. For such families, finding a decent home becomes more complicated.

A long queue is always waiting to get into the three movie houses in town, each seating about 550. Only other entertainment: in Leesville, a boisterous carnival; two miles from town, a roller-skating rink.

Restaurants are usually jammed. Menus are limite meals are poorly prepared. Many Army wives, rooms with primitive cooking facilities, complain th restaurant prices are "awful — they change daily

To clinch the story of the Army wife's difficulties in Leesville, writer, editor and photographer agreed on a final spread to be devoted to the town itself and to the opinions of officers, men and wives living there. The article could have concluded with the experiences of our heroine on the preceding page, but the decision was that additional force could be obtained from an epilogue in which other persons in

NO PLACE TO GO . . . BUT LEESVILLE

Just for a change of scene—and maybe a beer—thousands of men like these will pack the town, walk aimlessly for hours.

urday afternoon, the boys line up for the eight-bus trip. Eager for a bit of fun, they find little of it in Leesville. And knowing what Army towns are like, many a soldier discourages his wife from joining him. "When there's a war on," observes one corporal, "for women, there's no place like home."

OULD YOU BRING YOUR WIFE TO LEESVILLE?

wouldn't want my wife and two children in an overcrowded town like this one. It sure is tough on the people who have to live here."—Lieut. Elmer Kaiser, Collinsville, Ill.

I've been married only 11 months and my wife's working in Cherokee, Iowa. But, without a decent place for her, I wouldn't bring her here."—Sgt. Robert J. Glow, Storm Lake, Iowa.

"Why should I even consider it? There are no conveniences here, and my two kids would go completely nuts. A private can't afford $50 rent."—Pvt. Wm. Johnson, Ava, Mo.

"Sure, I'd rather have her here with me. I think she could manage somehow, though I wouldn't want her to live in something uncivilized."— Pfc. Tom Wanner, St. Louis, Mo.

I miss my wife and two youngsters but I don't want them in Leesville. Living conditions are terrible, prices are high, there's a food shortage."—Lt. Maurice L. Smith, Russell, Kan.

WHAT DO YOU THINK OF THIS ARMY TOWN?

came down to beat my husband up every night, so I like it here. What they need in this burg is places to go — especially a swimmin' pool."—Mrs. Edith Green, Brooklyn, N. Y.

"We were lucky to find a room the first day; they told us 'you're close to God.' What do I like about Leesville? Are you kidding? I think it stinks!"—Mrs. F. Radford, Enid, Okla.

"I've followed my husband to four other camps before this, taking my baby with me into 25 states. This is the worst Army town we've hit."—Mrs. Jeanne Grant, Gardner, Mass.

I and three girls share a nice, cool cabin and I like it. I'd go through any inconvenience to be with my husband. So far, I've seen him two week ends."—Mrs. I. Miles, Louisiana, Mo.

"I've lived in five places since I arrived last July. Leesville's a dive. There isn't a decent place to eat. I wouldn't live here unless I had to."—Mrs. Anne Turner, Philadelphia, Pa.

the same circumstances would affirm the typicality of her experiences. This, of course, forced a departure on the final spread from the narrow, personalized focus of the remainder of the story. Primarily because of this, a layout continuity device—subheads reversed on dark panels—was added to the repeated-identity and chronology continuities employed in the first five pages.

It's in the Bag

← **This fuchsia** quilted pouch slung on a black vet cord gives a "1944 look" to the L-85 silhoue

This is a sample of the "prediction" story so popular with editors and readers—a forecast of things to come. The original idea, suggested by a fashion writer, was to predict increasing importance of fashion accessories in a war year because of government restrictions on manufacture of garments. Accessories include gloves, belts, bags, scarves, costume jewelry and so on. "Too diffused," said the editor. "Get the focus down

...er soft, and supple enough to drape like velvet ...s this smartly luxurious, roomy shoulder bag.

A plaid pouch adds color to sports costumes. It may be worn with a matching suit or with solid-color tweeds.

Hand-tooled cowhide postilion bag, although expensive, is a lifetime investment.

...lder bags like this smart mocha cocktail carry-...uld be "fitted" to the arm length of the wearer.

Telling accent for the plain suit is a sleek, fitted, fur pouch which leaves hands free to push perambulator.

Her heart-shaped felt shoulder bag does not interfere with this young lady's play:

...oulder bags, exciting accessories ...ll dramatize the 1944 silhouette

By GERTRUDE BAILEY

Fashion editor, New York World-Telegram

...e drama of dressing in 1944 will lie in the ...xaggerated role of accessories — such as ...lder bags, now an established part of the ... silhouette. When the WPB made rule L-85 ...iting yardage), it shrewdly admitted "if ...ut American women in barrels they'd slit ...n up the side, trim them with lace." WPB ...ained from limiting style or size of hand-..., length of gloves, design of belts. Women will discover that whopping duffel

bags are as convenient as they are smart; that gloves will lend daytime conventionality to the bare backs under boleros, to almost sleeveless dresses due to appear on city streets by summer; that hats, so tiny they are at a vanishing point, are apt to cost more than dresses with which they are worn (milliners are enjoying the biggest boom in 14 years); that blouses will zoom to the proportions of entire wardrobes; that belts, no longer a mere definition of the waistline, will assume the importance of panniers and peplums; and that jewelers will celebrate a veritable diamond jubilee. The girls will make a few basic dresses do the work of more extensive apparel, but they will splurge on "the little touches"—no longer as "little" as they used to be.

The 1944 "look" has sneaked in without outdating last year's dress, yet is different as the neat new hairbuns. Heads are sleek, shoulders almost normal, color a major consideration. Watch for Mardi Gras prints this spring in flower colors or adorned with familiar objects like matchbooks.

The new look lacks the subtlety of prewar Parisian styles that depended on intricate draping, unlimited yardage. Ours is the direct approach. American designers, working under restrictions, have shaken themselves free of French nostalgia. They are on the track of a new, forthright style which, once achieved, may well prove to be the beginning of American fashion independence—even after Paris is back in the picture.

to one kind of accessory." Consequently, the fashion editor concentrated pictorially on bags with shoulder straps, using a variety of bags on several types of models for her pictures, originally reproduced in four colors. The resultant picture article, held together by the repeated identity of an object, is complemented by text presenting a more generalized forecast.

Prejudice in its ultimate form means violence—last resort of vigilante action and terror against our "second-class citizens." This Negro being assisted by two white men was stoned in a race riot by other white Americans demanding segregation at a Detroit housing project. In general, the process of intolerance may start with comparatively harmless social snobbery, give way to active denunciation of a minority group, and lead to serious street fights and riots

THESE ARE THE EVILS: Segregation . . . Poverty

Underlying our prejudices, whether racial, religious or cultural, is fear—the fear of being overrun, changed or diluted, done out of our jobs or social positions. Thus prejudice is a defense of our particular status quo, our "pure" race, our "right" faith. Too many Americans who should know better shy away from people who appear to be "different" and deliberately or unconsciously wall them off.

Segregation—Shame of Democracy

Probably the most common symptom of our malady is segregation. The South's Jim Crow caste system, at odds with all democratic principles, separates the Negro on trains and buses, excludes him from parks, hotels, restaurants, beaches and schools frequented by whites, seats him in a "nigger heaven" balcony at the theater. Even in our armed forces, Negro enlisted men are often kept apart.

To a lesser extent, Filipinos and Mexicans on the West Coast are barred from "white"

restaurants, segregated in theaters. Chinese are apt to be confined to "Chinatowns."

Advertisements for resorts or for the sale or rent of property often stipulate "Protestant Only" or "White Only" or "Gentile Only." Restrictive clauses in property deeds, agreements among neighborhood associations and real-estate agents set up the equivalent of a "No Dogs Allowed" ban against the unaccepted. Even wartime-housing projects are likely to discriminate. In Northern cities, colored ghettos have become worse, rather than better.

By-products: Disease, Poverty, Crime

One effect of physical segregation in slums and "shacktowns" is overcrowding, which in turn produces poverty, squalor, disease, crime and ignorance. Here, even such elementary needs as garbage disposal and fire prevention are generally inadequate.

Illness of almost every kind is pronounced in the Black Belts of virtually every city where

Negroes have settled. Pneumonia and scar[let] fever, for instance, hit their highest peak the[re] Infant mortality among Negroes in Chicago [is] twice as high as it is in the rest of the ci[ty] Among the *Hispanos* (Spanish-Americans) [of] New Mexico, the tuberculosis death rate is ab[out] three times the national rate; in San Francisco Chinatown, it is three times the city's avera[ge]

In supporting segregation, as *One Nati[on]* points out, America is subsidizing social ev[ils] When diseases in slums break away and beco[me] epidemic, when anti-social behavior created [by] slum living turns into a crime wave, or wh[en] race tensions explode into riots and bloodsh[ed] the entire population pays the bill.

Wanted: Equal Opportunities

Reinforcing the fencing-in process, e[co-] nomic discrimination resists the efforts of [our] sub-citizens to rise out of their "class." A nu[m-] ber of business firms will not employ Catho[lics] or Jews. The South recognizes "white me[n's]

A book by Wallace Stegner, *One Nation*, was the basis for this magazine picture-text combination entitled *Prejudice: Our Postwar Battle*. As usual with article ideas based on books, the chief trap to avoid was the tendency to do too much. The final decision was to use five pages, organized as follows: an introductory page; a spread depicting the evils of prejudice, pictorially and textually; and a final spread giving

yal Japanese-Americans may now return to the West Coast states, but
ring their absence in relocation camps anti-Japanese feeling—as this sign
ows—has grown worse. Jingoistic groups foment much of this hatred.

Hoodlumism may take the form of knocking over tombstones in a Catholic
cemetery—like this one in New Jersey—or vandalism in synagogues and
churches. Disagreement with any religious belief never justifies such action.

ti-Jewish feeling in America is not often violent, but prejudice in Nazi
oring crops out in such signs as this on a railroad underpass in New York
y. They indicate youthful gangs have been infected by rabble-rousers.

Bad housing retards families such as these Mexican migrant farm workers.
Segregation from "white" residential areas prevents the underprivileged from
escaping the slum evils of disease, crime, ignorance, vice, delinquency.

ence ... Job Discrimination ... Hate Propaganda

s" and "nigger jobs," the latter being the vile, the low-paid and the unpleasant. irty-two labor unions either exclude Negroes ehunt them into Jim Crow locals. Hate strikes ve broken out against hiring and upgrading Negroes, in the North as well as the South.

Highly trained Chinese and Japanese have en forced into menial jobs. Mexicans and Fili- os generally have been confined to back- eaking migrant labor. Although the man- wer shortage and the President's Fair Em- yment Practices Committee have recently ded to even up work opportunities, wide- ead discrimination persists.

Schools Are Hand-me-downs

As with jobs and homes, education is of- ed to some minority groups only on inferior separate terms. Certain colleges and profes- nal schools have "quotas" for Jews and the ored races. The system of separate schools for ored children, prevalent in the South, shows

signs of spreading to the North. Southern schools for Negroes are crowded, inadequately equipped; colored teachers draw salaries lower than those of white teachers. Mexicans in Los Angeles and other Southwest communities have similar educational hand-me-downs.

The Law, Too, Is Prejudiced

Inevitably, legal discrimination has become part of the pattern of keeping the sub-American "in his place." Police protection for minorities is frequently a farce. "Law and order" too often is applied according to the ruling caste, class, color and faith. When hoodlums attack a minority group, victims rather than aggressors are jailed —"for protection." Voting procedures like the poll tax in seven Southern states, or direct in- timidation at balloting or registration places, rob Negroes and others of their franchise.

The ultimate stage of the sickness known as prejudice is violence. It may take the form of hoodlumism, vigilante action or terror. Recent

incidents directed at Negroes, Jews, Japanese, Mexicans and Filipinos have a clear relationship with the Nazi philosophy of hate; the difference is only in degree.

Hate Mongers Use Nazi Methods

Feeding these fires of discord is the slimy propaganda shoveled out by the demagogues who spread their lies via whispers, chain-let- ters, mass meetings, pamphlets and periodicals. Their poison infects all sorts of people. A decent, well-meaning American is likely to swallow the most whiskered myths and generalizations— canards about Catholic "opposition to scientific progress," Jewish "monopoly," Negro and Mexican "shiftlessness," the Filipino "threat to young American womanhood," unfair Chinese "competition with white labor."

The task of checking group tensions, before they break out into a postwar battle, is Amer- ica's challenge. How can we meet it?

(Continued on next page)

the reader specific suggestions on what he can do to help combat these evils. Above is the spread setting forth the evils, with photographs used as confirmation for con- tentions in headline and text. Such pictorial evidence, shocking in its revelation of poverty, violence and discrimination, brings home the evils of prejudice with impact far beyond the power of mere words.

A Negro teacher in a classroom of predominantly white children, as in this New York school, should not be a rarity. Equal opportunity will lift the blight from the lives of minorities, give them a chance to develop as citizens. Not lack of ability but prejudice blocks them from economic, educational and so[cial] progress. Even under handicaps, Negroes, Jews, Catholics, other groups c[on]tribute much to American life—in science, business, education, medicine, a[nd]

WHAT YOU CAN DO: Expose the Lies ... Legislatio[n]

At no time in recent history have the American people been so conscious of racial and religious prejudice as they are today. Under the impact of war and its democratic aims, more has been done to combat discrimination in the past few years than in decades before. Over 200 inter-racial committees, created by public or private agencies, are tackling local issues. But the outcome of our civil war against intolerance must eventually rest with *you*, as a voting citizen, and with your community.

You can help bulwark your democracy against the enemy within. Here are some specific things you can do about it:

Facts Refute the Myths

1. Nail the lies. Refute the moth-eaten labels, libels and worn-out club-car jokes about members of minority groups. Generalizations about any racial or religious group are absurd. The Negro's achievements in the arts and science, in industry and on the fighting front,

blast the myth that he "can't do skilled work," that he is "a child, with a child's emotional equipment and dependence." If the Catholic Church "in politics" scares some people, you can point out that Catholics in America are of virtually every political persuasion.

There Is No Composite "Character"

The Jews are neither a race nor a nation; they are so mixed that generalizing about them is impossible. There is a higher percentage of Jews in the armed services than in the general population. Election statistics prove the Jew is not a Communist. Nor does a study of bank directorates indicate that he is an "international banker." The composite Negro or Catholic or Jew does not exist.

2. Support legislation, both local and national, outlawing the evils of intolerance. Legislative firmness not only can curb prejudice; it can help break down that prejudice by making people learn that the thing they have feared is

no more than an inflated bogey.

New York State has just enacted a law [de]signed to prevent discrimination in employm[ent.] There is need for a permanent federal Fair E[m]ployment Practices Committee, a federal a[nti-]lynching law, repeal of poll-tax statutes, a [ban] on discrimination in our armed forces, scho[ols,] trade unions, housing projects, medical care [...]

Give the Minorities a Chance

3. Help open up equal employment opp[or]tunity, in private industry and governm[ent.] This can be a real contribution to econo[mic] security of minorities and to better harmony[...]

During this war, our second-class citiz[ens] have demonstrated their ability to handle [any] and all jobs, skilled or unskilled, if they are [giv]en the chance of training and experience[...] you're an employer, give them the same kin[d of] chance in peacetime, too.

4. Participate, wherever possible, in e[du]cational campaigns to combat prejud[ice...]

In this final spread of the article on prejudices, text informs the reader of six ways in which he can help combat the evils thereof. Ideally there should be six pictures, each tied to one of the recommendations. But in this case, as they frequently do, editors had to compromise between the ideal editorial pattern and need for the best possible visual pattern. Pictures to achieve the former were either unobtainable or

God Bless America is sung by these children of 24 nationalities in a Los Angeles school. Youth holds the brightest hope for eradication of intolerance. Studies show children have no natural aversion to other races; they learn it, from parents and others. Education alone will not banish suspicions and fears; but it can bring home to American people the pressing need to improve our democracy on all fronts and help remove the threat to the future of our country.

ual Opportunity ... Education ... Know Your Neighbor

Through our schools and churches, young and old must be made to see prejudice not as white versus black, or Protestant versus Jew and Catholic, but as democracy versus fascism.

Schools should become a social pilot plant for the understanding of races, cultures, heredity. In most young people, merely going to school together breaks down the worst prejudices, unless they are subjected outside to propaganda fomenting distrust, snobbery and hatred.

Needed: More Springfield Plans

Schools can actively educate for racial and religious democracy. An outstanding example is the Springfield (Mass.) Plan. A few years ago, this city found that soon its schools would be attended mostly by children of foreign stock, rather than by Yankees. In a decade, these 'across-the-tracks' children, grown up, would run Springfield. Rather than look down on the "minorities," Springfield decided to make them full and equal Americans. So the school board

revised the curriculum, launched an experimental program to meet the problem.

Under the plan, students are given practical experience in working together. Pride in their backgrounds is encouraged. The Negro, Jewish or Polish child gets a chance to learn, write and talk about the contributions his group have made to America. Parents get the same chance through forums and adult classes. The many kinds of people in Springfield have been welded into a community.

Other cities are studying and copying the Springfield Plan. You should try to interest your town in adopting it.

They, Too, Are Fellow-Americans

5. Know your neighbor. Nobody knows so little about a minority group as the average American who has lived near it for years. Since prejudice feeds on ignorance, any sort of contact, any breakdown of the segregation wall tends to weaken or destroy it. Take part in

church, school and community-center get-togethers with people of varied cultural, racial and religious backgrounds.

6. Help marshal public opinion against intolerance. Get behind one of the many interfaith and inter-racial organizations, support your mayor's or governor's committee planning and promoting internal harmony.

Prejudice Endangers Your Own Welfare

You have a personal stake in a working democracy. Prejudice, through the evils it creates, undermines public health, public safety, religion, the home, business.

There is no magic formula to end intolerance in America. We can start with education, better jobs, better housing, more social freedom, more political freedom. Progress in one field advances others. But our basic, important mission is to guide the potential good-will of Americans into channels of working and living together as a nation united.

deemed dull for publication. Thus, two schoolroom scenes symbolizing the hope of eradicating the prejudices of future generations were selected. For many readers, these photographs had shocking impact, as attested by hundreds of letters of protest against showing Negroes and whites in the same classroom—additional proof of need for the article and others like it.

AMERICA EATS

The best-fed nation in the world counts its ration points, tightens its belt, lives tough, eats lean—to win!

Sacrifice on the home front

So you think it's tough, do you . . . meatless days and butterless lunches? Well, don't feel too sorry for yourself; the food you can't get is going to our fighting men

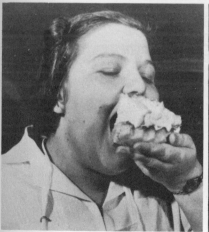

Happy memory! Pie and a mountain of whipped cream.

Umm! It's unrationed and good right down to the bone!

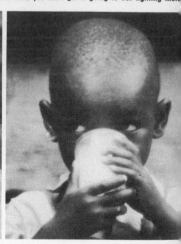

To build strong Americans—free milk for school kids

Both newspaper reading and personal experience prompted a picture-magazine editor to suggest the article of which this spread was a part. The papers were filled with rationing news, and some of his friends were forever complaining that they could not get sufficient meat, butter, or what not. Investigation showed that Americans, as a nation, were eating better than ever and that such home-front shortages

soldiers, sailors and marines—world's healthiest because Uncle Sam balances their diet. If you balance yours, you too can still be well-fed—even under rationing.

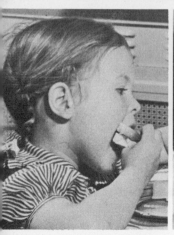

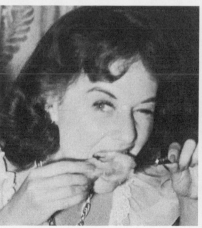

fare—the after-school peanut-butter sandwich.   Gone is Goddard glamour as Paulette gulps the last bite.   It'll always be America as long as you can get a hot dog.

as did exist were largely the result of increased demands from the armed forces. The editor plotted a story to be done with photographs emphasizing both facts, with the title, *America Eats*. Pictures were taken by staff photographers and obtained from the Army and Navy and various agencies. The result was an almost pure picture story, with text confined entirely to heads and one-line captions.

Russian-born dress designer is her own m

VALENTINA IN "BAUTTA" HAT

Valentina is a New York designer who dress smartest women in the U. S. Her best-know tomers are stage personalities: Katharine He Zorina, Lynn Fontanne, Lily Pons. Her best model is herself. Tall, slender and exotic-looking she launches her new styles on her own back York theater openings.

The next day she is besieged at her East 67th Shop by calls from eager customers who want th same thing for themselves. They pay soundly privilege of wearing Valentina dresses ($250 min but their reputation for smart attire is establish moment they mention her name as their dress Much of her fame comes from costumes she ha for the stage, notably *Amphitryon 38*, *Idiot's Delight* and *The Philadelphia S*

Born in Russia 40-odd years ago, Valentina conceals her family name and life. She fled the Revolution when she was 15 and on the way out met her futu band and business manager, George Schlee, in the Sevastopol railroad static was with White Russian army. After their marriage they lived in Athens and where Schlee ran a theater. In 1923 they came to New York. A feminine ac tance, admiring Valentina's clothes, which she designed herself, offered to se up in the dressmaking business. No sooner had they opened a shop than they their angel was penniless. Valentina then opened her own shop with 13 dresse her personal wardrobe. From this unpropitious beginning her dress sales for th year reached $90,000. She now operates a four-story salon employing a staf counts 2,000 customers. Among them are a number of working girls who ski all other items of their clothes budgets to be able to buy one Valentina dress

Husband George Schlee is Valentina's business manager. Here they play Chinese chec an evening in the cozy library of their brownstone house on New York's East 78th S

Valentina is a "natural" as the subject of a picture-personality story. Her exotic appearance, romantic Russian background and beautifully furnished home enhance the interest engendered by the clothes she designs for famous actresses. She has adorned fashion magazines, home-furnishing magazines and publications of general circulation. Above is the first spread of a picture story from *Life* which featured the

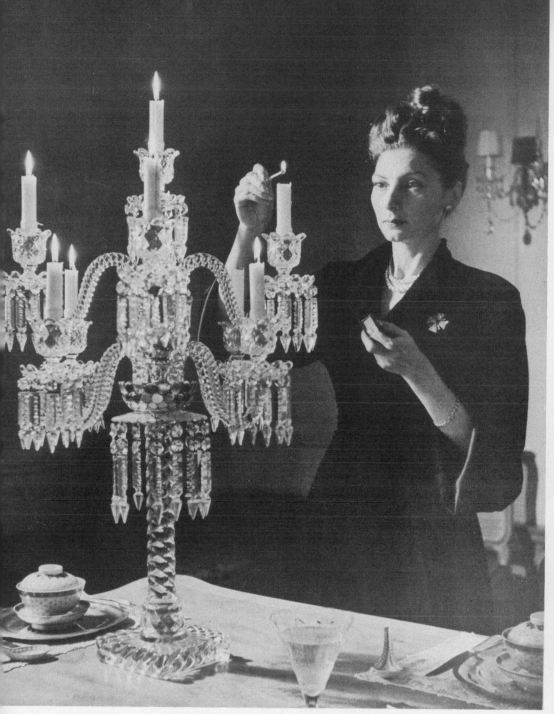

designer against the background of her own home. The charm and beauty of the photographs serve to emphasize the fact that an idea does not have to be brand-new to succeed. As a magazine subject, Valentina was "old stuff," but with a new approach, new situations and imaginative use of lights and background, a writer and photographer team built a new and interesting story around her.

127

CHAPTER 5

The Personality Picture Story

THE PERSONALITY ARTICLE is important to any modern mass-circulation publication. Any editor selling nonfiction to millions of readers knows that he can interest more of them with stories about people than he can with any other single device or combination of devices. That is why, today, nonfiction is an essential ingredient in national magazines—even in those which devote half or more of their editorial space to fiction.

The personality article, feeding a tremendous human appetite for information about human beings, has been the keystone of many a magazine's success. *The New Yorker's* high place in its own self-limited field is largely attributable to its profiles — smoothly written biographical sketches, frequently cruel and sardonic, usually satirical but almost always incisive, informative and entertaining. *Life* runs similar, but generally less biting, pieces under the heading "Close-Up." The *Saturday Evening Post, Collier's, Liberty* and most general monthly magazines all devote a considerable share of their nonfiction space to outright biography of one kind or another. To a lesser extent, so do women's service magazines and the leading fashion periodicals.

Picture magazines generally try to tell stories in terms of people—and in terms of *one person* whenever possible. The picture profile, if we may call it that, presents peculiar problems not applicable to the text profile, along with those common to both. The picture-story writer attempting a personality piece must do everything expected of a writer doing an all-text profile. In addition, he must plan and produce a picture story.

Personality article subjects fall into one of three categories:

1. The well-known personality.
2. The little-known personality who will interest millions of people because of his unknown accomplishments or his eccentricities. He may be either a hero or a screwball, but there must be something fascinating or exciting in his experiences to make him "worth a story."
3. The little-known personality through whom can be told a story of national or international significance. Example: an overworked elderly doctor whose daily life holds up a mirror to national conditions caused by a wartime lack of sufficient medical care in the United States.

Of the three, the well-known personality is editorially most important. Any number of tests have shown us that an article built around a known identity, a genuine national celebrity, will almost invariably attract more readership than a stylistically even more interesting piece dealing with a comparative unknown.

Consequently, the first criterion for evaluating any suggestion for a personality story is the answer to this question: How well known is he? Some writers make the mistake of assuming that a character well known to them and their friends is well known to everybody, or that a local celebrity is a national one.

The editor of a national publication cannot consider any subject really well known who isn't as famous in Sacramento and Chillicothe as he is in New York or Reno.

The second yardstick to be applied is summed up in this question: is there a good reason for doing an article on him at this time? (This time, of course, means two, three or four months hence, or whenever publication is contemplated.)

Once an editor is satisfied with the answers to both these questions, there is a personality article in the making. A picture-story writer assigned to execute it, if he proceeds properly, will take the following steps in the order listed:

1. Read everything he can find that has ever been published on his subject and make ample notes as he reads.

2. Talk to everybody he can find who knows the subject and will talk about the subject.

3. After digesting information obtained by reading and asking questions, consult his editor on the approach to be taken. "What's our angle going to be?" is the inevitable question.

4. Interview the subject, both orally and in writing, if possible.

5. Get his co-operation in the making of new pictures of himself, his family and friends, and make definite appointments for the photographer.

6. Decide, in collaboration with editor and art director, what the picture focus is to be. This usually will be narrower than the text focus, but neither can be decided upon until the writer knows a great deal about the subject.

7. Write a picture-shooting script for the guidance of the photographer, making sure that the photographer is familiar with the story angle and objectives.

8. Supervise the photography.

9. Collect any family pictures or news photos and agency pictures that may fit into the story.

10. Assist the art director in planning the layout of the story.

11. Write the article to fit the layout, blending text with pictures so that the combination will both depict and appraise the personality honestly in the light of what the writer knows about him.

Every step from No. 5 on is peculiar to the creation of a picture profile. The writer assigned to a purely text piece could start hitting the typewriter keys after the fourth step.

Of course, innumerable variations from this routine are possible, depending on the kind of article desired. If, for example, the editor wants a psychological study, the writer may consult psychiatrists before interviewing the subject, or afterwards. If some single action taken by the subject is the focal point of the piece, every effort will be made to discover why it was taken. One watchword for every writer working on any kind of personality story is this: as often as you ask what the person did, ask why.

This applies to the two categories of little-known personalities as well as to the famous ones. With the first of these, the personality who is interesting because of accomplishments or characteristics, the writer will face about the same kind of research job as with a celebrity, but less extensive because the sources will be fewer. The best procedure on this type of article is to get onto one exploit or one unusual facet of character and "ride" it hard.

With the personality who is to be used as a vehicle for a story of general importance, the writer faces these special problems:

1. The individual must be typical, or at least representative, of a large group.

2. He (or she) must look the part. Examples of all three types of articles, presented with a variety of techniques, appear on following pages.

Fifty Years Behind the Footlights

Ethel Barrymore, First Lady of the American Theater, stars simultaneously in a play, a movie, a radio show

At an age when most women are content to embrace grandmotherhood, Ethel Barrymore is at the peak of her career. She is leading a triple life professionally, not to mention a busy private existence. As Aunt Teta in the Theater Guild's rich dramatization of Fránz Werfel's religious novel, *Embezzled Heaven*, Miss Barrymore plays a part she considers as

memorable as that of Miss Moffat in her 1940 triumph, *The Corn Is Green*. Sunday afternoons she becomes mellow Miss Hattie, a sort of female Will Rogers, over the Blue Network's *Lighted Windows*. And her mobile features—said to resemble her late brother John's when gay, brother Lionel's when dark—appear as Ma Mott's in the current Clifford Odets-RKO screen version of Richard Llewellyn's *None but the Lonely Heart* (reviewed on pp. 74-76).

Understandably, 65-year-old Miss Barrymore, in her fourth and private life, is bent on hoarding her energy. While working she makes

social engagements rarely, grants interviews discriminately as a queen does audiences. S philosophizes: "Learn not to waste your se and energy and brain on the little things . . . gnats of living . . ."

She currently spends her few spare m ments in a big Manhattan duplex apartme which belonged to her late friend, author Alice Duer Miller, and to which Miss Barrymo has imported her grand piano, her books an charcoal portrait of herself as a girl by Jo Singer Sargent. Her relaxation is reading lending library dry, plus old favorites Dicke

Born in Philadelphia in 1879, Ethel Barrymore is shown here in an early photo with her mother and brothers.

At 15 she made her stage debut in Montreal in *The Rivals*. Her grandmother, Louisa Drew, played the lead.

Ethel's father was dashing, Oxford-educated Maurice Barrymore, matinee idol of the Elegant '80's and Gay '90's.

In 1896 she played with her John Drew in *Rosemary*. Off she yearned to be a concert pi

Her fate was decided in 1901 with the part of Mme. Trentoni in Clyde Fitch's *Captain Jinks of the Horse Marines*. Ethel wept when she found that Charles Frohman had put her name up in lights one week after the New York opening.

The next year, in *Cousin Kate,* she was the toast of London and was rumored engaged to Winston Churchill.

Her most famous line—in S (1904)—was actually an ad lib: " all there is, there isn't any

She scored again in James Barrie's *Alice-Sit-by-the-Fire* (1905), became the "oomph girl" of the 1900's. Women fans copied her walk, her voice, even her posture. Playwright Ashton Stevens nicknamed her "Ethel Barrytone."

Wealthy, well-born Russell G. Colt won Ethel's hand in 1905. Separated 18 years later, they are still friends.

The three Colt children are (right) "Little Ethel" Barry Samuel Pomeroy and John

The life story of Ethel Barrymore is an oft-told tale, but in her fiftieth year as an actress the famous star became a subject for a picture article in a magazine of general circulation. The stage anniversary itself would not have been sufficient reason for publishing this story, but Miss Barrymore at the time was appearing in a hit movie and on a new radio program. Radio and motion pictures number their audiences in the high mil-

ificent Miss Barrymore celebrates her 50th anniversary on the stage this year with triple stardom, the gratifying knowledge that she is at the peak of her career.

Galsworthy play produced in ca, *The Silver Box* (1907), Ethel good at serious drama.

Mid-Channel (1910) won her fame as a dramatic actress. Never "typed," she absorbs a part until she is it.

In 1911 Miss Barrymore toured in *The Twelve Pound Look*. Today she has a New York theater named for her.

She played with brother John in *A Slice of Life* (1912), his first stage vehicle. Ethel was devoted to him.

lions; their "name" attractions have more appeal for national magazine readers than stage performers, with two or three exceptions. In the article of which one spread is shown above, Miss Barrymore's life was presented in a photographic "album," following her career from childhood. The album is one of the most popular picture-personality story devices.

HEDDA HOPPER STARTS GATHERING NEW GOSSIP AS SOON AS SHE GETS UP. AT 9 A.M. BREAKFAST SHE IS ON THE PHONE GETTING ITEMS. DOESN'T STOP WORK TILL MIDNIGHT

HEDDA HOPPER

SHE BECAME A LEADING HOLLYWOOD COLUMNIST BY TELLING WHAT SHE KNEW ABOUT HER MOVIE FRIENDS

by FRANCIS SILL WICKWARE

The former Elda Furry of Hollidaysburg, Pa. is planning to write her memoirs when she has some spare time and she already has selected an ideal title for them—*Malice in Wonderland*. Malice is an important ingredient of the column called "Hedda Hopper's Hollywood" which Elda Furry produces for readers of nearly 100 big-town newspapers and many small-town weeklies throughout the U. S. It is among the intangibles, psychological and otherwise, that make Elda Furry—or Hedda Hopper—perhaps the most influential female in that area called Hollywood which includes Burbank, Culver City, Beverly Hills, Santa Monica, Westwood, Palm Springs and a good many points in Manhattan.

There are about 325 individuals who properly can be called Hollywood columnists, including those who contribute to the fan magazines and the industry trade papers like *Variety* and the Hollywood *Reporter*. They fall roughly into two groups—professional journalists, who report soberly on production plans and the affairs of the studios generally, and the gossipists. The serious reporters heavily outnumber the gossipists, but any one of the latter can cause more commotion in Hollywood than all these reporters put together. Until the ascendancy of Hedda Hopper there was the unique phenomenon of a great American industry cringing and genuflecting before the redundant figure of Louella "Lollipop" Parsons, a Hearst columnist whose power at one time was so great that she could not only de-

mand—and get—a 24-hour break on every important news story in every studio, but who could —and did—bully the biggest stars in the business into appearing without pay on her radio program, *Hollywood Hotel*. The Screen Actors' Guild eventually put a stop to the latter practice, and Hedda Hopper was largely instrumental in breaking Parsons' strangle hold on the studios. Louella Parsons is not a has-been, but neither is she any longer the ringmaster of the Hollywood circus. Hedda Hopper has a whip of her own and cracks it more expertly.

Hedda Hopper's rapid emergence as a great voice in Hollywood was mainly due to her knowledge of the place and the people. The Hopper record runs back nearly 30 years. Twenty-eight

CONTINUED ON NEXT PAGE

HEDDA HAS FIVE PHONES SPOTTED IN HOUSE WITH EXTENSIONS FOR PATIO AND POOL. ON ACTIVE DAY SHE GETS NEARLY 400 PHONE CALLS, SEES 50 PEOPLE IN LINE OF BUSINESS

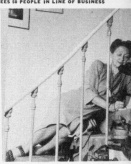

This page introduced a *Life* "Close-Up" of Hedda Hopper, syndicated Hollywood columnist. When the writer discovered Miss Hopper had five telephones in her house and another at her swimming pool, he wisely had her photographed at the telephone in several situations. The result was a picture story, combined with text, with a double continuity device—repeated identity of an individual and an object.

132

Undersecretary of War Patterson, a thorough Spartan from his close-cropped head down to his GI shoes, alarms even generals with his win-the-war zeal.

The Man Behind the Squeeze

Frugal Bob Patterson fights the battle of supply as GI Robin Hood, takes from civilians so soldiers can have enough

By RICHARD WILSON
Chief of LOOK's Washington Bureau

Washington's No. 1 war zealot is Robert Porter Patterson. As Undersecretary of War, he wears no uniform. But his Spartan civilian abnegation and his frenetic demands for an all-out war effort by the home front would put many a Pentagon-Building general to shame.

Patterson was the man who brought about the closing of the race tracks and the suspension of conventions for the duration. He considers these extremely mild sacrifices for a nation at war to make; and he becomes purple with impatience when people disagree with him. Patterson himself never visits race tracks. He spends his spare time at the nearest Army camp, where he goes whenever he can in order to live the life the American doughboy lives in the field.

Undersecretary Patterson is a lawyer by profession but a soldier by instinct. He was a judge of the Federal Circuit bench when President Roosevelt appointed him to the War Department in July, 1940. But the appointment did not reach him at his court chambers; for Patterson, a volunteer buck private, was peeling potatoes at the Business and Professional Men's Training Camp at Plattsburg, N. Y. The colonel in charge saluted Private Patterson, still in his fatigue uniform, and informed him of his appointment as Undersecretary of War.

(Continued on next page)

Beside a statue of Perseus he parks his hat in his rush to get to work.

Robert Patterson, Undersecretary of War, was profiled by LOOK in a picture-text combination, the focal point of which was Mr. Patterson's zealous compression of our civilian economy in order to speed the winning of the war. The large picture on this first page of the article is noteworthy for two reasons: 1. The camera angle (photographer shot from the floor); 2. The notations printed on the picture.

He takes no vacations, relaxes at Army camps and the fighting fronts

He fires a rifle grenade on a visit to Camp Lee, Va., always investigates new weapons himself.

In World War I, Patterson (left) reached rank of major in the Infantry, was awarded the DSC.

Between wars, he acquired this permanent home at Cold Spring, N. Y., on Hudson River.

On a war-front trip, Patterson met Yugoslavia's Marshal Tito. A girl interpreter translated.

News of his appointment as Undersecretary came while Patterson was busy on K. P. duty.

With General MacArthur, Patterson listens to 5th Air Force's Maj. Gen. Ennis C. Whitehead.

Back home, the Pattersons like to entertain wounded veterans. Guest is Lt. B. R. Shepard.

Patterson learned to fly while Undersecretary. On war-front trips, he often subs for pilot.

THE MAN BEHIND THE SQU

continued

Patterson's one-track insis
that fighting needs must be
leads to "war-as-usual" crit

Ever since then, the lean, energet
year-old Judge has spent 78 hours a
snapping the kinks from the Army'
production program. As Undersecret
War he is America's minister of mu
And in this capacity he has strained
utmost to squeeze civilian productio
raise war production.

It is not generally understood, even
that the War Production Board is rea
a production, but a resources board. It
tion is to allocate raw materials, to
civilian or military uses. But Patterse
ognized this at once, took over the actu
duction problems in the name of th
Department and began to organize in
for all-out co-operation in the war ef

He's a Champion Spender

Then he went ruthlessly to work
WPB, whipsawing it into denying ma
for civilian production and granting th
war production. He was in a position
this because he made and signed th
contracts. Patterson signed 45 billion
of war contracts as a starter, then del
this chore to a subordinate. The Jud
directed the spending of more money
any other man in our history.

Some critics call him a mere tool o
Brehon Somervell, chief of the Army S
Forces. But if so, Patterson is a tool w
sharpest of cutting edges. His zeal is
that he is often accused of having milit
the country's industry on behalf of the

While the WPB's businessmen - tu
Government - officials worry about c
clothing, the Judge is quite content to
$22.50 suits, $3.50 shoes and GI wool
summer and winter. He spends no mo
speak of. Last January he cashed a che
$50. Two months later, he still had $:
in his billfold. The other $30 had been s
dered, at the rate of $3.75 per week, fo
non-essentials as cigarets, chewing gu
the occasional lunches he eats away
the War Department restaurant.

He Quit Law for the Army

Judge Patterson was born and brou
in the comfortable little city of Glens
N. Y. He graduated from Union Colleg
from Harvard Law School, where he h
honor of serving as chairman of the a
Harvard Law Review. He entered a p
nent New York law firm immediately
graduation, in 1915.

Young Bob Patterson seemed to be
for a lifetime in Wall Street law lib
But within one year he resigned—t
the Army for Mexican Border servic
to give rein, for the first time, to his m
yearnings. He was a born soldier.

In World War I, while serving as a
fantry captain in France, he won the I
guished Service Cross for stirring u
German machine-gun nests, when he es
alive only by playing dead one whol
under a broiling sun. But his biggest
War memory was the difficulty and i
tance of bringing up ammunition to the
lines every night. Unquestionably, t
partly responsible for his present-day p
for all-out war production. He wants ne
suffer from the lack of any weapon.

The picture article on Undersecretary Patterson and running text are continued in combination on this spread, with the text interposed between an eight-picture album and a full-page shot showing Mr. Patterson in his office with weapons of war and veterans of the campaign in the Philippines. Every photograph on these pages serves to strengthen the textual reporting of Mr. Patterson's wartime frugality, his interest in

ortar and several machine guns are part of the private arsenal Patterson ps in his office to brush up on his knowledge of modern arms. Here he fondly exhibits guns to Rangers and Scouts who rescued 513 prisoners from Cabanatuan prison on Luzon last January. **(Continued on next page)**

things military, and his determination to force prosecution of the war to the limit. Because the album has this focus, it was edited to begin with the subject's service in World War I, instead of with his childhood, and to feature soldiers throughout, including two very famous ones—General MacArthur and Marshal Tito. Such known identities invariably increase readership.

Visitors wait while Patterson talks war production on phone. Here it's Maj. Gen. Donald H. Connolly, who wants to discuss liquidation of surplus war goods.

In Patterson's busy day, every luncheon is a war conference. Here, he c fers with his recently resigned potent special assistant, Julius H. Amb

Patterson calls frequently on Chief of Staff Gen. George C. Marshall. Now that Germany is beaten, they chart a war-production course to finish Japan.

All day long, from 8:30 a.m. to 8:30 p.m., war-production officials pou and out of Patterson's office. The atmosphere is informal, not at all mili

Business-as-usual is the enemy he fights

Between wars, Patterson married, raised four children. Commuting to New York from his home and chicken farm 50 miles up the Hudson, he made a brilliant legal reputation which finally led him to the bench of the second highest of all federal courts.

Today in Washington it is his wife, the former Margaret Winchester of Baltimore, who runs the household. One morning not long ago, impatient with the Judge for failing to bring home household money, she gave him only carfare when he left for work. Mrs. Patterson thought this would force him to cash a check. But the ruse did not work.

With all the non-essentials cut away, Judge Patterson is free to labor 12 hours each week day, and half-time on Sundays, at the occupation he gives A-1 priority over all things: winning the war on all fronts.

Patterson openly favors any restriction on civilians aimed at this objective. Thus, whenever the Government adopts some galling measure, Patterson gets blamed. He did inspire closing the race tracks and he put the kibosh on conventions. He stopped cold all plans to reconvert industry in the fall of 1944, when Gen. George C. Marshall thought the Germans might possibly collapse within three weeks. This iron resolution led to the canard that Patterson fights a war too tough for the military.

The Judge was also blamed for Justice Byrnes' midnight night-club curfew, but he actually had nothing to do with it. Patterson does not oppose drinking, gambling, horse racing or petting. He merely feels that these activities could be carried on without gasoline, tires or electricity.

He Wants the Army to Have Tires

Any sign that Americans are not all-out for war vexes the Judge. Once, in the company of a WPB official, Patterson spied a truck unloading soft drinks at a drug store.

"My God," he exclaimed, "there's your civilian economy. Tires and gasoline are used to haul soft drinks when we can't get enough stuff for the commanders at the front!" He was original advocate of the plan to appropr seven million used cars for their tires, thought no automobile needed more than f during the war.

Patterson has no authority to issue ord to draft farm workers or even one-eyed wei lifters in blooming health. He himself car ban conventions or close race tracks. He c recommends, spurs, goads, annoys until so official with the authority acts.

He feels the American public dotes fondly on its belly. He is out of patience w complaints of food shortages and spouts figu to show that the average American is eat more than ever.

A year ago he insisted that all danger real food shortage was passed and that it time to haul into the Army upwards of 500, farm youths being held on the land by d policies. Today he still cannot understand these men were not drafted, and asks if it is wonder 18-year-old boys have had to go the line with less than a year's training.

Patterson was in the ring in Washington bloodiest bureaucratic battle royal, in 1942.

Pictorially, the final spread of the Patterson article is devoted to activities in and around the Undersecretary's office. Here the attempt is to take the reader behind the scenes in the Pentagon Building and show him some of the hour-by-hour routine of the operational head of the War Department. This is a valuable element in any article on an important or colorful personality. The more truly you can give the reader an il-

Undersecretary thought Rubber Czar Wil- Jeffers was dawdling with the critical tire em, and he showed his ire when Jeffers ly installed a tire inspection system and all drivers to turn in extra spares.

'inally, at a WPB session when Patterson n his most virile win-the-war mood, Jef- aid his hand on the Undersecretary's shoul- nd murmured: "Now, sonny boy, take it or you'll bust a blood vessel." President evelt then issued his ukase against public -letting by feuding war administrators.

'he Judge's fervor causes many less ex- g public officials to pray nightly for his cal demise. Contemptuous of luxury, un- ng of his own time, Patterson is a paragon rsonal rectitude who confounds and annoys ore leisurely gentry of the war-production —and there are plenty of them.

A few months ago, a plot hatched in Wash- n to pack Judge Patterson off to Berlin as ican High Commissioner. Two purposes d have been achieved: he could practice eal on the Hun; he would be ditched in the ersion period after the German war. Patterson spiked this plan with the discon- certing logic that the Nazi occupation requires ruthless application of military discipline by a high Army officer answerable only to General Dwight Eisenhower.

Reconversion Is a Hot Issue

Patterson's most infuriating taunt to indus- trialists has been that at least some of them want "business-as-usual." Now they are mak- ing the bitter rejoinder that Patterson wants "war-as-usual" even after Germany's defeat.

The issue is a hot one. The Undersecretary's detractors have ceased talking of him as hard and zealous, now dub him emotional and im- practical. Behind these gibes lies a bitter and significant conflict.

Is a large part of industry to lie idle and stand by until the military finally is satisfied it has enough munitions to lick Japan? Or will there be a rapid move back to peacetime pro- duction? Over all lies the suspicion constantly raised by industrialists against Somervell and Patterson that, wittingly or not, they are paving the way for new and dangerous postwar controls of industry and business.

Patterson snorts at this supposition. But Congress takes the other view and that is why it killed national-service legislation, although the Army and Navy had called it essential.

The Judge calmly assumes reconversion to peace is a military job. He says: "Of course I am in favor of converting to civilian production where possible after V-E Day. In time of peace, the Army prepares war plans, including indus- trial-mobilization plans. But it doesn't talk about those plans. In time of war, we must always plan for peacetime reconversion and in- dustrial demobilization. We have been prepar- ing those plans for two years."

The problem will be a continuing one. With Germany beaten, war production will be main- tained at the rate of 60 billion dollars annually until the Japanese war is won. Patterson will make it his objective, provided he isn't moved out of the War Department, to keep the nose of American industry to the grindstone until the war is won on all fronts.

His motto will be the same, whether as Undersecretary of War, Secretary of War or Postwar Administrator in London:

"There is no time to spare. There is no easy way."

---

lusion of really meeting and getting to know the subject, the longer you will hold him. In text, a favorite device for achieving this is the anecdote, such as the one above about the truck unloading soft drinks. However, the writer is cautioned against using an anecdote for its own sake; it is justified only if it carries the story forward or helps delineate character.

As a naïve 20-year-old in *The Affairs of Susan*, Joan Fontaine falls in love with Broadway-bored produ[cer] George Brent (left). To express this personality, she wears little make-up, an Alice-in-Wonderland hair[...]

Joan Fontaine Gets Four Men

Produced by HOLLY McGRANAHAN • Photographed by DOROTHY TAYLOR

A versatile actress, she does it with four changes of personality in her latest picture, *The Affairs of Susan*

Unlike most motion-picture stars, Joan Fontaine does not play herself. Whereas an audience is rarely unaware of the identity of Greer Garson or Betty Grable or Ingrid Bergman, on the screen Joan Fontaine completely submerges her personality in the role she is portraying. This rare ability stands out vividly in Hal Wallis' forthcoming production for Paramount, *The Affairs of Susan*. (For synopsis and pictures, see this and the next three pages). In this gay romantic comedy, she tosses off a quadruple characterization with the finesse of a chameleon, confirming a remark she once made: "I live each part I play."

As Susan, Joan portrays a wide-eyed 20-year-old, a devastating divorcée, a tailored intellectual and, finally, a fine figure of a lady. And because she has never permitted herself to be typed, Miss Fontaine interprets all four personalities convincingly.

The mercurial five-foot-four winner of the 1941 Motion Picture Academy Award (for h[er] performance in *Suspicion*) did not achie[ve] success easily. A deep-rooted inferiority co[m]plex—planted in childhood by ill-health, nu[r]tured in her teens by the abounding succe[ss] of her older sister, Olivia de Havilland[—] makes every motion-picture assignment a tr[a]vail. Nevertheless she is now a crack spor[ts]woman, skilled flier and super cook—and s[he] has also topped her sister's professional su[c]cess. With all this, and beauty too, Joan Fon[-]taine remains emotionally insecure—and [an] ace actress.

Although not a personality story in the strictest sense of the term, this picture-text article on Joan Fontaine is included because it provides a combination of interest in a known, glamorous personality with fashion and movie appeal. The "peg" was the fact that Miss Fontaine was to appear in a movie in which she attracted the adulation and attention of four different men by playing four different kinds of women—a naïve young-

or No. 2, a lumber king on ⟶
pree (Don DeFore, below),
kes sexy, glamorous gowns.

The Affairs of Susan, Joan di-
orces her producer - husband
orge Brent, opposite page) aft-
e has made her into an actress,
ts a wealthy Western lumber-
 who is backing one of her
ws. Stung by her ex-husband's
usation that she can't "adapt"
self, Joan decides to go all out
 the lumberman. Playing the
astating divorcée, she assem-
 a wardrobe dripping with se-
ns, low-cut gowns and glamour
ample: right). They dine at
v York's snappiest restaurants,
ce in the ritziest night clubs.
 proposes between rumbas, in-
 that she give her answer upon
 return from a flying business
 to Montana.
his gown and Joan's quadruple
drobe were designed by ace
amount stylist Edith Head with
eye to carrying out each of the
ods Joan creates on the screen.

ster, a sophisticated divorcée, a tailored intellectual, and an upstage *grande dame*. For
each characterization, of course, she had to have a special wardrobe. Above is the
opening spread of the article, showing Miss Fontaine in two of her roles, each with the
man who shared it. The lead text block is devoted largely to an analysis of the star's
versatility as an actress.

While strolling in the park one day, Joan picks up Dennis O'Keefe, writer and revolutionary thinker. She dines with him in Greenwich Village and they discuss romance. "A kiss," says he, "is a catalytic agent of a high spiritual communion." After a few old-fashioneds, O'Keefe becomes more personal. When she proposes, he accepts. But after getting him before the Justice of the Peace, she changes her mind, leaves him flat.

For this romantic excursion into the high intellectual planes, Miss Fontaine turns tailored (right), wears a slim wrap-around skirt, a sporty turtle-neck sweater and a checked jacket. Her ash-blond hair is drawn into a smart, severe knot at the nape of her neck—a style touted by Faye Emerson, Mrs. Howard Hawks and Liz Altemus Whitney

To snare No. 3, intellectual Dennis O'Keefe (above), Joan dons mannish garb, slicks her hair.

The second spread of the Joan Fontaine article is presented in exactly the same layout pattern as the first; hence, the piece has visual as well as repeated-identity continuity. Because of its varied appeals, this kind of story is a joy to any picture-magazine editor. Most magazines are made up to include subject matter covering a wide range of basic reader interests, categorized by such titles as national affairs, sports, fashion, food,

No. 4, Walter Abel (below), a Washington biggie, is intrigued with this woman of the world.

On the rebound from her Bohemian romance, Joan accepts the marriage proposal of correct, cut-and-dried Walter Abel, Washington alphabet man. Picturing herself in the role of his charming wife and gracious hostess, she assumes the air of a *grande dame*. She is about to pack her trousseau when, through circumstances seldom encountered outside the movies, suitors 1, 2 and 3 all converge on the scene, demanding an answer to their proposals. Having proven herself a versatile actress, Joan then makes her final decision.

To play the *grande dame*, Joan's wardrobe must undergo another change. The naïve, the sexy and the arty influences are replaced by elegance and good taste. Typical of this phase is the low-cut (but not too low) black velvet gown with a bustle of ermine tails (at right).

entertainment, science, home-making and so on. In this article a well-known personality has been employed to help cover at least three categories: fashion, entertainment and sex interest. The last named is a category which some editors won't admit having, but it is a basic ingredient in any successful publication, although some magazines deal with it more delicately than others.

JOHN P. MARQUAND AT HIS HOME IN NEWBURYPORT

In this first spread of a "Close-Up" of John P. Marquand, *Life* combined a staff-made portrait of the noted New England author with two small albums—one of his distinguished ancestors and another of his early life. The title, subtitle and introductory text appear between the albums. *Life* frequently publishes long personality pieces running to as much as 5,000 words (the Marquand story above is an example), but invari-

Governor Joseph Dudley of Massachusetts Bay was an ancestor of Marquand.

Transcendentalist Margaret Fuller, New England intellectual, was a great-aunt.

Author Edward Everett Hale (*The Man Without a Country*) was another relation.

Fuller family photograph shows Marquand's maternal grandfather (*right*). The Fullers were mostly clergymen and lawyers.

JOHN P. MARQUAND

AMERICA'S FAMOUS NOVELIST OF MANNERS WOULD MAKE A WONDERFUL CHARACTER IN ONE OF HIS OWN BOOKS

by ROGER BUTTERFIELD

It was June and high-school graduation time in the old seacoast town of Newburyport, Mass. The year was 1910 and the place was the box-shaped brick town hall just down the street from the high school. The graduates, in white dresses and best blue suits, had gathered in nervous groups in the basement, and now they were marching up the stairs in boy-and-girl file, under the admiring scrutiny of their parents and relations. Presently they found themselves standing on the stage inside, with programs in their hands, singing the class ode which had been written (to the tune of *Fair Harvard*) by Judge Simpson's daughter Lillian:

Oh golden and rosy the dreams of our youth
And bright are our hopes for success.
We look to the future with wide shining eyes
And to failure we'll never confess.
Oh beckoning dreams and confident hopes,
Starry visions your ardor reveals.
In your soft lustrous haze all is beauty and joy
Every peril the future conceals. . . .

Presently also they were listening to the class prophecy, recited in a high monotone by Miss Gladys Whitson. In the back row a boy with sandy blond hair suddenly swallowed hard as

John Phillips Marquand has written four of the outstanding American novels of recent years: *The Late George Apley, Wickford Point, H. M. Pulham, Esquire* and *So Little Time.* Critics have called him "America's foremost satirist" and "our leading contemporary novelist of manners." He has just been elected a judge of the Book-of-the-Month Club.

Gladys declaimed: "Marquand's great dictionary is a marvel to behold, A day's perusal in its depths would make a boy grow old. . . . (But) Miss Simpson, famed philanthropist, doth with weighty brow, the lexicographer entrap with definitions wise enow. . . . " He stole a quick glance at Lillian Simpson and saw that she was blushing too. People in the audience were snickering and looking at both of them.

At that moment John Phillips Marquand, aged 16, would have welcomed death.

Not that there was anything at all between him and Lillian Simpson. He had only been to

see her once, in her family's big Victorian gingerbread house on High Street. After they had sat for awhile on the porch Mrs. Simpson invited them into the parlor to have "a dish of cream." He had never heard of having a dish of cream and couldn't imagine what it was; he sat there in a dreadful silence until it appeared. It was homemade vanilla ice cream. He gulped it down and made his escape and never went back to the Simpsons' because he felt he had shown inexcusable ignorance about the dish of cream.

He didn't go back after the high-school graduation either; he never saw Lillian Simpson again. The following year he entered Harvard, where he continued to be self-conscious and lonely. After he got his degree he worked for a while on the Boston *Evening Transcript* and soldiered in France and did some more newspaper and advertising work in New York, and then he became a professional writer of fiction. He wrote short stories and serials for the *Saturday Evening Post* and *Collier's* and *Good Housekeeping*. He invented Mr. Moto, a Japanese adventure-story hero who was quickly bought by Hollywood. The movies made six Mr. Moto pictures, paying Marquand $4,000 for each picture and not even

CONTINUED ON NEXT PAGE

J. P. Marquand, aged 3, sits on his father's lap and ignores the book. He was a backward reader.

Also at 3, he went riding in a dogcart drawn by Mack (the poodle) and Nick (the setter) at family's summer home near Newburyport. His long curls were cut next year.

At 21, he posed for this solemn-looking Harvard graduation picture. He was on the *Lampoon* staff.

- -

ably employs some form of picture story on the opening page or spread. LOOK, as a general rule, tries to combine pictures and text throughout. Most other popular publications carrying long profiles use pictures chiefly as illustrations or decorations for text. Editors are agreed on only one point: however they are used, pictures stimulate increased reading of any given article.

Joan Gladding is fitted for one of six $275 costumes she wears in her first Broadway show. With a chance at Hollywood, she still sighs to sing with a name ba...

Ashtabula to Broadway

Produced by PATRICIA COFFIN, Editor • SPRAGUE TALBOTT, Photographer

A small-town girl gets a chorus job in a New York musical, *Up in Central Park*, and lands on LOOK's cover

Nineteen-year-old Joan Gladding of Ashtabula, Ohio (see cover), came to New York last winter, landed a bit in a Broadway hit with her first try. As a member of the chorus in Mike Todd's musical period piece, *Up in Central Park* (based on the N. Y. *Times'* exposé of Boss Tweed), she makes $60 a week, is prac-

tically guaranteed a year's stage experience. Daughter of an Ashtabula defense-plant executive, Joan used to star in local school plays, took music lessons in nearby Cleveland. Seven months after she'd landed a job there, singing with a hotel orchestra, she was invited to New York for a 20th Century-Fox screen test. Encouraged by her mother, Joan came to the big city, was tested, told to come back after a year on Broadway.

"I was shopping for a hat as usual, although I never wear one," curvaceous, gray-

eyed Joan relates, "when I saw some girls en tering a stage door. I followed them." Insi she found Mike Todd casting a new sho Treading where Broadway angels hesita Joan auditioned with aplomb—got the job.

How she became a coruscant cog in a maj Broadway production is shown on this and t following five pages. LOOK's picture tre which included a side trip to Philadelph culminated in the appealing color shot whi appears on the cover of this issue.

Here, in modern dress (and undress) is the Cinderella story, as appealing to the current younger generation as it ever was to their grandparents. Focused on an unknown personality whose dreams and ambitions typify those of millions of American girls, this picture article is the ever-popular tale of the small-town girl making good on Broadway. Editors have to be eternally vigilant against press agents trying to "plant"

During signing of contracts, tough, cigar-chewing Mike Todd—Broadway's youngest successful producer at 39—gives Joan the once-over in his plush, private office. Contract specifies $2 fine for tardiness (money goes into armed-forces fund), a minimum salary of $15 weekly during rehearsals. Although the show is spectacular, astute Todd produced it with economy.

Before entraining with company for Philadelphia, set designer Howard Bay (right) color-checks a prop against Joan's pink-and-lavender costume (her favorite). Joan tries to chit-chat with designer, gets monosyllabic answers. Bay and a paint crew of more than 100 men worked five weeks covering 34,000 square feet of canvas with stunning Currier & Ives-type backdrops.

The show goes into rehearsal

It tries out in Philadelphia

When rehearsals begin, Joan meets Noah Beery, Sr., who plays Boss Tweed in the show, and he treats her to coffee in a Broadway diner. He advises: "Keep fresh and unaffected. Don't shove." The cast rehearsed for four weeks in heatless New York theaters; girls came to work in slacks, star Wilbur Evans sang while wearing a muffler around his ears.

Dancer Natalie Wynn limbers up as Joan, perched on a prop, watches. Final Philadelphia rehearsals lasted until 2 a.m. and dress parade took place before critical gaze of producer Todd, composer Sigmund Romberg, book and lyric writers Herbert and Dorothy Fields. Committed to do a society benefit, first performance actually was dress rehearsal.

---

stories of this sort, but when they find the genuine article they know they have something that will interest the majority of their readers. In this story, the heroine's charm and sex appeal are heightened by her pictorial association with known personalities (producer Mike Todd, actor Noah Beery) and several photographs giving readers backstage glimpses of a big musical show.

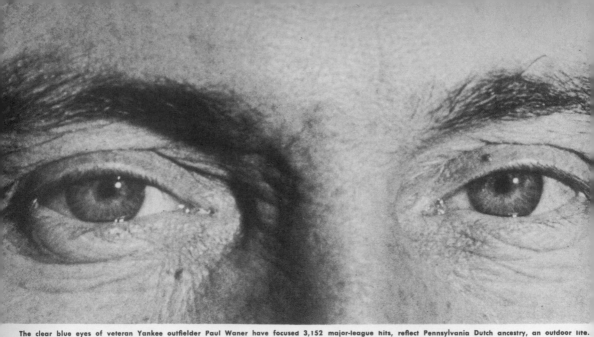

The clear blue eyes of veteran Yankee outfielder Paul Waner have focused 3,152 major-league hits, reflect Pennsylvania Dutch ancestry, an outdoor life.

The Sharpest Eyes in Sport

They belong to Paul Waner, one of seven major leaguers ever to make 3,000 hits

By TIM COHANE
Sports Editor of LOOK

One spring evening 37 years ago, Ote Waner, a Harrah, Okla., farmer, returned home from a baseball game in Oklahoma City which he had pitched and won. He brought presents for his sons: two bananas for Ralph, 11, a banana and a baseball for Paul, 5, a banana for Lloyd, 3. After Paul had eaten his banana, he offered to trade his baseball for one of Ralph's bananas, and Ralph agreed. But when Paul had eaten the second banana, he regretted the trade and cried for the baseball. Pa Waner made Ralph hand it over.

Now 42 and one of the seven immortals to make 3,000 or more major-league hits, Paul Waner still gets pretty much his own way where a baseball is concerned. His pinch-hitting record of 16 hits and 15 walks in 63 times up, for a .333 average and a .492 reached-base percentage (with the Dodgers and Yankees last summer), is one of the most remarkable in the annals of the game. But it is not surprising. As veteran scout Ted McGrew sums it up: "As long as Paul is able to drag himself and a bat up to the plate, he'll be able to hit that ball."

Only Ty Cobb, Tris Speaker, Hans Wagner, Eddie Collins and Nap Lajoie made more hits than Waner's 3,152. Fabulous Pop Anson, whose 3,081 was surpassed by Paul in 1943, completes the ultra-select 3,000-hit lodge. Ultra-select is the adjective. Babe Ruth, George Sisler, Rogers Hornsby, Lou Gehrig, Willie Keeler, Jimmy Foxx, Mel Ott, Al Simmons, Fred Clarke, Ed Delehanty and Zach Wheat don't belong.

The sharpest eyes in sport—even though the advancing years have forced them behind glasses off-and-on since 1942—are the principal reason for Waner's 19-year major-league average of .332 and those 3,152 hits. As pictured on these pages, this gift of eyesight is supplemented by strong, sinewy wrists,

Now 42, pinch-hitter Waner confidently faces this, his 20th season in big-league baseball.

Virtually the narrowest possible focus was used in this picture-text combination of Paul Waner. The text focuses on Waner, the picture story on his eyes, with secondary emphasis on hands and wrists. The attention-compelling picture on the first page, of course, is the closely-cropped shot "blowing up" the eyes. It ties in directly with the title and is repeated in smaller size on the next page, which features magic-eye camera

146

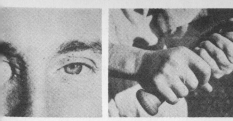

These eyes, and these strong hands and sinewy wrists, account for Waner's batting prowess. Developed pitching 90-pound bales of hay, his hands wield bat lightly. Pictures on this page analyze Paul's swing.

Hitting to left, the "opposite field" for a left-handed Hitter, Waner (1) grips bat an inch from the end, (2) shifts weight early to his right foot.

He controls arc of bat with left wrist (3); as a result, his left elbow points toward belt buckle. He meets pitch well out in front of plate (4).

His left wrist, taut forearm (5) "steer" ball into left field. His eye follows its flight (6) as he completes "opposite-field" swing in rhythmic balance.

Occasionally, he would strike out on purpose

Forearms and shoulders, an intuitive sense of timing, split-second muscular reaction and a knowledge of technique from long, conscious study of batting form.

Thrice batting champion during his Pittsburgh-glory days, Waner always has been the toast of his contemporaries. When the Giants visited Forbes Field, Bill Terry, a great hitter himself, and Carl Hubbell would stand behind the cage during Pirate batting practice. "Hit one to left, Paul," Terry would say, and Paul's liner would scare up a flurry of lime from the left-field foul line. "Now pull one to right," Hubbell would request, and Waner would obligingly nick the right-field line. Small wonder such a champion refused to accept a scratch hit from the official scorer for Number 3,000 at Boston in 1942! Number 3,000 should be faultless, and was—a smash to center two days later, against Rip Sewell.

Like any authentic genius, Paul never took his gifts for granted. He studied each pitcher as a separate problem. He kept a little black book on strengths and weaknesses. Occasionally, he'd strike out on purpose to make a pitcher believe he couldn't hit that type of ball. Then, later, perhaps with the game at stake, the hurler would feed him that pitch again, and Waner would be ready for it.

(Continued on page 64)

Hitting to right, Paul is set for the delivery (1), yet is not tensed as pitcher begins wind-up. He holds elbows loose (2) and well away from body,

keeps right arm from elbow to wrist parallel with ground (3) in order to maintain level swing, delays shift of weight (4) from left to right foot.

For driving power, he turns his body, from left wrist to left foot, into swing (5), turns left wrist all the way over in bringing bat around (6),

employs right foot as anchor (7) during the follow-through (8) which is in contrast to the short, "opposite-field" swing shown at top of the page.

sequences showing how Waner hits to left field and how he pulls a ball into right. (As originally published, these pages did not face each other—the eye shot was repeated as a layout continuity device.) The story continued with other photographic sequences showing how Waner's sharp eyes and co-ordination make him adept at golf, hunting, fly-casting, parlor magic.

After each correct sports prediction in his column, Roundy modestly wears this old silk hat and sign.

He's Only a Hi
Sports Writer
but...

Roundy Coughlin, screwball sag
Madison, Wis., is a famous institu

The most famous—and the least gramm
—of all bush-league sports writers is J
Leo ("Roundy") Coughlin. His unique co
"Roundy Says," appears in the *Wisconsin*
Journal of Madison, Wis., where today the
his only serious rival for public attention.

Roundy doesn't confine himself to spor
the war, he philosophizes: "Keep your sh
we will have our field day. Them babie
fighting America don't forget that and whe
start hitting all the devil will be poppin
ain't going to sign no peace terms this tim
sit around table in dress suits and medals
the way this time folks and how."

The war has affected him personally, to
writes: "I read where men might have to
shorts due to the shortage of wool. You
have to go to the movies it will be the fu
thing you ever saw. I am going to cover my
up if I got to put burlap around them. I'll lo
my readers if I go down the street in short

Happy Though a Hick

The world's only author of such strange pr
about 50 (admits to 44). Bright-blue Irish
and a quick smile make him look younger
6 feet, well-upholstered amidships, weigh

He is a pal of sports celebrities. He v
"guest columns" for newspapers in many
He has had handsome offers to work in the
time" but turned them down. Roundy exp
"I have got that Wisconsin look on my fac
I am going to keep it there. I always want
near the cows I want to see my milk whe
laid on the back porch. I'm still a hick write
I'm going to keep on being one."

Triumph! "Great Prognosticator" was right o

Picking winners, Roundy asserts, is his long suit. "That's why I'm called the Great Prognosticator." Actually, the title is self-bestowed. Some 15 years ago, Roundy really predicted the outcome of 52 football games in a row. Immodest to a fault, he bragged daily in his column. Some-body taunted him: "You think you're quite a prognosticator!" It was meant as an insult—but Roundy didn't see it that way. He adopted it, along with his "victory hat," which you see above. Nobody loves a winner more than Roundy, especially when the winner was Roundy's choice.

They call Roundy the Sage of Mad and the Sage of Mendota. The latter title him; for, while it is the name of a local lake, also the name of a mental hospital. Roundy not remember who gave him these names how, in boyhood, he came to be called "Roun

Joseph ("Roundy") Coughlin, subject of the article shown here, is a small-town sports writer with a big reputation in the vicinity of his native Madison, Wis. He has been profiled by two national magazines, not because of his local fame but for his eccentricities. As the photographs show, he is the kind of personality known as a "character." Coughlin is a writer with little knowledge of grammar or punctuation; an "expert"

ndy wails continually that he is
e verge of destitution. For instance:

etween what I give away and keep the
going it just keeps the sheriff off the porch.
 to keep my money in a safety deposit box.
ox is still there but the banker and money
e."

s true he kept his money in a safety deposit
ecause he wouldn't trust a bank with it. In
a lot of people quit laughing at him for that.
 he has any money saved today, the chances
 is still in that box, because he was never
n to open a bank account.

undy drives a 1941 DeSoto coupe. He lives
our-room apartment with his two widowed
s, and Roundy claims it is for their sake
e has never married. A better explanation
 fact that he is somewhat afraid of women,
gh he makes frequent references in his
n to one "piperoo" or another.

h as Roundy Writes It

Lowell, the distinguished Boston poet, once
hat Roundy wrote "the real American lan-
." Here are some typical Roundyisms:

aw pictures last night of a society woman
now smokes a pipe for fashion. Well that is
ast straw on this earth when a woman
es a pipe. By jeebers that is awful."

xaggeration ain't a crime. When a broader is jumping in right direction he can't go
ar."

aw four co-ed riding around in an old car
day — if they don't know less when they
ate than when they started to school then I
e best English writer in the world."

here is just one thing I got against peanut
r is I can't eat it."

he best football game Roundy ever saw
 in a tie score. Roundy's comment was:
t more could be fairer?" That question has
repeated in his column a thousand times
 It is Roundy's way of indicating approval.

undy is partially deaf. Last summer, he ob-
a hearing device which helped him tremen-
y. "Folks," he wrote happily, "I am starting
 life it is pretty nice to have two lives."
K Photographer Bob Hansen went to Madi-
nd brought back pictures of the happy hick
 his second life.

Roundy interviews two Wisconsin coeds—prom queen Priscilla White (right) and Dawn Herbuveaux.

y, left, spars happily with Jack Dempsey, ex-U. S. heavyweight champion.

of the first celebrities to be a Roundy fan was the late
Frank, who became President of the University of Wisconsin about
ne Roundy became the Great Prognosticator. When Dr. Frank pub-
a pretentious book on the state of the world entitled "Thunder and
" Roundy tried to read it, then wrote tersely: "He should of called it
og." More erudite critics said the same thing in hundreds more words.

Roundy is a pal of Red Grange, football immortal, who likes Roundy's column.

Roundy's all-time hero was Knute Rockne, Notre Dame football
coach who died in a plane wreck. Roundy wrote: "Gee—Knute Rockne. His
sudden death dazed me so I can hardly see. Just think of it when Southern
California played in Chicago here was biggest crowd ever in history of football, he sick man in wheel chair and team on his hands and he was worrying about two tickets for Roundy—I never got over that and never will."

on world affairs who never finished the fifth grade; a "great lover" who is afraid of
women. Yet, with all his handicaps, he has entertained thousands with his devastating
wit and weird mannerisms, personal and professional. He is a fit subject for a national-
magazine article because in him and his life and his fantastic writings is a story of basic
interest to others.

149

Bacall comes from dramatic school, magazine pictures, fashion-modeling, stage walk-ons.

Janet Gaynor and Charles Farrell made 10 pictures based on wholesome, unadorned romance. In *Seventh Heaven* (1927), both were 21.

Greta Garbo and Jo won screen love-team on tempestuous love. I *the Devil* (1927), she w

To add to the already heavy reader interest in the famous movie team of Lauren Bacall and Humphrey Bogart, two picture tricks were used in this article. At the time, Miss Bacall and Mr. Bogart would not pose together except on a movie set; consequently, separate photographs were juxtaposed to create the illusion that the lovers are gazing fondly at each other. To this was added a strip of smaller photographs showing love

Bogart comes from Phillips Andover Academy, U. S. Navy (World War I), Wall Street finance, stage-managing, stage leads, tough-guy roles in the movies.

Bacall and Bogart

They are headed for a prominent place
among the screen's famous love teams

Because even Hollywood's magic can create them only infrequently, a hit team of screen lovers is a producer's dream. The latest to achieve this film bonanza is Warners'—with Lauren Bacall of the come-hither eyes and tough-guy Humphrey Bogart. LOOK herewith presents studies of 1945's happiest combination (their next: *The Big Sleep*) and some of their predecessors.

low and Clark Gable
portrayers of violent
sm. In *Red Dust* (1932),
, he 31. She died in 1937.

Greer Garson, Walter Pidgeon
found a warm wartime response
to mature, tender affection. In *Mrs.
Miniver* (1942), she was 30, he 44.

Ingrid Bergman, Gary Cooper
also built team reputation as tender lovers. In *For Whom the Bell
Tolls* (1943), she was 27, he was 42.

Lauren Bacall and Humphrey Bogart
hit team-heights trail with a combination
of sex, action, humor. In *To Have and
Have Not* (1944), she was 20, he was 46.

scenes between five other noted motion-picture teams and a "clinch" between Bacall and Bogart in their first screen triumph, *To Have and Have Not*. The story thus acquired the "pull" of twelve well-known personalities instead of being limited to the appeal of the two leading characters. From a strictly design standpoint, it is cluttered, but it ranked high in reader tests.

Zeke Curlee (on desk) is a man who likes to try things. Texas-born, he ran away at 14 to join a circus. After a spell as a cowboy, he toured Mexico with Richard Harding Davis. He then went to col-

lege. Later he became a reporter, an aviator, a salesman, a singer, a press agent. He made $272,000 in four years from a West Virginia auto agency, lost it overnight in a Florida publishing venture, recouped

it in miniature-golf courses. Five years ag— tired" to then-drowsy Albany, Ore. Thr— later he was managing the Chamber of Cor— on the strength of recommendations he wrot—

OREGON FIREBALL

Carl "Zeke" Curlee felt tired. He chose quiet little Albany, Ore., as a fine spot to rest. The quiet got on his nerves, Zeke got restless—and so today, at 54, he's the busiest small-town booster in America.

Zeke's main interest now is building up Albany. He checked logs for 72 hours in a Washington freight yard, found most of them came from his part of Oregon, got three plywood mills to move to Albany.

Leading citizens love Zeke. Here (white shows how he flagged a through train, talke— ficial into getting off, won Albany a civilia training program meant for Portland, 80 mile

Newspapers are Zeke's dish; he's been fired from 182 of them, from New York to Singapore. Here he's "planting" a Chamber of Commerce story in Albany's one paper. Zeke is paid $275 a month, and earns it.

Directors of the C. of C. usually meet in Zeke's kitchen; they admire his wife's cooking. Here Zeke (holding model) talks up a plywood-plane project. A grandfather, he has a weakness for sporty clothes.

Thanks to Zeke, Albany is having a w— (albeit his figure here is a bit optimistic) in civilian defense, rationing, war housin— selling, the USO, he affirms, "I'm not bac—

Like "Roundy" Coughlin (see pp. 148-149), Carl ("Zeke") Curlee, subject of this one-page article, belongs, from an editor's viewpoint, in the category of interesting screwballs. Although nationally unknown, he had country-wide appeal because of his dynamic performance as a one-man booster club for Albany, Oregon. The story is notable for the amount of pictorial and textual information it packed into small space.

To Bing Crosby, the Screen's No. 1 Entertainer,
LOOK Presents Its Male Motion Picture Award
for Achievement in 1944

is rare unsmiling picture of Bob Hope and Bing Crosby, caught as they listened to a general's speech at an Army base, was made by LOOK photographer Theisen.

Bing Crosby: Father Time's Older Brother

By BOB HOPE, with Marginal Notes by BING CROSBY

EDITOR'S NOTE: Continuing its new kind of magazine biography, LOOK submitted this article to Bing Crosby before publication. Crosby's comments appear beside Hope's manuscript.

SAYS CROSBY:

First time express ever came through via second-class male.

I have been asked to express my opinion of Bing Crosby. How do you make that kind of a noise on a typewriter?

Bing Crosby—that's the large, economy-size Sinatra. Funny, the way I met him. I was at Lakeside golf course. He sauntered up with a number three wood sticking out of the sag of his pants, and said: "Need a caddy, friend?" How could a guy of his standing and position be so cheap as to caddy for a few extra bucks? Walking up and saying: "Need a caddy, friend?" What made me really mad was that he didn't say it to me, but to the guy I was caddying for.

The next time I saw him was at New York's Paramount Theater. Outside the box office stood the longest line that has gathered in one spot since Lady Godiva quit the bridle paths. I turned to a couple of fellow vaudeville assassins and asked them what the excitement was about. Before they could answer every woman in the house started to squeal.

"It's Bing!" the girls screamed. The other actors and I just stood there, star-

SAYS CROSBY:

A true statement by a man who personally attended both events.

The format of this personality piece on Bing Crosby is unique with LOOK in the United States, although it has been copied by an English publication. It is a picture-text combination to which the subject of the text supplies marginal notes spoofing or denying what the author has written about him. The picture is the only known photograph in existence of Crosby and Hope caught completely off guard.

Born in 1904, Crosby began his singing career at Gonzaga University in Spokane, Wash. (1), then joined Al Rinker, Harry Barris to form Paul Whiteman's Rhythm Boys (2).

In his fourth picture, Paramount's *Too Much H* (1933), he sang *The Day You Came Along* to Judi (3). An ardent sports spectator, he is notoriously lang

Radio's ace gag artist, Old Shovel-face tees off

SAYS CROSBY:

Proof positive that Hope had help. The paucity of his knowledge of psychology and etymology is epic. The largest word he could collar is delicatessen.

Pure self-aggrandizement! The man who has to plan to steal a scene from this self-centered girdle-bender is still playing bits for penny grind machines.

This is too tough a task for an unarmed man to tackle when confronted with a coterie of unpaid mercenaries who seek to curry favor with this aging glamour-boy by bombarding him with moth-eaten bons mots which he proceeds to palm off as spontaneous witticisms.

ing and shaking our heads. We had hoped it would be a man.

Actually, it's about time I exposed old Bobby Socks. He gives an impression of laziness that makes Rip Van Winkle look like the original perpetual-motion kid. His languor is as apparent as his hair piece. People say he is so lucky he won't even stop for a clover with less than eight leaves. They claim he's as casual as a croupier at a crooked roulette wheel.

Well, I'm a guy who tells nothing but the truth, so here is the real dope. What people don't know about Tonsils is that he is actually about as casual as a Long Tom at 20 paces. Why, the Machiavellian plotting that goes on under that thinning thatch that is supposed to cover the Crosby cerebrum would make a Jap propagandist turn pale. The Crosby you've been taught to know is nothing but a hoax.

Actually, when he sneaks off the set for a supposed nap, he is really seeking solitude in which to dope out a scheme for pick-pocketing the next scene. If he isn't trying to steal the girl, he is burglarizing the ad libs. If he's lucky, then so is Einstein. Let's not even talk about his laziness.

Since 1932, he has appeared in 31 pictures. Through personal appearances and congratulatory wires, he has been able to corrupt exhibitors to the point where he has eased himself among the 10 top box-office characters for seven of those 12 years. This gives him a .600 average and a head so big it interferes with camera angles.

And that egg on the back of his head is not where he hit himself—it's what happened when he heard that he won LOOK's 1944 male actor's Achievement Award. His studio might as well start tying a paper

bag over his head—when he sees this story in the magazine his brain will burst.

Crosby also dabbles in radio. For 15 years he has annoyed radiomaniacs with a purported program. He has been stealing money from cheese-eaters since 1934, and ranks among the 10 top Limburgers in every known rating. Since Pearl Harbor, he has put in appearances at Army camps, worked on a weekly short-wave radio show beamed overseas and sent entertainers out on a self-sponsored USO tour.

Then there are his phonograph records. Now, every male has piped a song or so while soaping in the shower. Crosby sings the same numbers in the same style, but with a difference—he's not embarrassed. The kid has cut some 500 discs, most of them suitable only for shying at strange cats, but one (*White Christmas*), which has hit 3,500,000 in sales, is still driving more Iowans to California.

While I'm on the subject of singing, there's a lot of talk that Tonsils and Frankie sing alike. That's ridiculous. Bing and Frankie each has an entirely different way of singing. There is absolutely no similarity between their styles. Sinatra sings through his left nostril, Bing sings through his right.

Crosby has changed a lot. He used to smoke a pipe. Now that Sinatra's around, he just smokes. Actually, the boys are very good friends. Frankie even visits at the Crosby house. He started to play once with one of Bing's kids. When the others saw that, they yelled: "Hey, Pa, if Gary can have one, we want a new doll, too!"

At this point I'd like to give you the lowdown on the sport shirt that walks like a man. I won't say that Bing's clothes are loud, but one of his fans rushed up to him

SAYS CROSBY:

To keep the facts from becoming as distorted as th confused statistician's pro boscis, the association be gan in December, 1935.

The implication that m quartet of gang buste dallies with dollies ma mean mayhem, should th author of this encyclope dia of malicious misinfor mation drop his guar near my diggings.

Hope tells a joke, Crosby cracks back, Hope salaams out as they entertain 25,000 airmen at the Santa Ana (Calif.) A

The second spread of Bob Hope's article on Bing Crosby was presented with photographs bordering text at top and bottom. The numbered sequence at the top is an album bringing Crosby from his college days to the beginnings of movie stardom. At the bottom of the left-hand page is a picture panel showing Hope and Crosby cavorting together at an Army air base, and at the right is another depicting a motion-picture

o is married to pert ex-actress Dixie Lee, takes continual kidding from
eres about his four sons (5, taken in 1938), just as Eddie Cantor is
out his five daughters. Owner of the Del Mar race track, not now in
operation, Crosby is shown (6) broadcasting a race from a fencetop. By 1938,
when he appeared in *Sing You Sinners* (7) with Donald O'Connor and Fred Mac-
Murray, the crooner had really begun to sizzle. They are singing *Small Fry*.

roaner—who gets in a few potshots himself

SAYS CROSBY:

*modest but effective de-
se against being knifed
he back.*

*mbing was invented
this type of joke.*

*e fantasy! Anybody
plays better golf than
wouldn't even be seen
a rug auction with the
enous hacker.*

the other day and tried to tear the shirt off
his back. The fan got an awful shock—the
wiring short-circuited. You know, those
shirts are so hot that Crosby is the only
man I know who wears Unguentine for un-
derwear. Yet Tubby really considers himself a *bon vivant*. He kids me about my
shape, but take a good look at him. I won't
say he is exactly big around the stern, but
he is the only guy I know who carries a tail
gunner in his back pocket. He's built like a
house. I won't say what kind of a house, but
I don't see many of them any more since
they invented plumbing.

Considering his equipment, Crosby isn't
a bad golfer. The last time I played with
him, he got a birdie on the first hole, and
he got a birdie on the second hole and he got
a birdie on the third hole. After the fourth,
he made his caddie keep quiet.

I played in a match with Crosby and a
couple of better golfers recently. I'm certainly not playing with Crosby any more.
Would you play with a guy who cheats, and
when nobody is looking picks his ball up
and throws it toward the hole? Of course
you wouldn't. And neither will Crosby.

And I won't say Crosby digs divots—he
just goes down the course carving out new
hazards. Universal set up a camera out at
Lakeside and one of Crosby's divots was
the flying carpet in their picture, *Ali Baba
and the Forty Thieves*. Another time Croz
sent the follow-through of his mashie shot
flying over the Lockheed plant. The foreman pointed at it and yelled to his men:
"Get busy, boys—look what they're turning
out over at Douglas."

Crosby used to live near me in North
Hollywood. He owned a big, flimsy-looking
house, sort of a barrel-stave Taj Mahal. It

was the showplace of the orange-crate industry. It's a very unusual style of archi-
tecture even for California — imagine, a
stork nest with a patio.

I used to go over and play with Bing's
four kids—but he caught me one day and
took away the dice. Then, after he examined
them, he made me give back the two veloci-
pedes and the kiddy car.

What a host that guy is! I had dinner at
his house once. It was supposed to be steak.
I'm not saying it wasn't, but for two days
after—every time I passed the sign of the
Flying Red Horse my tummy whinnied.

One day I passed the house and saw
Crosby lying on the front stoop, reading a
fire-insurance policy. The next day I passed
and the house was in flames. The neighbors
were busy pulling the furniture out, and
Crosby was busy throwing it back in. It
seems the furniture was insured, too.

That's how Crosby's house accidentally
burned down. And just in time, too. He only
beat the North Hollywood Board of Health
to it by three days. Now Crosby has a beautiful new home in Holmby Hills. It has 10
gables and 14 insurance policies, and Bing
walks up and down in front of it with a
can of kerosene and a flame thrower. The
only thing that's holding up matters is that
he hasn't been able to persuade Sinatra to
come and spend a week end in a specially
designed windowless room on the top floor.

By this time, the Crosby life story is as
well known as a Grimm Fairy tale—spelled
with one m. Most Americans are aware that
despite all he says to the contrary, he was
born in Spokane, not Tacoma, on May 2,
1904, was christened Harry Lillis, is now
40 years old. He was air-borne into a seven-
child family and he got into the average

SAYS CROSBY:

*I fell asleep on the stoop as
Sickle-snout says. The fire
resulted from a comical
hotfoot—one of Swirl-
snozz's minor methods of
bringing down the house.*

*An idea that could only
come to a vindictive sadist
bent on the plans this li-
belous lout is mulling for
Red Skelton.*

*This is an example of how
Hope labors a point to such
an extent as to insult his
audience's intelligence.*

e makes love languidly

In one of his rare love scenes (*Here Come the WAVES*), Crosby kisses Betty Hutton with all the enthusiasm he can muster.

love scene played by Crosby and Betty Hutton. With these three picture elements and
two text elements all to be blended into a cohesive whole, the layout artist who designed this spread was faced with unusual difficulties. It seemed to the editors that he
solved them fairly well; at least he avoided "visual conflict" by arranging the elements
so that no one gets in the way of another.

In corset and bloomers, Melchior wipes face clean of ruddy make-up worn in first two acts. In Act III dying Tristan wears sickly pallor, with deep lines in hands and face. Melchior has only 18 minutes to effect complete change before curtain rises to show him on his de He has to work fast because Met must pay stagehands $300 overtime if final curtair

This picture spread from an article in *Life* on Lauritz Melchior demonstrates that a well-known personality can also be put in the "screwball" class. Mr. Melchior, who sings on the radio and the screen as well as at the opera, is not averse to publicity even if it means posing for a *Life* photographer in corset and bloomers. From a publicity standpoint, he is wise, because there is no gainsaying the additional reader interest

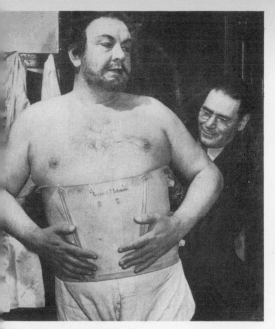

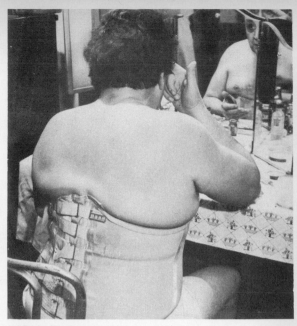

or is strapped into his corset by Dresser Angelo Casamassa. He wears it not for reasons ~~ty~~, but support. *Tristan* is exhausting, requires its hero to be on stage almost four hours.

Melchior avoirdupois overflows top of corset which he never wears off stage or on concert tour. It was designed by him, has suspender attachment and four buttons to hold up armored pants.

~~SSING~~-ROOM SCENE ALSO
~~S~~ HIGH DRAMATIC PITCH

The excitement and tension backstage between the acts of *Tristan* almost equals that of the performance on stage. In a dressing room once occupied by the great Enrico Caruso, Melchior encases his 250 pounds in a formidable corset and applies his own make-up. Racing against curtain time, he works fast and silently.

Worried stage manager darts in and out with watch in hand, urging him to greater speed. Mrs. Melchior and the dresser, Angelo Casamassa, stand ready to help him into his trappings. Melchior alone maintains a stately dressing-room calm, says that it is because his nerves are buried so deep inside him they don't show.

~~ed~~ tunic goes over Tristan's coat of mail. Next he buckles on his sword, places winged ~~on~~ his brown wig. He never goes on until Mrs. Melchior pronounces costume perfect.

Mrs. Melchior follows Tristan to stage carrying train. She watches performance from wings, sends him on with fond "*Hals und Beinbruch*" ("May you break your neck and your legs").

engendered by these behind-the-scenes shots. In addition to the "inside information" flavor such photographs give an article, they provide many readers with the psychological satisfaction of being able to feel superior in some way to the celebrity about whom they are reading. That is a basic reason why the flaws and foibles of the subject are important in personality pieces.

A Boy and a President, 1933-1944

1933

On March 4 Franklin Delano Roosevelt rode to his inauguration as 32nd President of the U.S. with ex-President Hoover. The nation was in a crisis. Totally unaware of this, Thomas Reilly Dibble of Englewood, N. J., a quiet, introspective boy of 10 who loved the out-of-doors and was known to his friends as "Dibbs," was vacationing in Cape Cod with his family.

1934

Trying to lift the national economy by its bootstraps, F.D.R. and G Hugh Johnson made the U.S. alphabet-conscious with NRA. Again summ ing in Connecticut, Dibbs (left) formed a strong attachment to his aggress cousin Chad (Charles) Mason. Dibbs' sister Julie Lou "tagged along," a the inseparable boys victimized her, getting her to do all their wo

1935

Roosevelt, shown at Hyde Park with his son, Franklin, collided with the Supreme Court, which began invalidating New Deal acts. In Englewood, Dibbs played with his dog Sandersfield (born in Sandersfield, Mass.). The dog followed Dibbs everywhere, even to school, waiting by his bike. One day Sandersfield was killed by a car. Dibbs went to his room, shut the door, cried.

1936

Campaigning vigorously, the President won re-election for a second ter Now in Tenafly, N. J., Dibbs' family had political discussions with th breakfast, but Dibbs took no part. Chad (left) moved in with the fam for a year. Dibbs announced to his alarmed parents a plan to buy a b constrictor and "raise young ones." It took four hours to dissuade hi

1937

Roosevelt went fishing in May; more important, he aroused the country by proposing a reorganization of the Supreme Court. Meanwhile, Dibbs' interest turned to pelts: he bought traps, began arising at dawn; it was a family joke—until he caught a mink in New Jersey's Palisades. He was growing taller, and when beside his mother (above) he stood very straight.

1938

In Chicago, F.D.R. called upon the world to "quarantine the aggressor Ethiopia, Spain, China were in flames. Dibbs' family moved to Manchest Vermont, and his father (above) drove them to school every day. Early o morning their house caught fire, and Dibbs rescued Julie from her burn room; praised, he gave all credit to his dog, Legion, who, he said, woke him

In the spread shown here, the parallel-contrast continuity device (Chapter 3) was employed in a double album featuring the late President Roosevelt and a young man who was 10 at the time of his first inauguration, an American soldier at the time of his fourth. The story, timed to appear during the week of the 1945 inauguration, was, in a sense, a condensed history of Mr. Roosevelt's years in the White House. The pictures

939

rom a vacation at sea Roosevelt sped to Washington as Hitler prepared to
vade Poland. Though beginning to be conscious of the impact of world
ents, that winter Dibbs thought mostly of skiing. Loathing school, still
ving the out-of-doors, he told his parents dramatically: "Just give me a
an and a knife and a horse and that's all you ever have to give me."

1940

While the U.S. teetered on a precarious neutrality, F.D.R. inspected defense
plants. Dibbs graduated from high school into a world at war. The next
night he went out with another boy, returned tipsy; in the morning his father
offered him some gin, watched him grow ill, and let it go at that. The family
moved to New York, and Dibbs enrolled in the Art Students League.

941

rving a third term now, the President reached the year's climax when
signed a declaration of war on Germany, Japan, Italy. But months before,
bbs had begun thinking maturely about World War II, concluded that it
d a personal meaning for him; at 18 he enlisted in the American Field
rvice and on March 9 sailed for North Africa as an ambulance driver.

1942

Roosevelt called for unheard-of quantities of arms and inspected training
camps. Dibbs returned from North Africa. He walked into his home unexpectedly one July evening at 11 o'clock, kissed his mother, sat down and
talked until 5 a.m. He registered in the draft, spent a few months at home,
then joined the merchant marine, sailing as an ordinary seaman on tankers.

943

he President flew to Casablanca, Quebec, Cairo, Teheran. Dibbs returned
me, had his picture taken with his mother, father, and Julie—now an art
udent and a Conover model. Dibbs' war experiences had changed him;
ll quiet, introspective, he was now more self-assertive, he had opinions and
ve them. He wanted to be a pilot and enlisted in the Army Air Forces.

1944

Franklin Delano Roosevelt on November 8 was still President; he was also
Dibbs' commander-in-chief. The AAF sent Dibbs to Scott Field, Ill., to
become a radio technician; there he celebrated his 21st birthday. Roosevelt
the President, and Dibbs the soldier, who typifies the millions of youths
who have grown up with F.D.R., now together face four critical years.

Beginning his fourth term, F.D.R. faces his greatest responsibility to youth: victory, and lasting peace

show him growing old, tired and haggard under the tremendous burden of his re-
sponsibilities; captions provide a running summary of the momentous events in which
he participated, played against a similar chronicling of the peaceful, happy childhood
of the boy in the snapshots. Neither sequence, published alone, would have nearly the
reader appeal of the parallel sequences.

CHAPTER 6

The Picture Story in Drawings

WHEN A MAGAZINE editor decides that a picture story should be done with drawings, he has convinced himself that it cannot be well done with photographs. Other things being equal, he would almost always prefer the photographic technique: there is no substitute for photographic realism.

However, there are stories for which no photographs are available and for which none can be obtained. Other stories can be made more graphic, more exciting or more accurate with pen or brush than would be possible with a camera. In a few instances, photographs and drawings are combined, but it is difficult to find many examples of successful blendings of two visual techniques.

A writer assigned to the production of an article to be told with drawings faces many of the same problems as a writer working with photographs, and some additional ones. In each, the same kind of preliminary preparation is needed: thorough research, a basic decision on story angle, a narrow focus, a detailed shooting script. When drawings are to be used, these steps, of course, are taken in consultation with the art director and staff artist assigned to the story, whose understanding of every detail should be as complete as the writer's.

Generally speaking, a writer working with an artist has to do much more careful advance research on minute details than a writer working with a photographer; he has also to do more preliminary writing

and editing. In compensation, he is not required to do the amount of field work that confronts the producer of a story done with photographs.

Early and earnest attention to minute details is a "must" requirement, for the artist can put into the pictures only what the writer supplies. The photographer relies on the camera to reproduce the subject's smile, or the angle of a rifle, or the nature of a gesture; but for such important minutiae the artist must depend, in almost every instance, on information supplied by his collaborator. This is not a discussion of "creative" art—an artist's own interpretation of a person, scene or event—but of the art of illustrating actual happenings with a minimum of distortion.

Assume, for example, that an article is to be prepared on the brilliant exploit of an American fighter pilot who shot down five Japanese planes in one engagement. It is the writer's responsibility to discover every fact about that engagement which can be gleaned from any source—from the pilot himself, if possible; failing that, from his commanding officer or fellow pilots, from newspaper dispatches, War Department records, the pilot's friends and relatives, anybody who has a fragment of information.

Moreover, the writer must learn a great deal about the plane in which the pilot did his fighting. If it was a P-47, it must look like one in the illustrations. The locale of the action must be known and studied; likewise, the kinds of enemy planes involved, the objectives of the attack, the individual story of each Japanese defeat, and a hundred other pertinent details.

Having amassed such information, the writer has to convey it to the art director and the artist. This can be done in conversation, but not nearly so satisfactorily as in writing. The best procedure for the writer to follow at this stage is to write a complete text article — 3,000 or 4,000 words, if necessary. This does not have to be tight, polished prose, but should be comprehensive.

If the writer has done his work well up to this point, his manuscript can be the basis for everything that follows. It should be read carefully by both staff artist and art director, and gone over, sentence by sentence, in consultation with the writer. From such discussion will emerge the story angle, the visual approach to be taken and a list of picture situations. Whether the artist is to make wash drawings, work with pen and ink or lithograph crayon is a decision usually made by the art director.

The writer, however, should help decide how many pictures are to be used, which situations are to be eliminated and which pictures are to be "played up." It may be that his text will supply 25 possible pictures. By combining some situations and eliminating others, he can perhaps reduce the number to 10 or 12. As a general rule, the absolute minimum required to tell the story is the largest number that should be suggested in the script from which the illustrator will work.

This is a major way in which an article done with drawings differs from one done with photographs. The reason is largely one of economy. In preparing a script for a photographic picture story, the writer should include every situation at all likely to be considered in the final selection of pictures, especially if the story is to be produced at any distance from the office. Film and bulbs are cheap compared to time and traveling costs, and often it is impossible to get a picture if it is missed the first time. On the other hand, the picture script for an artist must be whittled down to absolute essentials if the cost is not to be prohibitive. The best illustrators are paid by the drawing—and very well for each—and it is ruinous to the art director's budget to order more drawings than will be needed.

With the script and the writer's text, the illustrator usually receives a rough layout design which shows him what size each picture will be in reproduction and the visual relation of each to the others. In completing his part of the story, he will have to make a number of decisions on his own: for example, which details to include in any given picture and which to leave out. His visual translation of the writer's facts has to be convincing and accurate, but not necessarily 100 per cent literal.

To get the proper emphasis, the illustrator must "edit" every drawing, just as the writer edits his text in selecting basic picture situations from it.

The illustrator also must decide, largely on his own, which pictures are to be close-ups, which are to be presented at longer range, and the angles from which they are to be drawn. An experienced writer will be able to provide guidance on such details, but a wise one will let the illustrator have his head on a purely illustrative problem, just as he will usually yield to a photographer on a technical photographic question.

Customarily, the artist submits rough sketches for approval before finishing his drawings. At this stage the writer gets his final opportunity to check visual details against his own facts and ask for corrections if they are needed. All he has to do then is condense his 3,000 or 4,000 words to the few hundred allowed him, and make sure they blend with the pictures into a cohesive, comprehensive, interesting picture story!

Mark Wayne Clark: Super-Spy

He led the dangerous secret mission which cleared the way for American troop landings in French North Africa

STORY BY DON WHARTON—DRAWINGS BY FRED LUDEKENS—
17TH IN LOOK's SERIES OF ARTICLES ON AMERICAN HEROES

1 **In the dead of night** General Clark leaves London on the war's biggest undercover assignment. With him are General Lemnitzer, Colonels Hamblen and Holmes, and Navy Captain Wright — all volunteers for the daring mission. Dressed as civilians, they set out in a curtained auto, transfer to a blacked-out train, speed toward Scotland. They switch to a plane, fly to an undisclosed base, transfer to a ship. At sea the ship keeps a rendezvous with a submarine and the mission transfers again. While the marine heads for Africa, Clark checks plan. three young Commando officers skilled at ing enemy shores. Clark is 46, a tall, a West Pointer who at 21 led troops in F

4 **Vichy police,** tipped off by a suspicious Arab servant, start for the isolated conference house. Word is flashed that the police are on the way. Maps disappear, French officers hurriedly change back into civilian clothes, take flight in every direction. One French general makes his change in a minute flat and leaves through a window. Clark and his staff gather up their papers and equipment, furtively make their way to the safety of the empty wine cellar.

5 **Clark hears the police** questionin house-owner overhead. While one Com do chokes off a cough, Clark fingers a ca He wonders whether to shoot or bri police if they enter the cellar. Finally, th

---

An exciting historical episode of World War II, unrecorded photographically because of the secret and dangerous nature of General Clark's mission, is re-created above in a sequence of wash drawings. Fred Ludekens, one of America's leading magazine and advertising illustrators, made these drawings as realistic as possible, working from photographs of principal characters and from descriptive data provided by the writer, Don

shore in North Africa, Clark watches for a re-arranged signal—a light from an isolated ouse. The signal hour comes, but the house ays dark. Clark's men lie low for 24 hours, g into iron rations. Then the light flashes.

3 **Inside the house** Clark finds French officers who have changed from civilian clothes to full uniforms. The owner reveals he has sent his wife away on vacation and given his Arab servants a few days off. Clark begins con-ferences which last all night and day. He de-termines which Frenchmen will be friendly to American occupation, secures military data, arranges for Algiers airfields to be delivered as soon as American troops start landing.

ack on the beach, everyone fears the surf is too heavy for rubber lifeboats. Clark ets out anyway—with Commando Livingstone. Their boat is spilled and Clark ses $18,000 in gold. After more boats are overturned there is a long wait in the old, dark night. The boats are lightened for another try. Just as the last boat aches the submarine, Vichy police cars drive up to the conference house.

7 **In London, Clark confers** with Lieut. Gen. Dwight Eisen-hower. Three weeks later, Americans land in North Africa without prolonged land resistance. Clark's work saves thou-sands of American lives, much valuable time. He is made a Lieutenant General—youngest in the United States Army.

Wharton, after weeks of careful research. The article is presented as a narrative chron ology, based entirely on fact but with the structure of fiction—a dramatic beginning, development of suspense and a climactic ending. The writer's preliminary outline for this article developed dozens of possible picture situations, of which the seven shown above finally were used.

THE YANKS TAKE OVER ...continued

Here is a city just captured from the enemy. Recent battles, and prolonged Axis rule, have left chaos. U. S. Army civil-affairs officers are given this command: Turn chaos into order.

DRAWINGS BY EDWIN EBERMAN

SUPPLIES TO

DAM WRECKED BY ENEMY

RADIO STATION

VIADUCT UNDER REPAIR

RAIL ST

HEAVILY BOMBED AREA

TEMPORARY OCCUPATION HQ

BOATS BEING RECONDITIONED

BOMB-BATTERED DOCKS

TRANSPORTS UNLOADING

SUPPLIES

This might be any city in any Axis-held country. After an all-out assault, climaxed by American occupation, Army authorities are moving in and to

First step in governing is to post notices (printed weeks ahead) telling the populace what U. S. occupation means and what must be done to help restore order. Tone of the notices is firm but friendly: people are confused, helpless, not sure the fighting is really ended. For some time U. S. military police will guard the city.

Soldiers will feed the starving. Local stocks of food and needed materials will be taken up, accounted for, paid for by civil-affairs officers. If these stocks are insufficient, Army supplies may have to be diverted to civilians. In any case, strict rationing will guarantee fair distribution of whatever is available.

To prevent epidemics, medical office ordered to inoculate the population with serums; Army nurses will help Civilian been living underground to escape bomb ill from malnutrition and poor sanitation. supply system will probably need to be

The future, as well as the past, can be dealt with in drawings—and obviously the camera is not even a possible rival for the illustrator in the field of prediction. In the spread shown above, the artist (Edwin Eberman) projected the occupation and management of an enemy city by the American Army long before any such city had been captured by our troops. In this type of article the artist's imagination is permitted

164

SUPPLIES TO FRONT

GE UNDER REPAIR

SUPPLIES TO FRONT

AIRPORT BACK IN SERVICE

PONTOON BRIDGE

T. BUILDINGS WRECKED

BOMBED GAS TANK

BRIDGE UNDER REPAIR

BOMBED POWER STATION

SCUTTLED ENEMY SHIPS

TEMPORARY DISPENSARY

nemy retreats over the horizon, transports unload arms and supplies to speed pursuit. For what is going on behind the lines, note the panels below.

must be sheltered. As material becomes e, they will repair their own homes (with elp where needed). They will also do general uction work under Army supervision; when g for the Army, they will be paid. U. S. ex- ll run public utilities and essential industries.

Radio stations, necessary to public information, will probably be closed to local people at first. Signal Corps technicians will man control panels; Army officers will make public announcements, tell the population when to stay off the streets, direct them where to report for food, work and assistance.

Schools will reopen — after necessary repairs have been made — and children will go back to their usual classes under their regular teachers. American super- vision will be light. The Army's main concerns will be restoring normal classroom routine and seeing that all traces of Axis doctrine are eliminated from text materials.

more leeway than in the narration of actual history, but it is nevertheless held within the realm of probabilities. The city in the large drawing above is wholy imaginary, but it is completely lifelike. The activities depicted in the smaller drawings were exact- ly those contemplated by our military leaders when the conquest and occupation of Germany were in the planning stage.

EIGHT MEN ON TWO RAFTS

The Army Air Forces conducts a scientifically controlled experiment in the problem of survival at sea

A bomber limps toward home after a successful attack on an enemy harbor. Two of the four engines "conked out," the controls of the flak-riddled ship half shot away, it sinks ever lower over the tropical sea. Her crew prepares for "ditching." Do these men have the best possible chance of living to fight again another day?

That's what the Army Air Forces wanted to know.

In the Gulf of Mexico twenty miles out of a Florida base, a few weeks ago, drifted two rubber life rafts, to all appearances occupied by survivors of a crash landing at sea. They were volunteers—officers and enlisted men—testing the life rafts, equipment and rations carried on AAF bombers. It was on a Sunday afternoon that nine men, wearing summer flying suits, fatigue hats, socks and shoes, went overboard from the Army crash boat P-269 into two fully equipped life rafts of latest design.

Eight of these men (one became seriously seasick) remained in their rafts six days and nights, coming aboard the attending ship a few minutes each day for medical tests. The experiment, illustrated on these pages by T/Sgt. Greg Duncan, gained information of great value to the airmen who fly and fight in enemy skies.

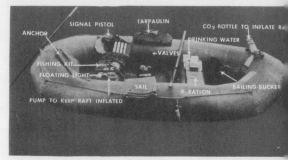

Some of equipment carried on latest type inflatable life raft furnished U. S. bomb

DRAWINGS BY T/SGT. GREG DUN

A 38-year-old officer went without food or water for four days and nights, felt no ill effects because, before boarding the raft, he drank more than three times his usual daily intake of fluids (which were apparently stored up by his body) and refrained from smoking. Others, on short rations, suffered more.

During the first day, men in one raft protected themselves from the sun w a tarpaulin; men in the other raft, who did not, suffered considerably more fr dehydration. One man (with adhesive patch on back) tested various sunb preventives. Eyesight remained normal despite constant exposure to the s

This article tells the story of a test made by the Army Air Forces of life-saving rafts and equipment in the Gulf of Mexico. Sixteen volunteers stayed on the rafts for six days and six nights to give the equipment a thorough trial under conditions approximating those which would confront a downed bomber crew. Both photographs and drawings were made throughout the experiment, but the editors decided to construct

ere storms and squalls buffeted the men for two days. They caught rain r in pouches built into their tarpaulins for that purpose. By the second day, y complained of being weak, easily fatigued, showed poor judgment, confu- irritability; but they all returned to normal quickly when given water.

Two men with little fishing experience tested the life-raft fishing equipment. Selecting the largest hooks and lines, they fished for several hours without a catch. Then, trying the smaller hooks and pork-rind bait, they caught a small fish quickly, cut it up for bait, and within an hour caught two ten-pounders.

men tested a tempered-glass signaling mirror (left) and a Delano sun still listilling sea water. Frequent "dunking," keeping clothes wet, was found to ease greatly hardships due to exposure from sun; it also diminished weight and dehydration from perspiration; noticeably improved the men's spirits.

A pyrotechnic pistol was found valuable for signaling. Except for weariness and mental fatigue, the men had suffered few physical changes by the end of the week. But they lost over a pound a day on an average, the thinnest men at the start losing most, the fattest the least. All were happy to end the test.

the story with five drawings and one small diagrammatic photograph of a raft and some equipment. Air Forces censors had eliminated a number of photographs on the ground that they revealed too many details not yet known to the enemy. With these gone, the story would have been photographically dull. Drawings were more dramatic than photographs in this instance, and less likely to be censored.

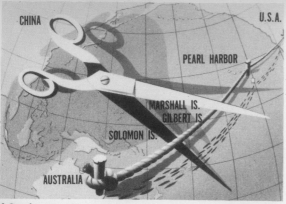

1 **Our chances** of a Pacific comeback after Pearl Harbor depended on our keeping open the lifeline between America and Australia. Japanese penetration of the Marshall, Gilbert and Solomon Islands threatened this lifeline in 1942.

2 **First offensive** move of the U. S. in the Pacific was the February raid on Kwajalein and Wotje in the Marshalls, using the one-two punch and sea bombardment to pound these outposts. Halsey led the ta...

Bayonet-pierced islands s...

7 **Now our great** Pacific offensive has come within range of Japan defenses. Our Navy strikes Japan and the conquered islands from (see pages 28-29); our Army's B-29's raid Jap industries from th...

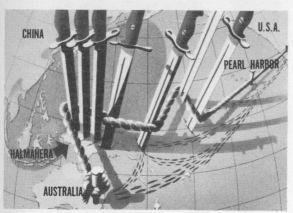

5 **Late in 1943** and early in 1944, Spruance's "triphibious" B-Squad forces took Tarawa and Kwajalein, driving the enemy from the Gilberts and Marshalls, and giving us bases from which to strike Japan's west Pacific positions.

6 **By July, 1944,** MacArthur had reached the west tip of New Guinea — in August, he started bombing Halmahera. The stage was set for a two-pronged offensive. The naval conquests of Saipan, Guam, formed the other prong.

In wartime, one important function of the magazine artist is the animation of maps. This is done in many ways—with ships, airplanes, trains, artillery, marching men, political symbols, caricatures of political and military leaders and so on. In the spread above, the artist has used symbols of familiar objects to help tell a visual story entitled *Our Coming Conquest of Japan.* The American "lifeline" between Pearl Harbor and

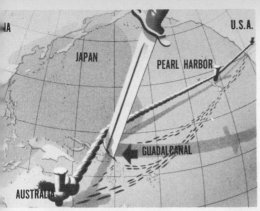

august, 1942, we began our island invasion strategy when we landed
~uadalcanal. The fight was hard but we learned much—in the air, on sea
land. Lesson No. 1: only bayonets can hold what air and sea fighting win.

Meantime, MacArthur's Australian-American Army had begun cleaning up
New Guinea. The Buna-Gona offensive was made possible by air transport
jungle jumps. Rabaul neutralized, our A-Squad lifeline was secured.

re our A Squad and B Squad have conquered the Japanese

Australia is a rope, and the Japanese threat to cut it is a pair of scissors. Our one-two
punch against the Marshall Islands is depicted with boxing gloves; leaping arrows
forecast the direction of future advances. The information on which the pictures
are based was supplied by the writer, the visual scheme was then worked out in consultation between writer and artist.

What the Nazis Think of Us

By JOHN GUNTHER

War correspondent, author of *Inside Europe*, *Inside Asia*, etc.

With a sampling of Dr. Goebbels' fantasies illustrated by cartoonist Carl Rose

The Goebbels plan was to drown us in a sea of falsehood. Following are 17 Nazi lies about U.S.:

1 Americans are "mongrels without nationality or culture"; the *Herrenvolk* are urged to regard us as weakling. . . .

2 . . . except when frightened by stories about American barbarians who commit atrocities and molest women.

3 The American soldier is a military moron who "relies for his strength on his knowledge of precision instruments."

4 He is also "broad-shouldered and tall . . . moves with catlike agility . . . carries a two-edged dagger." (Take your pick.)

5 And, oh yes, the Yank is a coward whose fighting is done for him by "Canadians, Negroes, Red Indians and Kaffirs."

6 Moreover, with a straight face, our men "lack the profound moral qualities so conspicuous in the German soldier."

7 Americans at home are arrogant and money-mad, our civilization characterized by refrigerators and built-in toilets.

8 But, in the next breath, "America is no longer the land of opportunity; instead it is a land of misery and sickness."

9 Our pilots are "convicts . . . [who] get great money rewards. After a few raids they can retire and live on their money."

10 "Americans, having no culture of their own, want to see that of Europe ruined." (So the Nazis "save" paintings!)

11 Our "outstanding social type [is] the gangster," produced by crossing "pagan backwoodsman and criminal Jew."

On these pages, the talents of a famous writer, John Gunther, were combined with those of a well-known cartoonist, Carl Rose, to produce a picture story blended with a text article. For his text, Mr. Gunther studied dozens of Axis broadcasts and propaganda pieces issued over a period of years. From these he garnered a long list of Goebbels' inconsistencies in his description of American attitudes and characteristics,

12

Our troops are "rather nice boys, not devoid of some courage," who think of the war "in terms of a football game."

13

However, American politicians are not simpletons but scheming imperialists who plan to annex the French empire.

14

In fact, we are Machiavellian Edgar Bergens of international politics—we dictate British policy in world affairs.

15

And—simultaneously, of course—we are neophytes in world politics, boobish puppets for Stalin and world Communism.

16

To cap the confusion, Europeans are told our wartime promises "are futile because [America is] unsure of victory."

17

In the next breath, they are warned that "America is planning to rule the world." (And there are more lies below.)

These are but a few of many Nazi propaganda lies recorded by two United States Government agencies

Pumped into the German people day by day is a picture of the United States so wantonly distorted that it takes the breath away, even though we have long known that Dr. Goebbels is one of the most masterful liars alive.

I have spent the last few days going through propaganda directed by the Nazis to their home front and overseas. All the quotations in this article are from the Office of War Information and the Federal Communications Commission. The numbered cartoons on this and the preceding page are accurate transcriptions of Nazi lies recorded by these agencies.

We're Harmless Dopes—or Murderous Demons

The German propaganda machine unremittingly presents two contrasting pictures of Americans. One is that we are ignoramuses, a degenerate race of mongrels; the other, that we are cruel savages, so brutal that the German people must learn to fear and hate us.

Earlier in the war the Germans scornfully pretended to picture us as pushovers. They stressed our "inferiority." We were "unskilled fighting men, lacking the professional touch." They laughed at Eisenhower and in general described American troops as "simple-minded creatures misled by their leaders."

In a word, the Nazis were contemptuous of our military qualities. Since the invasion, the laugh is on the other side of the mouth.

But even now they seek to minimize our prowess—though they cannot conceal it any longer—by emphasizing what they call our "terroristic tactics" and our "vandalism." We are charged with deliberate attempts to destroy non-military objectives. Our airmen are pictured as "gangsters, destroyers, killers without mercy, inhuman monsters who take special pleasure in singling out defenseless women and children for slaughter from the air."

Further, they say, we bomb churches as "great sport"—a totally preposterous lie—"but what else can one expect from American barbarians? When they see a sacred historical treasure, they burn with a lust for destruction—out of revenge for the fact that they have neither culture nor ancient monuments."

For a time the Nazis' mouthpieces sowed utterly outrageous lies about American soldiers having been killed or otherwise punished for sexual offenses against Italian women.

We're Plutocrats—and Impoverished

Behind this Nazi concept of the American soldier is something deeper, the Nazi concept of the United States itself. The main lines that German propaganda seeks to stress are our "materialism and worship of money," our "mongrel background" and "gangsterism," our total "lack of culture" and our "imperialism."

Dr. Goebbels set the tune for this in an article in Das Reich. He said—among much else—that in America "everything is borrowed, everything spoiled by the process of Americanization." We go in for Verkitschung (vulgarization), which makes slang out of a language, jazz out of a waltz. We have no Volksein —no "basic road of life." And, "after reading the United States papers," says Goebbels, "we want to let cold water run over our hands."

As to worship of money, the Nazis continually declare that we "regard this war as big business" and a fit field for shady profits. Our Liberty ships are called "Kaiser's Coffins"— unsound and unseaworthy—and the Germans claim that this is not a "simple case of American ineptitude and bad planning, but of deliberate wickedness on the part of Henry Kaiser. He knows his work is rubbish, but it brings in money." Rubbish, indeed!

A contrasting lie, also common, is that Americans aren't really rich at all, that "American economy is facing disaster," and that "80 per cent of Americans live in poverty."

We're Conquering the World—but Losing the War

When we get into political matters the German propaganda line is confused beyond the point of conflict. The Nazis tell their people:

That our government is "treacherous," "callous," "cowardly," "warlike," "corrupt."

That "Roosevelt has a nauseating appetite to gobble up British possessions."

That we cheat the Russians by sending them inferior lend-lease goods.

That Roosevelt "surrendered to Bolshevism at Teheran."

That "Eisenhower wants control of the British railways."

That we have no intention of respecting the rights of neutrals or small nations.

That the recent inauguration in London of the American Broadcasting Station in Europe was the first step "in the American plan to dominate European radio."

That Undersecretary Stettinius, "who is not even entitled to address his own Congress, addressed Britain's Parliament to make known his decision"—a wild untruth.

That we plan to take Formosa from Japan and rule China after the war.

That we plan to Bolshevize Europe.

That we plan a policy of imperialistic capitalism, with profit our sole aim.

All these lies give a kind of poetic justice to our coming victory. Because we are fighting the Lie. Because we are fighting for the Truth, as much as for any single thing in this war.

and set them down on paper. With the aid of the writer and of LOOK's art director, Mr. Rose animated these contrasts in his cartoons, which were presented in numbered sequence over two-line captions lifted from the text. Hundreds of tests of reader preferences have shown that this kind of combination of drawings and text is highly popular with readers of mass magazines.

The love birds: They pay good money to watch a torrid love scene, then get lost in one of their own—with sound effects. The rest of the audience, which has also shelled out considerable cash and would rather see the screen version, wishes they would get lost permanently. Whatever became of the rumble seat?

Movie Etiquette

Are you an antisocial movie-goer? Check your manners with those of film enemies Nos. 1-6

Chief thorn in the side of the American film fan is the cinematic pest, that social moron who can't or won't learn the ABC's of movie etiquette. Though he may be a well-behaved citizen away from the movie house, once inside, his techniques for disrupting audience attention are ingenious and manifold. Movie statisticians compute that there are 75,000,000 paid attendances weekly. Conservatively estimating one nuisance for every 100 admissions gives the prodigious figure of 750,000 pest admissions weekly. On these four pages, artist William von Riegen has depicted six of the more notorious types for your further identification.

The big inch: Here she comes—irresistibly, without warning and for all the world like a grimly determined tugboat. She always has packages. Inhale!

The picture-hat type: If you're too much of a gentleman to ask her to take it off, you can always go home and read the novel the picture is based on.

Satirical drawings are employed here to present graphically some of the pet peeves of millions of moviegoers. Conceivably, the story could have been done with "candid" photographs, but the difficulties are almost insurmountable. First, such an approach would require co-operation of a theater manager willing to risk the ire of his customers. Second, because movie theaters are dark and one flash bulb would give the

The squirmy set: They are the giggly girls who huddle 2 to 12 to the covey. They arrive in a tittering dither, inevitably and immediately find themselves more exciting than any picture, usually start a whispering campaign against it. A shouting counterattack, periodically repeated, may bring some relief.

Horizontal Harry: He attacks from the rear, pushes bony knees into your spine, rocks your seat. Usually a double threat, he also rattles candy wrappers.

The row hog: He's that insurmountable barrier impervious to all flanking attacks. A suggestion: retreat to the balcony, then depth-bomb him.

game away, the pictures could be obtained only with "black-out" film and bulbs. Third, the photographer would be invading the privacy of his subjects. Posed with models, the photographs would almost surely have a wooden, unreal quality. So the artist with a comic touch, able to distort for emphasis without losing realism, was given the writer's shooting script and sent to the movies.

"The Road to Serfdom"

By F. A. HAYEK
WHO SAYS:

"America is following the same road

Today, individuals and groups bent on planning our future are a feature of American life. But recent history proves that dictators follow "national planners" as surely as night follows day. What happened in Russia, Italy and Germany can happen in America, too, if we ignore the warnings outlined here ————————

IN ONE OF THE MOST CONTROVERSIAL BOOKS of a generation —*The Road to Serfdom*, published by the University of Chicago Press—Friedrich A. Hayek is making America take a long, hard look down the road he feels our "national planners" would have us follow. Economist Hayek knows this road: he has spent half his adult life in his native Austria, half in England and America. And he warns that he now sees at work in the democracies many of the same forces he saw produce totalitarianism and slavery in Europe. Among the major points he makes are:

DICTATORSHIP IS EASED IN. "The whole system will tend toward that plebiscitarian dictatorship in which the head of the government is from time to time confirmed in his position by popular vote, but where he has all the powers at his command to make certain that the vote will go in the direction he desires." This situation is close enough to the "spend and elect—elect and spend" philosophy to be grasped with no great effort of imagination.

OUR DANGER IS IMMEDIATE. Hayek says that nine out of ten of the lessons our "planners" want us to learn from this war are precisely those lessons the Germans *did* learn from the last war.

WE MUST PLAN FOR COMPETITION. This, says Hayek, is the one kind of planning compatible with democracy—because democratic individualism and freedom exist only under a competitive system. Such planning, he says, should include: 1) modernizing of business rules; 2) restoration of the free market by eliminating price favors to various economic groups; 3) an ending of the unpredictable, hot-and-cold improvising of "national planners" that now makes it so difficult for the individual businessman to plan ahead.

FREEDOM IS OUR GREATEST WEALTH. "It is only because we have forgotten what unfreedom means that we often overlook the patent fact that . . . a badly paid unskilled worker in this country has more freedom to shape his life than many a small entrepreneur in Germany or a much better paid engineer or manager in Russia." That is the central message in a book every American should read.

1. War forces "national planning" To permit total mobilization of your country's economy, you gladly surrender many freedoms. You know regimentation was forced by your country's enemies.

2. Many want "planning
Arguments for a "peace pl board" are heard before ends. Wartime "planners," w to stay in power, encourage

7. They try to "sell" the plan to all In an unsuccessful effort to educate people to uniform views, "planners" establish a giant propaganda machine (which coming dictator will find handy).

8. The gullible do find ag Meanwhile, growing nationa sion leads to protest meeti least educated, thrilled a vinced by fiery oratory, form

13. No one opposes the leader's plan It would be suicide; new secret police are ruthless. Ability to force obedience always becomes the No. 1 virtue in the "planned state." Now all freedom is gone.

14. Your profession is "p The wider job choice pro now defunct "planners" tur be a tragic farce. "Planner have delivered, never will be

---

The translation of important ideas on serious subjects into a cohesive picture story is often more successfully accomplished with drawings than with photographs. In the example above, writer and artist have combined their efforts to digest for millions the message contained in F. A. Hayek's *The Road to Serfdom*, a treatise on political economy that in book form is unlikely to be read by more than thousands. In such a project,

DRAWINGS BY FRED LUDEKENS

sia followed . . . Italy followed . . . Germany followed."

nners" promise Utopias . . .
lan for farmers goes well in
eas, a plan for workers is
in cities—and so on. Many
anners" are elected to office

4 . . . but can't agree on ONE Utopia
With peace, a new legislature meets;
but "win the war" unity is gone. The
"planners" nearly come to blows. Each
has his own pet plan, won't budge.

5. And citizens can't agree either
When the "planners" finally patch up
a temporary plan months later, citizens in turn disagree. What the farmer
likes, the factory worker doesn't like.

6. "Planners" hate to force agreement
Most "national planners" are well-meaning idealists, balk at any use of force.
They hope for some miracle of public
agreement as to their patchwork plan.

idence in "planners" fades
re "planners" improvise, the
ormal business is upset. All
People now feel—rightly—
anners" can't get things done.

10. The "strong man" is given power
In desperation, "planners" authorize
new party leader to hammer out a
plan and force its obedience. Later,
they'll dispense with him—they *think*.

11. The party takes over the country
By now, confusion is so great that obedience to the new leader must be obtained at all costs. Maybe you join the
party yourself to aid national unity.

12. A negative aim welds party unity
Early step of all dictators is to inflame
the majority in common cause against
some scapegoat minority. In Germany,
Nazis' negative aim was anti-Semitism.

ur wages are "planned"
ns of the wage scale must be
ary and rigid. Running a
d state" from central head-
s is clumsy, unfair, inefficient.

16. Your thinking is "planned"
In the dictatorship the "planners" un-
intentionally created, there is no room
for difference of opinion. Posters, radio, press—all tell you the same lies.

17. Your recreation is "planned"
It is no coincidence that sports and
amusements have been carefully
"planned" in Russia, Italy, Germany.
Once started, "planners" can't stop.

18. Your disciplining is "planned"
If you're fired from your job, it's apt to
be by firing squad. What used to be an
error has now become a crime against
the state. Thus ends the road to serfdom.

the heaviest burden is on the writer, who must distill the essence of the original work
into a simple sequence without changing its meaning. In addition to this condensation, he must solve the problem of reducing the essential message to a shooting script,
then he must work out, in collaboration with the artist, the visual pattern to be
employed in conveying his condensation to the reader.

THE FLYING FORTRESS

Cutaway sketches of the newest Boeing B-17 reveal little-known details of how the big bomber performs in action.

DRAWINGS BY HERMAN GIESEN. TEXT BY GROFF CONKLIN.

Labels in illustration: AILERON; RUBBER DE-ICER STRIP; NACELLE; GASOLINE TANKS; ENGINE No. 4; LANDING LIGHT; NACELLE; ENGINE No. 3; TOP WINDOW; CO-PILOT; PILOT; TOP TURRET; TOP TURRET GUNNER; R... OPER...; OIL TANKS; NOSE GUNS; BOMBARDIER; NAVIGATOR; NAVIGATOR'S TABLE; RADIO LOOP ANTENNA; PITOT HEAD (AIR SPEED INDICATOR); NACELLE; ENGINE No. 2; WHEEL, RETRACTED

With guns blazing to ward off enemy interceptors, this American Flying Fortress is portrayed headed for home base after a smashing bombardment.

Salient points of the Fortress: *Speed:* More than 300 m.p.h. *Altitude:* More than 35,000 feet. *Length:* About 75 feet. *Wingspan:* 105 feet. *Firepower:* 10–13 machine guns of .50 caliber. *Bomb capacity:* 3½ ton or more, in bomb bay. *Bombsight:* Not shown, th Norden sight (a military secret) is located in th

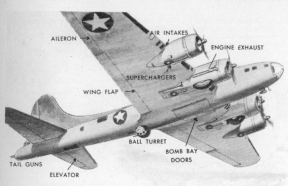

Labels: AILERON; AIR INTAKES; ENGINE EXHAUST; SUPERCHARGERS; WING FLAP; BALL TURRET; BOMB BAY DOORS; TAIL GUNS; ELEVATOR

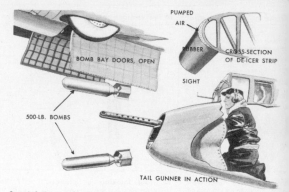

Labels: PUMPED AIR; BOMB BAY DOORS, OPEN; RUBBER; CROSS-SECTION OF DE-ICER STRIP; SIGHT; 500-LB. BOMBS; TAIL GUNNER IN ACTION

The underside of the B-17 is as well armed as the topside; guns from the ball-turret, tail, nose and waist can all fire downward. The four Wright air-cooled engines are equipped with turbo-superchargers, which compress the sub-stratosphere air so that the mixture of air and gas will be rich enough for the engines to operate. Wing flaps reduce landing speed. Ailerons help in banking and turning.

Special Features: Release of bombs from the bomb bay is controlled by the bombardier in the nose. To break up any ice that may form, a pump forces air into the wing de-icer strip, expanding and contracting it. Because it offers ideal visibility, the tail gun emplacement is most popular with Fortress gunners. The sighting mechanism is synchronized with the two machine guns

Drawings are employed in the kind of article shown on these pages because they can be made infinitely more informative than photographs. A photographer can shoot tiny segments of the inside of an airplane, but only an artist can "cut away" whole sections of the giant machine and show the entire interior in relation to the over-all exterior. (An artist can also show us an airplane of the future while it is still in the

DORSAL FIN RUDDER

ELEVATOR

TAIL GUNNER

ELEVATOR

CHEMICAL TOILET

WAIST GUNNERS

BALL TURRET GUNNER

NACELLE

AIR INTAKES

CYCLONE 9

ENGINE

AILERON

LANDING LIGHT

RUBBER DE-ICER STRIP

as nose, within the bombardier's reach. *Top l turrets:* power-operated, they enable gun- aim in any desired direction. *Gasoline tanks:*

they are self-sealing; if a bullet penetrates, a chemi- cal substance automatically closes the hole. *Protec- tion:* firepower, thick armor and extraordinarily

tough internal construction make the B-17 almost im- pregnable. *Crew:* usually 10, with every man except pilot and co-pilot responsible for two or more jobs.

BULLET-PROOF WINDOW

.50 CALIBER MACHINE GUNS

APE TCH

QUICK-OPENING WAIST WINDOW

OXYGEN MASK

AMMUNITION "RECEPTION"

.50 CALIBER MACHINE GUN

OXYGEN FEED LINE

INTER-COMMUNICATION WIRE

WIRE FOR HEATING SUIT

GUN STANCHION

all-turret, one of the hottest spots in a B-17, has room enough only all men—average height 5' 6". Except for his phone connections, the is completely isolated from the rest of the crew. Using a secret mech- the gunner is able to swing the entire turret around to any position he Actually, instead of aiming only his guns, he aims himself at the target.

Waist gunners operate their deadly .50 caliber Browning machine guns through the open side windows of the fighter bomber. In a steady stream, the wire mesh ammunition "receptions" feed shells to the guns from fixed ammunition boxes overhead. The gunners' oxygen feeder tubes (connected with secret oxygen tanks) and electrified flying suits protect them against rarefied atmosphere and cold.

drawing-board or "mockup" stage.) To do a good job on this kind of project, an artist must have extremely detailed information and the close co-operation of the writer, who should know almost as much about the appearance of the plane as do the engineers who designed it. The cross-section drawing is a favorite with publications which deal largely with science and mechanics.

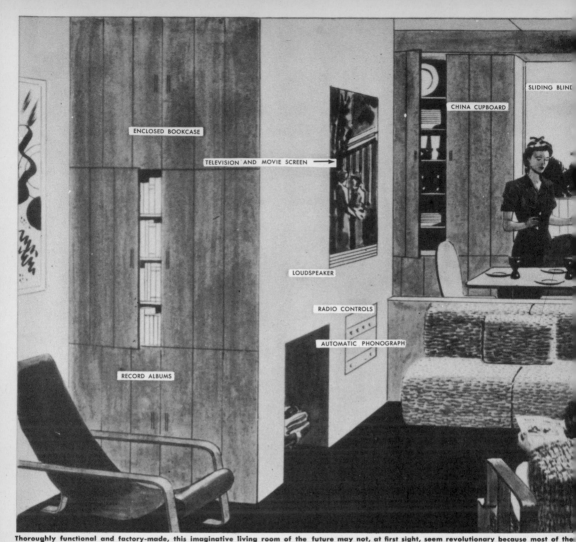

ENCLOSED BOOKCASE

TELEVISION AND MOVIE SCREEN →

LOUDSPEAKER

RADIO CONTROLS

AUTOMATIC PHONOGRAPH

RECORD ALBUMS

SLIDING BLIND

CHINA CUPBOARD

Thoroughly functional and factory-made, this imaginative living room of the future may not, at first sight, seem revolutionary because most of the

DESIGNED FOR BETTER LIVING

Your home of tomorrow will be more healthful, comfortable, attractive, durable — and cheaper

When this brave new world settles down after the war it will, sooner or later, live in a house of modern miracles. For technology and production know-how, spurred by war necessity, have telescoped decades of progress in the last few years. Your new home will reveal these developments wherever you turn.

Leading architects and designers agree that the home to come will be prefabricated and mass-produced, much as today's ships are being built. A house will come off the factory production line in neat packages and be assembled on the site like a jigsaw puzzle.

Construction, with materials such as plastics, plywood, glass, and light, noncorroding metals, will be stronger, cheaper than ever. Movable interior walls will enable you to enlarge or contract any room in the house as the occasion requires.

Air conditioning systems will permit the home owner to be his own weather man, will filter pollens causing hay fever and asthma. Acoustical tile or plaster will make the house soundproof, restful. Facsimile newspaper broadcasts, vanishing beds, countless other features will promote ease and efficiency.

The home sketched on these pages represents only one version of what we may expect within a few short years. It is a promise of America's productive and creative genius.

LIVING ROOM From the back of the bui couch, which cuts off the dining area, the table been pulled out. The chairs, upholstered with st proof and fireproof glass fiber, are movable. The also adjustable, swinging back at the press of a ton. Chair arms have remote controls for the st free radio, color television and record player (w can be slid out of the wall). **WINDOWS:** Sealed, breakable, they permit passage of the sun's vita carrying rays, keep dust out. Curtains operate single-rail track. **HEATING:** A "radiant" system, w may also be used for cooling in summer, consis pipes concealed in the walls and floor. **AIR CONDI ING:** The unit launders the air, keeps curtains walls clean, prevents drafts. **LIGHTING:** Indirect, rescent lights (their softness adjustable) line room just below the ceiling, are governed by an tric eye sensitive to outside variations in day! Ceiling spotlights can be turned on above the ch Hidden ultraviolet fixtures destroy air-borne teria. **OTHER FEATURES:** A central unit behind the place includes all electric inlets, air-conditic apparatus, water-supply and sewage connectio serve the entire house. The floor is of a nonslip ber composition; rugs are of synthetic wool. Th sulated plastic walls are crack-proof and the ce —of acoustical plaster—is sound-absorbent.

In the field of new housing, as in science and mechanics, the animated diagrammatic drawing is an important medium of communication. The problem in the example above was to present a panoramic view of a living room in one of tomorrow's prefabricated houses. Even if a sample room had been available, a photographer could not have distorted perspective to present it, *in toto,* as the artist did. And an artist

SPOTLIGHTS IN CEILING

INSULATED PLASTIC WALLS

INDIRECT LIGHTING

CURTAIN TRACK

CHINA CUPBOARD

CHAIR STORAGE

COLLAPSIBLE TABLE

COLLAPSIBLE CHAIRS

RADIO AND PHONOGRAPH CONTROL

TABLE STORAGE

ALL CHAIRS ADJUSTABLE

DRAWINGS BY ERIK NITSCHE

d to pleasurable, convenient living are hidden. It embodies only a few of the infinite possibilities suggested by recent technological progress.

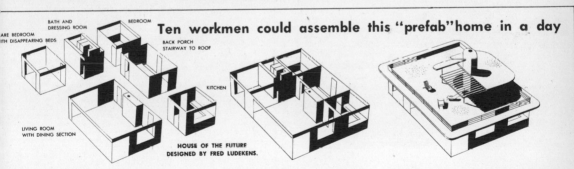

BATH AND DRESSING ROOM

BEDROOM

ARE BEDROOM
ITH DISAPPEARING BEDS

BACK PORCH
STAIRWAY TO ROOF

Ten workmen could assemble this "prefab" home in a day

KITCHEN

LIVING ROOM
WITH DINING SECTION

HOUSE OF THE FUTURE
DESIGNED BY FRED LUDEKENS.

A prefabricated home will come in room units such as these, which may be combined into any layout desired. Variety in homes would be attained by different sizes, designs, colors and textures.

The sections, with movable, interlocking partitions, are combined. Rooms may serve various purposes. The spare bedroom, with disappearing beds, could be turned into a rumpus room or a library.

The house is complete. Roof overhang allows for sun in winter, shade in summer. Other rooms may be added (or demounted) as needed. Theoretically, this house could be produced for $5,000.

was definitely required for the smaller cutaway pictures showing how the house will be assembled. The lettering on the pictures, calling the reader's attention to many small details, is a tested device known to increase readership of both pictures and accompanying text. It can be, often is, used in a picture story done with photographs, and is also employed effectively in advertisements.

How a Writer Presents Detailed Data to an Artist

Before he discussed the story of Solomon Parker with the illustrator, the writer prepared a 15-page manuscript detailing the pertinent facts about Parker's exploit which he had turned up during several weeks of patient investigation.

From the standpoint of construction and appearance, this is a very "rough" job, but it provided the artist with information he had to have before he could proceed.

SOLOMON PARKER: Rough Outline

THE EXPLOIT: Solomon Parker, Pharmacist's Mate in the United States Coast Guard, helped man one of the boats in the invasion of Sicily. He took troops in under machine-gun fire, raced out under both machine-gun fire and fire of German 88mm guns, got several more loads and took them in under bombing. Before the invasion of Sicily he had made the trip across the Atlantic in the tiny landing craft. Five weeks after the invasion began he was selected to become an officer---go to Coast Guard midshipman's school at New London.

THE MAN: Solomon Parker is 25; has dark eyes, hair, dark complexion, a little dark mustache. LOOK has photos made of him in the office. He was born in Queens Borough, New York. He went to St. Johns University in Brooklyn---the college of pharmacy, and took two years post graduate work. He entered the Coast Guard in January, 1942.

THE BOAT: This story provides an opportunity to show

---4---

Here's a closeup of an LCI. Artist should note locate of the No. 1 gun---for it was in that region that Parker spent considerable time under fire.

---5---

Here is another shot, showing American troops loading onto an LCI at Bizerte. The after part of the LCI is shown, with the armor for the gun crew.

Here are the first seven pages of the writer's preliminary draft for an article in LOOK's series on American heroes of World War II. (The remaining eight pages are on the following spread.) Before he presents this information to artist and art director, the writer has finished his research, learned all he can from any source about the hero and the exploit to be depicted. Because the LCI invasion craft is important in this story

much new material about the new landing craft: the LCI invasion
boat. Parker's boat was part of a ############ LCI flotilla.
His own boat was Number 96. It was an LCI (L) which means
a Landing Craft Infantry,Large. It is 150' long, has a beam of
15', draw 2 feet of water forward and about 4 feet of water aft.
This flat-bottom boat made its own way across the Atlantic with a crew of
4 officers and 30 men. In the rough weather in the Sicilian Strait
the night of the invasion it was rolling 30degrees. It did a job.

Here is a photo of one of the LCI's:

Painted on the
conning tower that
night of each boat
were strips indicat-
ing which beach
it was headed for.
Parker's boat was
heading for "YELLOW"
beach, thus strips
of Yellow, White and
Yellow as indicated
here. Flew the US
flag in action of
course.

I have indicated
with INK some of
the objects which
were hack-sawed off
before the invasion.

When the LCI touches the beach the ramps (you can see one
on the side) is rolled forward. It is down these ramps that the
troops rush into the water toward the beach. To get a clearer
idea of all this

look at this photo from the Infantry Journal. Here German and Italian
prisoners are boarding an LCI. Just reverse the men and you would
have a picture of our troops disembarking.

Here is another shot of the LCI's at Bizerte.

THE BACKGROUND: Parker's road to war began in Galveston
in March. On LCI no.96 he went to Key West, then to Norfolk,
then to Bermuda, Port Lyautey (north of Casblanca), Gibraltar,
and then along the Mediterranean Coast to Bizerte. He reached
Bizerte about the middle of June and began getting ready for
the invasion of Sicily.

The invasion was rehearsed on Cape Bon. Took load after
load of troops to the Cape,landed them, an all---to get the
timing right.

THE ACTION: As far as Parker was concerned, the invasion began
on July 7th when the Germans, discovering the accumulation of
ships at Bizerte, saw an invasion was coming. The German raided
Bizerte that night - -biggest air raid at Bizerte. Also biggest
anti-aircraft---thrown up by shore batteries and ships and all.
Whole place lit up with bombs, flares, searchlights, tracers from
the anti-aircraft. Shrapnel tearing into the sides of the
96.

On the morning of July 8 the LCIs began loading with troops. A
RCO Co (radio) came aboard the 96, marched to their bunks below.
Despite the smallest of the boat it still ad bunks for the more
than 200 men. The deck below was cut into four or five compartments.
About this time Parker was seeing that all of the crew of his boat,
and of no 95 and no 323, had their innoculations. He gave
tetnus innoculations to all the men and officers on these 3 ships.

When loaded the 96 pulled out into the middle of the lake. They
spent the day out there. Didn't want the soldiers too near to land.

Parker and the other Coast Guardsmen knew they were going to

invade something but weren't sure it was Sicily. When the troops
came aboard they knew: for the soldiers had pamphlets telling them
all about Sicily, with maps, and so on.

Next day, July 9, the 96 pulled out of the harbor into the
Mediterranean. It stood off the shore about 1 mile all day. That
day the skipper of the LCI (Lt (jg) Marshall Lee) called all the
crew into the boat's tiny messroom and gave them a pep talk; he
had a big map of Sicily and showed them what they were going to
do. Their beach was the "Yellow" beach east of Licata. Around sundown
they headed for Sicily.

Incidentally,as far as clothes were concerned Parker and the
other coast guards looked about like soldiers. Here is what
Parker had on:

Helmet : regular Army (new) helmet with
Red Cross in front.
Shirt: army, no tie
Life Jacket
Gas mask over left shoulder
Medical equipment slung over right shoulder
Trousers: Army---long.
Heavy Army brogans.

Suggestion: to artist, the life jackets will be about the only
item which will differentiate between troops and coast guards.

Incidentally, Lt. Lee had on Coast Guard kahkis, open shirt, his
rank bar (one silver bar).

of a Coast Guardsman, the writer has attached to his script several photographs of this
craft and has marked for the guidance of the artist various details which he believes are
worthy of note. On page 4, for one example, he calls attention to the location of the
No. 1 gun, in the region of which the hero of this story spent a large part of his time
under fire. Note writer's careful description of Parker's uniform on page 7.

No. 96 and the other LCI's proceeded in column, about 400 yards apart. No warships (cruisers, destroyers or anything) were nearby---they were all sweeping the seas up toward Sicily, etc. To the right and the left of the column were other ships---but they were so far away they were just dark objects on the horizon.

They hit rough weather about 10 o'clock that night. So rough many of the Coast Guard thought the invasion might be called off. They had crossed the Atlantic in these LCIs but nothing like this.

Dotted lines show how much the ship was rolling---as much as 30° to port and then to starboard. Flat-bottomed, with no keel, this might have meant turning over.

1 There was great deal of wind. Still, you could see the stars. Parker says doesn't remember seeing moon, and thinks it was moonless night---so planned by Eisenhower. Anyway, water was washing all over the decks---so much that Coast Guards were all ordered to wear lifebelts and also had to hang on to something to keep from being washed away. During this time Parker had to make his way about the boat, seeing everyone in shape.

He also had to go below to see that the soldiers' water supply was OKay. He found all 200 men---everyone of them---lying on their bunks. Most of them were sick.

This rough stuff kept up for about 3 hours.

2 Then the 96 began to pass the guide ships put out there to direct the landing boats. Fifteen miles off Sicily they passed a destroyer (guide ship). Then 10 miles off Sicily
3 they passed a PC boat acting as guide ship. Then about 5 miles off Sicily they passed a sub chaser which was the last of the guide ships.
4 They came close enough to these ships to yell across, bridge to

bridge.

5 In a few minutes Parker knew they hadn't surprised the enemy. His boat and the others ran into enemy searchlights. This was about 4 miles miles off LICATA. The enemy searchlights were sweeping the water. One of them picked up (way off to one wide) the USS Biscayne, which was the flagship of the whole invasion. It held the Biscayne in its searchlight for about 10 minutes---no shots through. Other searchlights were sweeping over the water. Now and then one would light upon 96. Parker He was up near No 1 gun at this time. says it was like a gangster moving picture---a gangster caught in a searchlight. Strange feeling, heightened by the fact that everything was quiet, no shells. Also by the fact that they knew the Italians somewhere there had a 14-inch mounted railway gun which could blow everything about of the water.

Then the lights all went out.

Meanwhile, of course, the boats were proceeding to their pretermined position.

6 The 96 then, about 2½ miles offshore, passed a LST boat unloading Higgins boats. These Higgins boats were going in, loaded with their part of the first wave.

The 96 moved on slowly. It was timed to reach the shore 30 minutes after the Higgins boats.

Then the 96 started moving in. Here is the layout:

hats at this stage. He is looking around, over the ship, to see if anyone is hit.

When the last soldier is off, the 96 beings pulling out. This is when the going gets really bad---for the enemy has had time to spot the ship. And here is where that anchor comes in:

Anchor cable

To get off the beach the fear anchor wench is put into action. As it pulls the cable this pulls the boat toward the anchor---hence off the beach. Parker goes aft. In 7 minutes after starting the ramp down this boat has gotten all its 200 troops ashore and is pulling out.

When the boat pulls itself out to where the anchor is, it pulls up the anchor and starts turning around. It is still dark. But this
12 kicks up so much foam that the enemy can spot it. In a few seconds the shelling begins. 88 mm. shells from batteries back beyond the beach.

Shells hit closeby. A piece of shrapnel tears through one of the no 1 gun crew. The executive officer calls for Parker. He
13 has to crawl to get to the man (space is so tight there) but gets there, tears off the man's life jacket and shirt, finds blood between

the shoulder blades, but not anything fatal. Parker puts on some antiseptoi.

Meanwhile shelling continues. The 96 is racing away. Shells falling all around. It sizzags as much as possible. Daylight is coming. Nearby a destroyer is running back and forth, firing. Several ships can be seen beached. One LCI is lying on the beach, on one side. It's no 88.

The 96 gets out, rendezvous with no 95. The men hang over the side swapping stories.

14 Then about 11 a.m. orders come to the 96 to move to an LST to help get its troops off. The 96 ties up alongside the LST. The LST throws its rope ladders to the 96, and men begin clammering aboard. About 200. While taking on these troops German bombers (2-motored) appear, and start bombing the two ships tied there together in open water. There are no US fighters to drive off the bombers. There are, however, aboard the LST some trucks which are headed for Sicily. These trucks have mounted on them some small anti-aircraft guns. These trucks are sitting on the deck. The troops rush to the these guns and there open fire at the German planes: a real FLYING guns on trucks, trucks on deck of ship, firing at German bombers.

Anyway, the bombers go on away. And 96 takes the troops right
15 into the harbor of Licata. While tied up to the dock there the German bombers attack again. No hits.

The 96 goes back and gets another load. Then another load, this one of radio equipment. All this in broad daylight---and with the skies NOT mastered by our Air Force as all the reports would have us believe.

16 Then the LCI (L) 96 starts back for Bizerte. On the way it joins up with other LCI's which are loaded with Italian prisoners.

In the final eight pages of the rough script on the story of the heroic Coast Guardsman, the writer gets down to the detailed action involved in landing troops on a hostile shore. He is as specific as he can be about such things as moon, wind and stars. With a rough drawing (page 8), he shows how much the ship was rolling, according to the hero's own story. On page 10, he diagrams the landing beach and the boats

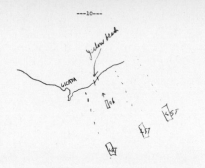

10

About 200 yards off the beach the 96 drops its rear anchor.
But the 96 keeps going in. (The purpose of dropping the anchor will
be explained later). Machine-gun fire has opened up from the shore.
Parker up there at No 1 gun can see the tracers. Then about 100
yards off the shore the machine-gun bullets begin hitting the

7 96. The executive officer, Lt (jg) John Whitebeck, calls out
"Get down on your bellies."
~~Abcmban~~ The soldiers are still below.
Parker can see the beach coming in toward him.

8 Then the 96 gets close enough to start to rolling out the
ramps. They roll forward their weight dropping them into the
water. Two Coast Guardsmen are standing by, stripped to their
shorts. They are J.W.Neece and Durward Nelson. Soon as the
ramps drop into the water their job is to run down them into
the water, and go on ashore. The purpose of this is to test the
depth of the water, make sure they have hit the beach and not a sandbar, &

---

9 thus not drown all the soldiers. About this time the soldiers
have been brought up from below. In the rain of machine-gun
bullets Neece & Nelso run ashore, and race back, reporting all
is okay. Then one of the grabs a ~~humann~~ raft made of 2 life belts
carrying a small (about 30 lb) anchor and takes it ashore. This
will provide a guideline for the troops. Here is the whole
situation diagrammed:

10
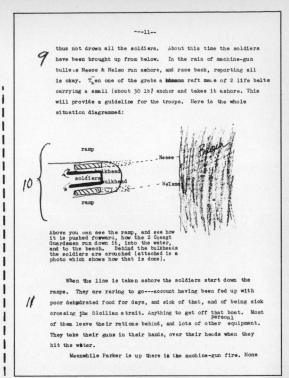

Above you can see the ramp, and see how
it is pushed forward, how the 2 Coasgt
Guardsmen run down it, into the water,
and to the beach. Behind the bulkheads
the soldiers are crouched (attached is a
photo which shows how that is done).

11 When the line is taken ashore the soldiers start down the
ramps. They are raring to go---account having been fed up with
poor dehydrated food for days, and sick of that, and of being sick
crossing the Sicilian strait. Anything to get off that boat. Most
of them leave their rations behind, and lots of other personl equipment.
They take their guns in their hands, over their heads when they
hit the water.
Meanwhile Parker is up there in the machine-gun fire. None

When they reach Bizerte you have this unusual PI TURE: Boats there
loaded with Italians and some of the LCI's loading up with
Sengalese troops in their fancy uniforms, with the little bags
hanging over their shoulders. These bags are for the Sengalese
to put the ~~hmm~~ enemy's ears in. These Sengaelse are paid by
the French 30 francs for each man they kill---and the ~~hmm~~ ears are
their proof.

NOTE: This is ~~mxhXXQM~~ essentially a Coast Guard story, showing
that Coast Guads put the troops ashore, run even greater risks
than the troops. Parker, like the other Coast Guards, did his
job. The story should be built around him, but the pictures should
bring in the other Coast Guards---manning their guns, getting the
ramps out, those 2 (Neece & Nelson) running down the ramps, etc, etc.
Parker is simply the instrument for getting unity of time, place and
action.

DON WHARTON
24 GRAMERCY PARK
NEW YORK

August 26, 1943

Dear Ed:
Here's the PARKER Coast Guard story.
You will see that there is more chance here,
for variety of drawings than in most stories we have done.
All types of situations.
Yours,
Don

1 {1. 96 rolling 30°
2 {2. Pass Destroyer
3 {3. Pass PC. boat
{4. Pass Sub chaser
{5. Caught in searchlights
4· 6. LST unloading Higgins boats
5· 7. 100 yds off shore being machine gunned.
6· 8. Roll out ramps
7· 9. 2 guardsman rush ashore.
8· 10. Soldiers rush ashore
9 11. Diagram
10· 12. 96 taking up anchor as 88mm. shells make near misses
11· 13. Member of gun crew wounds
13· 14. Takes troops from LST during aereal bombing
13· 15. 96 being bombed in Licata harbor
14· 16. Joins other ships loaded with Italian prisoner.

---

coming ashore. On page 11, he diagrams ramp and bulkheads. On page 12, he shows
how the rear anchor is used to pull the boat off the beach. He packs information into
every sentence, without much regard for style. Numbers in the margins are for picture situations culled from the script in the writer's conferences with artist and art
director. Of 16 possible situations, they used 12.

① ROLLING AT 90°, THE LCI 96 PASSES A DESTROYER
(PORTRAIT PARKER MAKING ROUNDS)

② THE 96 PASSES A PC BOAT (FROM BRIDGE OF PC)

③ THE 96, CLOSE TO A SUB-CHASER, IS PICKED UP
BY SHORE SEARCHLIGHTS - OTHER SHIPS IN
ENGAGEMENT IN BACKGROUND

④ THE 96 PASSES A LST BOAT, UNLOADING HIGGINS BOATS

⑤ 100 YARDS OFF LICATA, BEING MACHINE-GUNNED
(FROM #1 GUN)

⑥ COAST GUARDSMEN ROLL OUT PORTSIDE RAMP

The artist "roughs out" the story after reading the writer's text and conferring with writer and art director on the exact picture script to be followed. This is a rough on the story of the Coast Guardsman, Solomon Parker. Note that it was done with 14 drawings and that No. 9 is a diagram explaining the landing operation of the LCI. At this stage, writer and art director both get another chance to confer with the artist and to

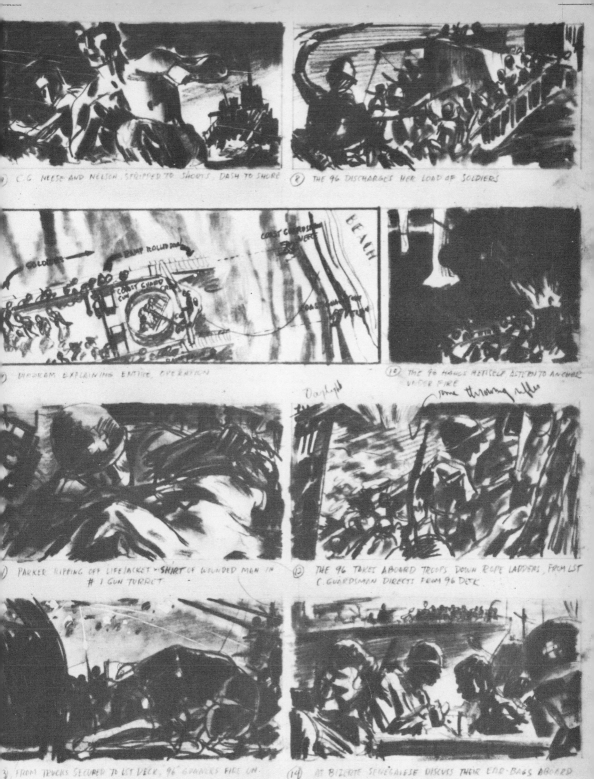

7) C.G. NEESE AND NELSON, STRIPPED TO SHORTS, DASH TO SHORE

8) THE 96 DISCHARGES HER LOAD OF SOLDIERS

9) DIAGRAM EXPLAINING ENTIRE OPERATION

10) THE 96 HAULS HERSELF ASTERN TO ANCHOR UNDER FIRE

11) PARKER RIPPING OFF LIFE JACKET & SHIRT OF WOUNDED MAN IN # 1 GUN TURRET

12) THE 96 TAKES ABOARD TROOPS DOWN ROPE LADDERS, FROM LST C. GUARDSMAN DIRECTS FROM 96 DECK

13) FROM TOWERS SECURED TO LST DECK, 96 GUNNERS FIRE ON 2 MOTOR CANNON BOATS & C GUARDSMEN HAUL ON

14) AT BIZERTE SENEGALESE DISCUSS THEIR EAR-BAGS ABOARD LST — BACKGROUND GROUP OF ITALIAN PRISONERS ON LST

make changes in the original plan if they think it is working out improperly. There is still time to reduce or increase the number of pictures, to correct mistakes, to add or eliminate details before the artist has drawn his pictures in final form. In this case, alterations were made after the rough drawings were submitted, as will be seen on the following two pages.

Landing Under Fire

Amid bullets, shellfire and bombs, a Coast Guard pharmacist's mate helps put U. S. troops ashore on Sicily

Solomon Parker, a 25-year-old New Yorker, was one of the Coast Guardsmen who landed our troops on Sicily. Parker's boat went in under machine-gun fire, put its troops ashore, raced out through machine-gun bullets and 88 mm. shellfire, picked up three more loads, took them in under bombing attacks. Throughout the action, Sol Parker did his work as pharmacist's mate, helped form one of the Coast Guard's smooth-running, unpublicized landing teams.

To prepare for the Sicilian invasion, the Coast Guard had sailed flat-bottomed craft across the Atlantic, rehearsed the landing diligently in order to perfect split-second timing. Before shoving off, Parker went through heavy air raids, gave tetanus inoculations to 100 Coast Guardsmen. After the invasion, he was selected as officer material, brought back to the United States, sent to Reserve Officers School at the Coast Guard Academy in New London, Conn.

AMERICAN HEROES

STORY BY DON WHARTON—DRAWINGS BY JOHN J. FLOHERTY, JR.—32ND IN LOOK'S AMERICAN HEROES SERIES

1 **The LCI's** (landing craft, infantry) run into rough weather in the Sicilian strait. No. 96 rolls wildly, threatens to capsize momentarily. Sol Parker goes below to check troops' water, finds 200 men in their bunks, most of them sick.

2 **Fifteen miles from Sicily** a destroyer bobs up, checks the landing bo see they're headed for the right beaches. Parker's boat passes two more ships: a PC boat anchored off Licata beach, then a subchaser closer to

3 **Four miles off Licata,** the LCI's run into enemy searchlights. One sweeps the sea, finds the invasion flagship. Another picks up No. 96. Solomon Parker, standing ready at his battle station, waits for the enemy to open fire.

4 **Moving on** toward the hostile shore, the LCI passes a ship spawning gins boats which race to the beach with first-wave troops. No. 96 p on slowly—timed to reach the beach a short time after the Higgins

5 **Enemy machine guns open up,** fill the sky with tracers. As No. 96 gets within 100 yards of the beach, bullets begin hitting. "Get down on your bellies," Lt. John Whitebeck calls. Parker keeps bobbing up—to see who's hit.

6 **The LCI pushes on,** reaches shallow water, begins rolling out its ra While troops below wait the signal to land, two Coast Guardsmen str to their shorts stand by under fire: J. W. Neece and Durward Ne

Here is the finished article on Coast Guardsman Solomon Parker, entitled *Landing Under Fire*. The number of pictures in the sequence has been reduced to 12, all now identical in size, and the diagram of the landing operation has been placed at the end of the story. This was done because all concerned, after viewing the original position, concluded that, as picture No. 9, it interfered with the flow of the narrative. The

a rain of machine-gun bullets, Neece and Nelson push ashore and
ack to No. 96—testing the water's depth. Then Neece grabs a raft carrying
30-pound anchor, takes it ashore to hold a guide line for the troops.

8 **While the Coast Guard** clears the way, the troops crouch behind pro-
tecting bulkheads. Now they come tearing down the ramps, hit the water,
press on to the shore. In his exposed position Parker watches for wounded.

n a few minutes after starting the ramps, the crew puts all troops ashore
nd pulls off—under fire from 88 mm. batteries far inland. The boat backs
ut by pulling a cable attached to an anchor it had dropped coming in.

10 **Shrapnel tears through** a member of the No. 1 gun crew. Whitebeck
yells for Parker, who crawls through a narrow opening, rips off the man's
life jacket and shirt, fixes him up. No. 96 zig-zags while shells land nearby.

Parker's boat rendezvous with other LCI's, then gets orders to go to the
aid of another landing boat. As No. 96 ties up, German bombers attack. In a
flash, troops climb into trucks on the deck, open fire with the trucks' guns.

12 **Several hundred** troops clamber down rope ladders, ride No. 96 into
Licata harbor—now in Allied hands. Parker's boat goes through another
bombing unhit, races back for more troops, puts four loads safely ashore.

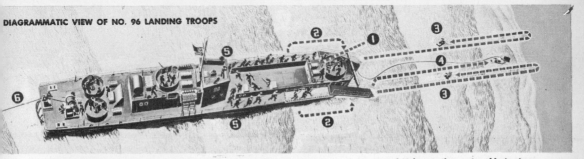

DIAGRAMMATIC VIEW OF NO. 96 LANDING TROOPS

1. Parker's battle station near No. 1 gun   2. Ramps rolling forward   3. Neece and Nelson testing water ship-to-shore
4. Neece taking guide line ashore   5. Troops heading for ramps   6. Cable to pull ship out of sand

writer, whose rough outline ran to nearly 3,000 words, has compressed the story into a
few more than 600, including a lead text block and 12 captions. In the lead, he has
presented the hero, told his story briefly, and relocated him at an Officers' Training
School. In the captions, he has integrated text with pictures to present the exploit in a
highly dramatic narrative.

HOW DISNEY DOES IT...

The Plot

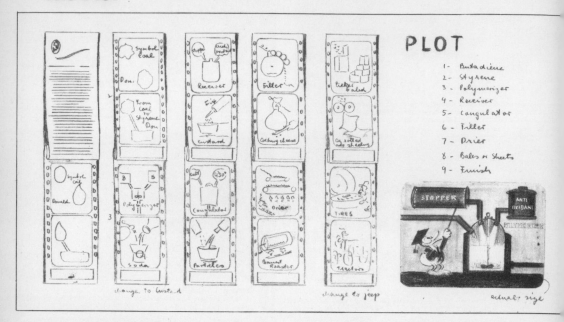

The Sketches

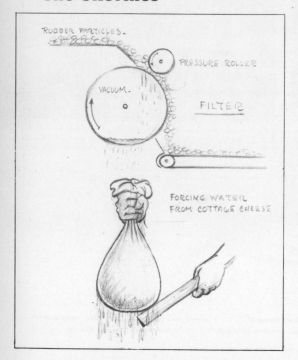

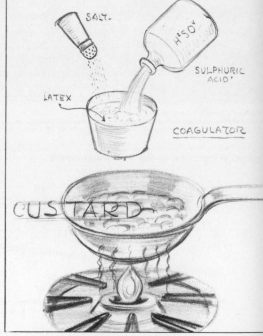

The sketches on these pages show the beginnings of an article on the making of synthetic rubber, done for LOOK by Walt Disney, greatest of visual educators. In the upper left-hand picture is the plan of the space to be used—five half pages. The plot of the story is that butadiene and styrene, combined in the right proportions in the proper solution, will produce a durable substitute for natural rubber. Disney's artists,

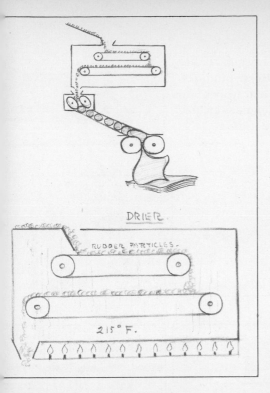

DRIER.

RUBBER PARTICLES.

215° F.

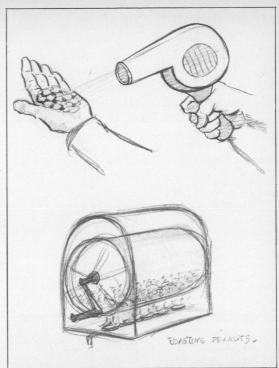

ROASTING PEANUTS.

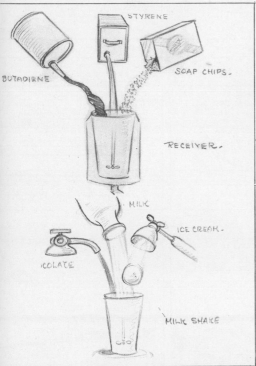

STYRENE

BUTADIENE

SOAP CHIPS.

RECEIVER.

MILK

ICE CREAM.

CHOCOLATE

MILK SHAKE

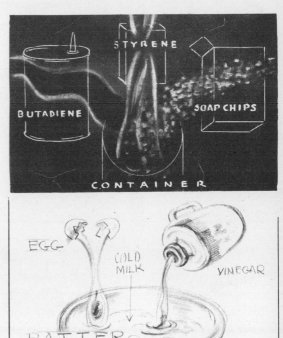

STYRENE

BUTADIENE

SOAP CHIPS

CONTAINER

EGG

COLD MILK

VINEGAR

BATTER

schooled in translating complicated scientific facts into understandable language, knew that they had to tell the story in terms of substances and experiences common to the everyday life of ordinary people. The rough drawings show that they thought of, and that they experimented with, such well-known and easily understood things as custard, milk shakes and a peanut roaster.

The Roughs

When the last pencil sketches receive the approval of writer and editor, the artist is free to execute a finished product—but not before. Between the completion of these drawings and the final "go-ahead" signal, there is always a conference at which the writer gets one more chance to ask for alterations.

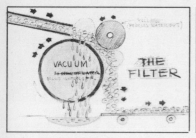

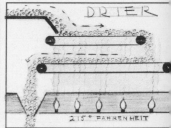

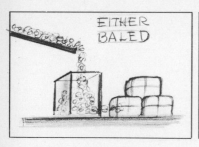

Just as the magazine artist roughs out a story for study, so does Disney. The small drawings on this spread are roughs made by Disney artists for the article on synthetic rubber. The story was plotted from information provided by a writer's research, as were all the others in this chapter. Disney has an advantage over the average illustrator: he has created cartoon characters as famous as any live movie star and can call on them

The Finish

➡️

DISNEY
Has Donald Duck Explain About
SYNTHETIC RUBBER

WHEN tomorrow comes, most Americans hope it will bring plenty of good, old-fashioned, rib-tickling Walt Disney cartoons. Which it will—with improvements. Currently, 90 per cent of the Mickey maestro's output is for training and propaganda purposes; this vital work is teaching him ways to make his future films funnier, more eye-appealing—and vastly more instructive—than ever.

On these pages is Disney's treatment of synthetic rubber—a serious subject for America, since on it depends our eventual freedom from reliance on the imported natural product.

Disney put two artists and five animators to work making these drawings for LOOK. They finally handed the job to Donald Duck, who herewith dons a professorial hat and proceeds to make a tough topic practically a cinch.

I'LL SHOW YOU HOW TO MAKE SYNTHETIC RUBBER!

Okay—we're off! One form of synthetic (or, better, *substitute*) rubber starts with oil as it comes from the earth. "Cracking" oil (1) gives gasoline, grease, many other things. One of these is *butadiene* (2)—pronounced *bu-ta-dy'ene*—a very complex gas composed of hydrogen and carbon.

for help in a case like this. Because he is so familiar to so many millions, Donald Duck was put to work telling the story. He provided both a well-known personality and a focus to carry the reader through the sequence. The first half page of the finished product is shown at the right, with Donald in the role of a professor. (Remainder of the picture story is shown on next two pages.)

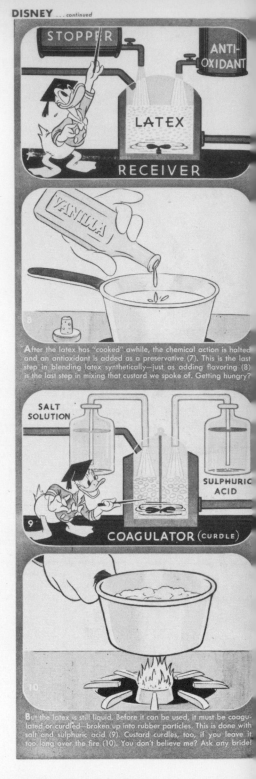

Leaving butadiene a moment, consider coal. Coal can also be made to yield a huge array of different substances (3)—raw materials of to-morrow's chemistry. One is *styrene* (4), a liquid and, like butadiene, a hydrocarbon—but of different molecular structure. That all clear?

After the latex has "cooked" awhile, the chemical action is halted and an antioxidant is added as a preservative (7). This is the last step in blending latex synthetically—just as adding flavoring (8) is the last step in mixing that custard we spoke of. Getting hungry?

Now we bring butadiene and styrene together—three quarters of the first, one quarter of the second—in a solution of soapy water (5). They combine to form a basic *latex*, similar to that of natural rubber. This is just about as simple as adding sugar and egg to milk (6) to make custard.

But the latex is still liquid. Before it can be used, it must be coagu-lated or curdled—broken up into rubber particles. This is done with salt and sulphuric acid (9). Custard curdles, too, if you leave it too long over the fire (10). You don't believe me? Ask any bride!

The article carries Donald Duck through a happy projection of the future. In as many panels as possible, the artists have compared the actual scientific problem with a common one of a similar nature. Thus, the mixture of three parts butadiene with one part styrene in a solution of soapy water is presented as akin to the combination of milk, sugar and an egg in the making of custard. The antioxidant used as a preservative in

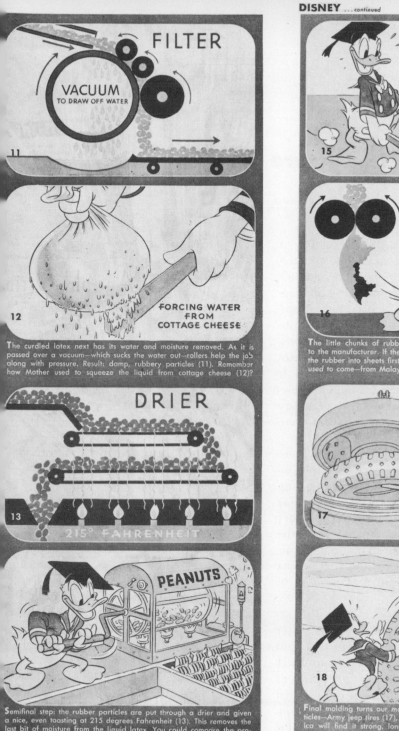

FILTER

VACUUM
TO DRAW OFF WATER

11

FORCING WATER
FROM
COTTAGE CHEESE

12

The curdled latex next has its water and moisture removed. As it is passed over a vacuum—which sucks the water out—rollers help the job along with pressure. Result: damp, rubbery particles (11). Remember how Mother used to squeeze the liquid from cottage cheese (12)?

DRIER

13

215° FAHRENHEIT

PEANUTS

Semifinal step: the rubber particles are put through a drier and given a nice, even toasting at 215 degrees Fahrenheit (13). This removes the last bit of moisture from the liquid latex. You could compare the procedure to roasting peanuts (14). Mmm—care to have a bag with me?

15

16

The little chunks of rubber are now baled (15), ready to ship to the manufacturer. If the manufacturer prefers, we can squeeze the rubber into sheets first (16). That's how it often comes—sorry, used to come—from Malayan and East Indian rubber plantations.

17

18

Final molding turns our man-made rubber into vital wartime articles—Army jeep tires (17), for example. And some day all America will find it strong, long-wearing, cheap (18). Imagine spinning down the highway on new tires right from the laboratory! Boy!

synthetic rubber is compared with the flavoring added to custard, and so on. For the Disney studio, a "still" picture story is a comparatively simple matter. In creating animated cartoons, Disney artists make thousands of individual drawings, working first from a written script and then from their own roughs. Their method and product are worth study by any writer—especially picture-story writers.

CHAPTER 7

Producing the Picture Story

THE VARIOUS STEPS in the production of a picture story are described in picture-story form in this chapter. The chapter outlines the procedure of only one magazine, a procedure not differing in any major respect from those of other publications using picture-text combinations.

Our story is done with thirty photographs. As with most picture articles, it could have been done with more, or fewer. It was edited to show every necessary step, but many possible pictures were eliminated to prevent "padding."

The article being produced in these photographs is not of earth-shaking importance. It is a simple tale of how young children absorb knowledge from play with building blocks. This type of story was chosen deliberately, to emphasize the fact that even the most modest of picture narratives requires the time, effort and close collaboration of a number of trained persons.

Studying the photographs in this article, the potential picture-story writer will see how important it is, in this kind of work, to consider oneself a producer and director during at least five sixths of the time it takes to turn out the finished product. This is not easy for writers to do, especially writers who have worked for years on publications requiring them to think only in terms of putting one word after another. The young writer with less experience may make the transition with less difficulty.

However, anyone interested in learning to create picture stories can benefit from the experience of those who have been struggling with the problem for years. From such struggles have come these general rules for the writer-producer:

1. Finish the preliminary, basic research on your subject before you plan a picture. It is important that you be as thoroughly informed as possible on every aspect of the story before you try to outline it or write a picture-shooting script for it.

2. Be sure of your "angle" and focus before you get down to the script. The best way to do this is to think in terms of the title or headline that seems best to tell the story you want to tell.

3. Make your shooting script as detailed as possible. If in doubt about a picture or camera angle, include it.

4. Confer with the photographer about the script and other phases of the story until you are sure that he understands its objectives and planned structure as well as you do.

5. Make certain that the photographer takes every picture provided for in the script, but don't let it be a strait jacket for him. In the field, let him shoot any picture appealing to his imagination, whether you have planned it or not. No amount of planning in an office can establish every picture situation which will occur when you are on location. Sometimes the best shot of all will pop up unexpectedly.

6. Arrange a shooting schedule and adhere to it as rigidly as circumstances per-

mit. Do your utmost to see that the photographer adheres to it. When you ask people to be in a certain place at a certain time, it is not only courtesy but good business for you to be there on the dot; you cannot get good results from subjects who are inconvenienced by your tardiness.

7. Don't be ashamed to do some of the menial tasks almost always required of a picture-story producer. The Hollywood film director has flunkies to move furniture, adjust lights, arrange clothing and so on, but chances are you will have to do most of this sort of thing yourself.

8. Be patient.

9. Be relaxed.

10. Be co-operative.

It is impossible to overemphasize the importance of these last three admonitions. By and large, picture-story production is not for the restless, the hasty, the impetuous, the intolerant or the excessively temperamental person.

To succeed at it, you must obtain the co-operation of other people, and this is impossible if you are not patient, relaxed and co-operative yourself. On almost every story you will find provocation to lose your temper, snarl at somebody or give up the whole thing as a lost cause, but obviously you can't do any of these things often if you hope to stay in the profession.

Frequently, one of the writer's biggest problems is how to deal with his own photographer. Almost any good photographer is likely to display temperament at times—to state the case mildly. On such occasions, the writer has to be his most unruffled self, capable of all the tricks of diplomacy to avert failure. The photographer who can be browbeaten is rare; the vast majority of creative cameramen are artists — sensitive beyond ordinary standards and extraordinarily responsive to praise.

The picture-magazine photographer has a tendency to regard his own part in the production of a story as all-important and to view the writer-producer as his "helper." It is generally futile to debate this point. The seasoned writer "plays up" the photographer while they are working together. If he is asked to hold a light for a shot, he holds it; and he otherwise co-operates as necessary for the good of the product and the good nature of the person being photographed.

We do not intend to convey the impression that there is an endless running feud between writers and photographers working on the same article. Frequently, they work harmoniously for days on end. However, the opposite is true often enough to justify warning the writer of the need for patience and diplomacy.

The successful writer in this field also needs an actively inquiring mind, and diligence in the pursuit of facts. These are attributes essential to the good reporter in any field, but doubly so in the case of the picture-story writer, who must compress a large number of facts into relatively small space and yet give his sentences flavor and sparkle.

It is a tremendous help to accumulate small, pertinent, colorful details — the color of a pair of eyes, the significance of a gesture, a startling statistic, a background fact which gives the reader a feeling of being taken behind the scenes.

Any or all such information may be obtained through library research, but it is more likely to be obtained in personal interview with those actually appearing in the pictures and with experts in the field being covered. With busy people, it is sometimes helpful to prepare written questions in advance of an interview. But, whatever his technique, the writer must keep everlastingly at his fact-finding.

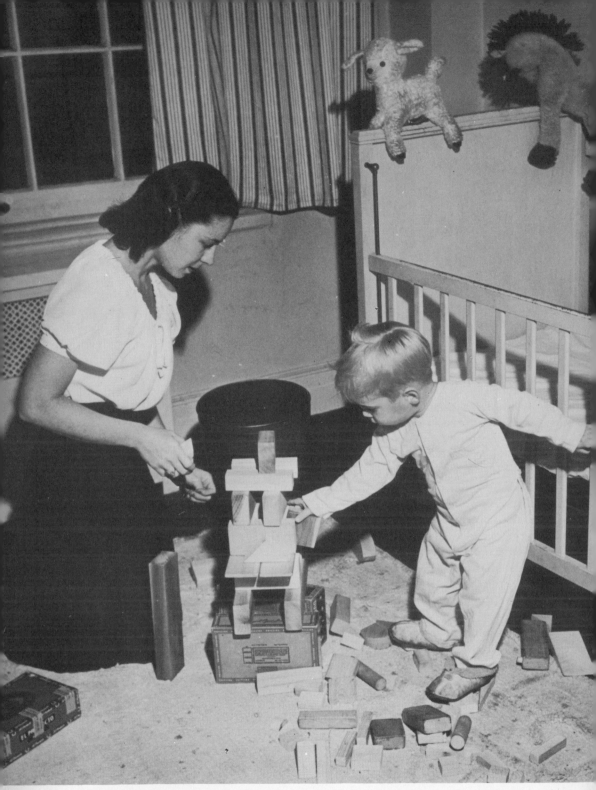

1. A picture-story writer, fascinated by watching her child at play, gets an idea for an article.

Every article begins with an idea, and, as we have seen (Chapter 4), ideas for picture articles come from several primary sources. This one came from the writer's own experience as the mother of a small boy. While watching her son play with wooden blocks, she wondered how much knowledge could be conveyed to a youngster through the scientific use of such playthings and whether child psychologists had done any

CATEGORY:
    CHILDREN

SUBJECT:
    YOUNG AMERICA BUILDS
    (building blocks)

SUGGESTED BY
V. Forsythe

DATE
Sept. 4

Parents worried about the effects of war play and alarmed at the glee with which their kids shout "You're dead – you're a Jap – ack – ack – ack" do well to offer building blocks as a toy. Approved by educators and psychologists, used in nursery schools and loved by all children, blocks are constructive, creative play material, teaching everything from design to math. Children may have tanks rolling over their block bridges, and they may "bomb" a skyscraper right down to the floor-- but they spend much more time building up.

    And it offers wonderful picture possibilities. For example:

    1. Two-year-old: One picture showing mother helping him build a tower (this age likes help). Another of him knocking it down, joy at noise, etc.

    2. Four-year-old: One "process" shot of him building--very absorbed in his work, strange position, tongue sticking out as he concentrates, etc. Another of his finished structure--usually this age likes a big, impressive structure, doesn't care much about it s "architectural accuracy."

    3. Six-year-old: This age is analytical, accurate, demands that its building be structurally sound, realistic, etc. Then he plays with it as in real life--if a bridge, he runs cars and trains over it, etc.

    4. School project: This should be the big picture, full page if good enough, showing group of children building. I have in mind the Dalton School where the 6-year-old group does really amazing stuff. Was up there the other day, and among other things they were climbing up on tables and chairs to get the top on a skyscraper.

DECISION:

Assigned to Forsythe

HK/fj-3-21-44-5000-ss

---

2. The idea, bulwarked by preliminary research, is submitted in written outline to the editors.

research on the subject. When she found that such work had been done and that the experts considered building blocks extremely valuable in child training, she turned in a written suggestion for a picture story on the subject. This included a possible structural plan for the story and a suggested locale for the pictures, a nursery school where children are taught to play with blocks.

3. The editorial board approves of the idea; (4) managing editor assigns it to the writer.

5. The writer calls for more detailed data then (6) gets research assistance from the library.

Shown on these two pages are eight of the preliminary steps in the creation of a picture story for a magazine. Before the writer can go ahead, her idea must be presented to and approved by the magazine's editorial board (3), which stamps its O.K. on only a small fraction of the suggestions it receives. After definitely getting the assignment (4), the writer gathers more background information from a variety of sources (5, 6,

7. She interviews the head of a nursery school and (8) consults an authoritative psychologist.

SHOOTING SCRIPT FOR CHILDREN'S BUILDING BLOCKS

1. DALTON SCHOOL
   A. The 6-year-old group goes in for it with great vigor - when up there the other day saw a very photogenic project. All in one room they had built a ceiling-high Empire State Bldg., much Radio City, and several lower, more rambling structures to represent movie theater, railroad tracks and station, etc. Each building has a sign saying what it's supposed to be. I think this would make a good take-off picture, probably full-page. Aim to get several of the children, plus teacher, at work on these buildings. They climb up on chairs and/or tables to reach tops of buildings - very active.

2. TWO-YEAR-OLD
   A. This young a child likes the cooperation of an adult to help him on hard balance problems. One picture will show him building a low tower, with the help of his mother. Have very cute child and attractive mother lined up.
   B. He also shows great glee when he knocks over same - such a young child is not too terribly "constructive," enjoys the noise and confusion when blocks tumble down all over floor. Second picture will show the knocking over.

3. FOUR-YEAR-OLD
   A. This age shows considerable imagination and sense of design, likes to work alone, is not too exacting about his building being sound structurally - he likes a pretty big structure, I suppose giving him a sense of power or something. First picture shows child busily building, much absorbed in his work. He is pretty strictly "constructive," doesn't care too much about knocking down, gets mad if anyone destroys his handiwork.
   B. He also likes to play games or etc. with whatever he's built. Second picture to show him playing some kind of improvised game with same - rolling marbles on railroad tracks, or etc. Have a very cute, bright-red-haired, definitely pure boyish boy for this one.

4. SIX-YEAR-OLD
   A. He's pretty likely to be of the analytical variety, demands that his building be absolutely sound structurally, as much as possible duplicating "real life." First picture will show him building whatever project he wants to build - might be a group of buildings, houses etc., into which he will introduce toy people, cars, etc. Or a bridge, or railroad station and railroad tracks.
   B. Second picture will show him at "realistic" play with same - for example, if it's a railroad business, he'll want to run his trains over it.

9. With the managing editor and art director, (10) writer prepares a detailed shooting script.

7, 8) before conferring with the managing editor and art director (9) to plan her picture script (10). The art director or one of his assistants is usually consulted at this stage because of his knowldege of visual techniques and because of his ultimate responsibility for the physical appearance of the article. The more these men know about the planning of a story the better.

199

11. A conference with photographers precedes (12) beginning of actual work in the field.

13. The writer must help in moving the furniture (14) and with the coiffure of a photo subject.

"Why does it take so long to do a picture story?" is a question frequently asked by neophytes. These pictures show some of the reasons. The writer has to explain her shooting script and her problems carefully to the photographer (standing, right) and photographic director (11) before tackling the field job. On location, she must serve in many capacities (12, 13, 14, 15). It is here that her patience is often badly strained

15. She has to get down on her knees to arrange blocks and keep a youthful model happy.

and her ingenuity put to severe tests. But it is also here that she finds opportunity to improve on her planning, to add unanticipated elements to the story, to deal with models so that they will co-operate with the photographer, and to leave them with so good an impression of her tact and friendliness that they will be happy to co-operate again with her and her associates.

16. The writer sprawls on knees and elbows to help keep a youthful camera subject natural.

17. Art director (left) and an editor help the writer select pictures to be used in the layout.

The field work is finished (16) and the actual construction of the story begins (17, 18, 19). Only a few samples of field experiences are shown here, but the writer and photographer really were on location through most of four days. They returned with 120 photographs for the consideration of an editor and art director (17), who helped to cull the pictures to be used and to plan the layout design. This is a crucial session

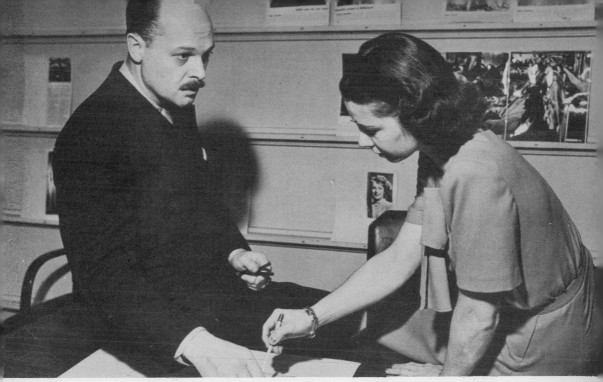

18. Art director gets writer's final instructions together with her own rough plan of the layout.

19. This man is pasting the actual layout together. Writer is asking for more text space.

on every story, and it sometimes lasts for hours, with much give and take of opinion. The editor taking part in it frequently has to arbitrate differences between the writer and the designer on the amount of space to be devoted to text. Even then, the writer is likely to back the art director into a corner and plead for "just two or three more lines" here and there.

20. A two-page spread is space allotted to the story. One picture gets the left-hand page.

Above is the "layout" for the article as it goes from the art department to the writer after getting editorial approval. The two-page spread is the exact size of a spread in the magazine, and the photographs, here pasted on cardboard, have been cropped to appear as they will in print. The text block and caption spaces are marked with figures giving the writer the number of lines for each space, and the exact number of units

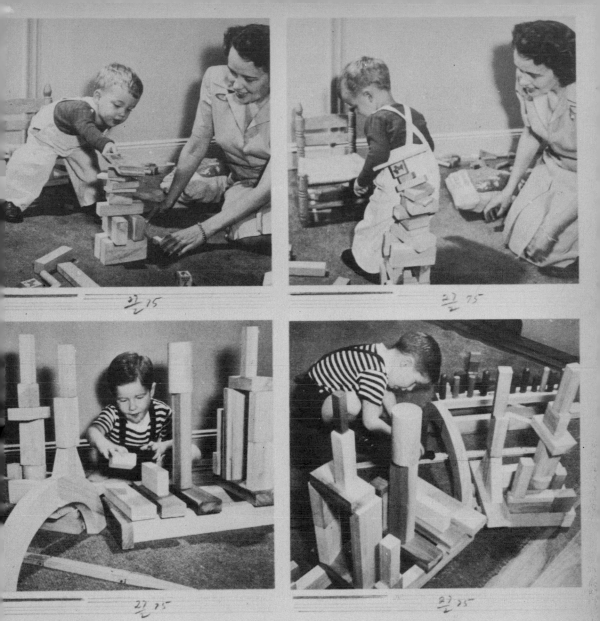

Young America Builds

pt futura bold low case 25½ picas 97 characters futura bold tower case futura bo

On the right-hand page are four smaller pictures and a text block of about 300 words.

(letters and spaces) for each line. The copy must be written to fit the unit and line count—a phase of picture-story writing most discouraging to writers who are unaccustomed to it. To simplify this task, most publications using picture stories now supply writers with ruled paper on which the lines are numbered in the margin and a unit-count scale is provided at the top.

21. The editorial board inspects the layout; (22) after approval, it goes back to the writer.

23. The copy department edits the manuscript, (24) polishes phrases then corrects the proof.

Of the eight pictures on this spread, only one (22) shows the writer at her typewriter. Only after she has gone through all the steps previously shown and has obtained editorial-board approval for her layout (21) does she start to put down one word after another. She spends no more than one sixth of her time in actual writing for publication. However, it would be a mistake to minimize the importance of this

25. Art department pastes proofs on layout; (26) several editors then check finished article.

27. Production department prepares to ship. (28) It's in the package, headed for the press.

part of picture-story production. For the writer, this is the climax, the culmination of days or weeks of effort, and to fail here is to fail completely. Copy for picture magazines is prepared and handled as carefully as for any other publication. Almost every article is rewritten two, three or more times before it meets standards of the copy department and is passed on to the editor.

CHAPTER 8

Trade Journals and House Organs

A GLANCE at any newsstand in America is enough to convince anybody that magazine publishing is a very big business in the United States. Yet, even the largest newsstand tells only part of the story; for, in addition to the 2,800 general magazines competing for consumers' dollars, there are thousands of specialized publications never offered for sale to the general public.

Most of these are either trade journals or house organs. A trade journal, defined for purposes of this chapter, is a magazine published in the interest of a given industry, trade or profession. Under this definition, the *Journal of the American Medical Association* is a trade journal, and we so regard it, knowing full well that its aggressive editor, Dr. Morris Fishbein, will boggle at having it classified in a group which includes *Leaks and Drips,* a worthy publication devoted to the welfare of the plumbing business.

In this group of trade journals are roughly 2,300 publications with a combined total of more than 75 million circulation. There is at least one journal for nearly every trade, profession or industry.

A house organ is a magazine published in the interest of a single business firm or group of firms operating under common ownership. Best estimates place the number of house organs published currently in the U. S. at 6,000 or more and their combined circulation at 50 millions. In format these publications range all the way from mimeographed pep sheets to

handsome, well-printed, modern magazines. Almost all are circulated free to employees, dealers, or customers of the companies paying the bill. Better employee relations is the prime objective of most house organs. A few are designed to improve dealer or customer relations.

With a few exceptions the basic difference between these two groups and the general media magazines, so far as picture-story publishing is concerned, is a simple matter of the budget. While such magazines as LOOK or *Life* can and do maintain teams of writers and photographers who spend weeks and travel thousands of miles developing a single picture story, few if any of the business publications and only one or two of the house organs can afford this expense as a regular procedure.

Yet the picture story is as valuable a publishing technique for both of these groups as it is for the general magazines. And both business publications and house organs regularly use the picture story, often with good effect.

Business publications generally are concerned with two similar kinds of information—how somebody did something, and how to do something. It is obvious at once that this is a natural and fertile field for the picture story, since this technique gives the reader information most quickly, most accurately and in a form that enables him to remember it longest.

The how-to picture article is the form most used in business publications. They

208

also use the related-picture sequence in connection with text and they employ all the other categories — personalities, contrasts, planned chronologies — and make full use of drawings, graphs, charts, maps and illustrations in their ever-increasing attempts to strengthen both the appearance and the service of their pages.

To get these results without budgets that can support the writer-photographer-researcher teams used by general magazines, business-paper editors and house-organ editors must rely largely on ingenuity and the willingness of their industries or their sponsoring firms to co-operate with them. This co-operation is generously given in most instances, because business and industrial firms have learned that honest information well presented in the trade press is valuable publicity that justifies considerable effort and expense.

In practice, therefore, the business-paper editor or staff writer who visits a plant and finds there some new process or procedure that is worthy material for his publication frequently can arrange with the company's public relations man to have an experienced industrial photographer take specified pictures that will provide the proper sequence or continuity. Often the preliminary writing is done for the editor by the plant personnel.

In the case of small plants, construction projects and merchandizing establishments, there is likely to be no public relations man and no regular company photographer. The editor must then arrange with company officials either to take his own pictures or to bring in an outside photographer to make the pictures he wants. And he must take notes from which he will prepare his copy.

Because this situation is so general in many of the fields covered by industrial and trade journals, a great many editors have found it necessary, or at least highly desirable, to become expert photographers as well as writers. They visit plants, stores or construction sites fully equipped with cameras, tripods, lights, film and filters and make their exposures as they make their notes. The views they want involve such technicalities that no outside photographer can be expected to succeed in taking them properly without the editor personally checking on the ground glass to insure that angle, lighting and included area are all correct.

In the house-organ field, the editor of a company magazine, if it is at all a pretentious publication, usually has at his command the services of the public relations or industrial relations department and access to pictures either made by the company's own photographer or by a good commercial or industrial photographer from a nearby studio.

Up to the point where pictures and raw materials for copy are in hand, the business-paper or house-organ editor must run the show alone. He may get a great deal of help from the people at the source of the information, and even the photographer may surprise him, but he cannot afford to rely on either of these aids. Generally, the result will be no better than his own vision, enthusiasm and ingenuity make it.

With the pictures and the rough copy in hand, the editor can enlist the help of his art director—most profitable business publications have one, and most house organs that are at all pretentious have access to one. From this point on, the best procedure will differ but little from that outlined for general magazines.

Naturally, in selecting pictures for a business publication, accent will be placed on pictures that reveal information clearly, but pictures that are also human and pictorially good are that much more valuable.

Picture stories do a large share of the job for the best modern house organs. Examples from some of these, and from a variety of trade journals, will be found on the 12 following pages.

HAT STUFF

IT GIVES our fighting men a kick to get into civvies when they can, but to date the movement has just come to a head. The boys shown here have thrown their service hats in the ring temporarily and donned various types of lid for the benefit of the cameraman.

DERBY DAY. This corporal celebrated when he found a battered bo Normandy and struck a pose like a knight of the road. His buddies say hobo, though, when it comes to chasing Nazis.

FRENCH STRAWS. They don't fit so well, but these skimmers, picke by American engineers after liberating a French town, certainly must given the natives a laugh.

FELT GOOD. A part of the spoils of war were the felt hats found at St. Lo, France, and shown in the top picture. The distinguished looking gent above is an air squadron commander.

ROMAN HOLIDAY. When these three GIs reached Rome they helpe citizens celebrate their liberation by blossoming out in straw lids.

This one-page picture story, designed for comic effect, was compiled from agency photographs for *Picture News,* a house organ distributed to customers of the Sinclair Oil Company. Recipients of this publication get their copies from their own dealer, whose localized advertisement is printed on the back cover. The inside pages are given over to picture stories, with short text blocks and captions.

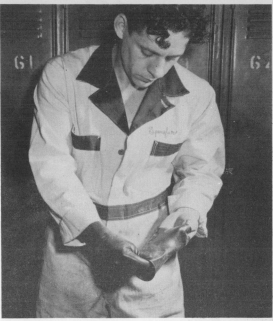

Photographs and directions by courtesy of The B. F. Goodrich Company

Don't pull rubber gloves off the way a dress glove is usually removed. By exerting pressure on the fingers the rubber glove is put under an extremely severe strain and is more than likely to tear

Peel gloves off the hand like this. Simply take hold of cuff and peel the gloves off inside out. Rubber gloves create a suction effect when fingertips are pulled, and may snap off at finger ends

Take Care of Rubber Gloves

Rotate gloves in use. Keep two pairs available, and wear them every other day. They last much longer if they are given a 24-hour rest between wearings

Patch tears and snags. Investigate the practicability of patching rubber gloves as soon as a tear or snag develops. It is not considered safe, however, to patch fingers or palms of electricians' gloves, or rubber gloves that are used by workers in acid

114

FACTORY MANAGEMENT and MAINTENANCE

Excellent use was made of the how-to picture-story technique in this article from *Factory Management and Maintenance,* a trade journal whose objectives are well stated in its title. Pictures and caption material were obtained from the B. F. Goodrich Company. Simple, lucid captions, packed with information, help photographs do their instructional job. Neither pictures nor text could do it alone.

Ammonia Synthesis At TVA

"**N**ITRATE PLANT NO. 2", a veteran World War I plant built at Muscle Shoals, Alabama, and now contributing to World War II, was taken over by the Tennessee Valley Authority in 1933. With the outbreak of war in Europe, plans were made and completed by December 1941, for rehabilitation and modernization.

Process operations in the ammonia producing plant are divided into six main parts, namely: semi-water-gas manufacture, hydrogen conversion, gas compression, gas purification, ammonia synthesis, and ammonia storage. Coke is unloaded from railway cars into hoppers and carried by an inclined belt to a rotary screen. The fine coke is removed for use in phosphate smelting furnaces. Oversized coke is then stored in bins located over the semi-water-gas generators which supply nitrogen in the blow-run gas. Watergas and blow-run gas are mixed and scrubbed with water, then pass through a sulphur removing process enroute to a three-lift 1,000,000 cu.ft. gas holder. Additional hydrogen is then produced catalytically by reacting the carbon monoxide of the mixture with steam. Four synchronous motor-driven compressors proceed to draw the gas from the converted gas holder and put it through six stages of compression for purification and synthesis. Purification includes removal of the carbon dioxide with water scrubbing at 17 atm.; and the elimination of carbon monoxide, oxygen, and residual carbon dioxide by scrubbing the gases with cold ammoniacal copper formate solution at 121 atm. Final compression is to 350 atm.

Purified synthesis gas is then mixed with the circulating gas and any foreign materials filtered out. The combined volume of new and recirculated gases is refrigerated in an ammonia-cooled condenser. Freed from liquid ammonia by a separator, the gas goes through a heater to the ammonia synthesis converter. The converted gases are then put through a water-cooled condenser, after which a second similar separator removes the ammonia which condenses, and the remaining gases pass into the recirculating system by way of the circulator-compressors. Liquid anhydrous ammonia from the separators flows through a pressure reduction valve into elevated spherical weigh tanks. Finally, the weighed ammonia is piped into spherical storage tanks prior to shipment.

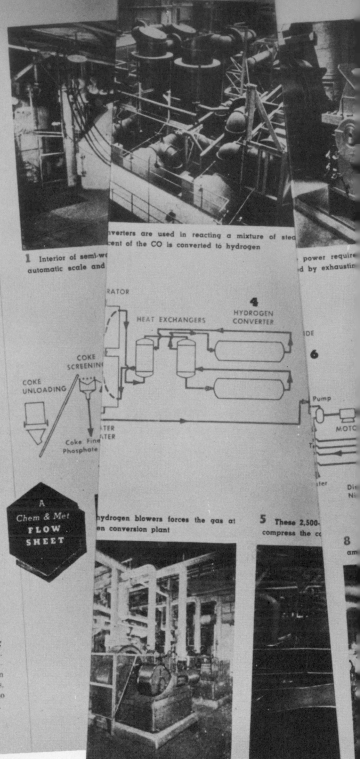

A combination of visual devices was employed here on an accordion-fold insert to simplify a highly technical article appearing in *Chemical and Metallurgical Engineering,* a first-rate technical trade journal. The article tells how liquid anhydrous (free of water) ammonia is produced at one of the big TVA plants in Alabama. The story is told in both text and photographs. But because the photographs are complicated d gas from

er into the CO
ton wheels

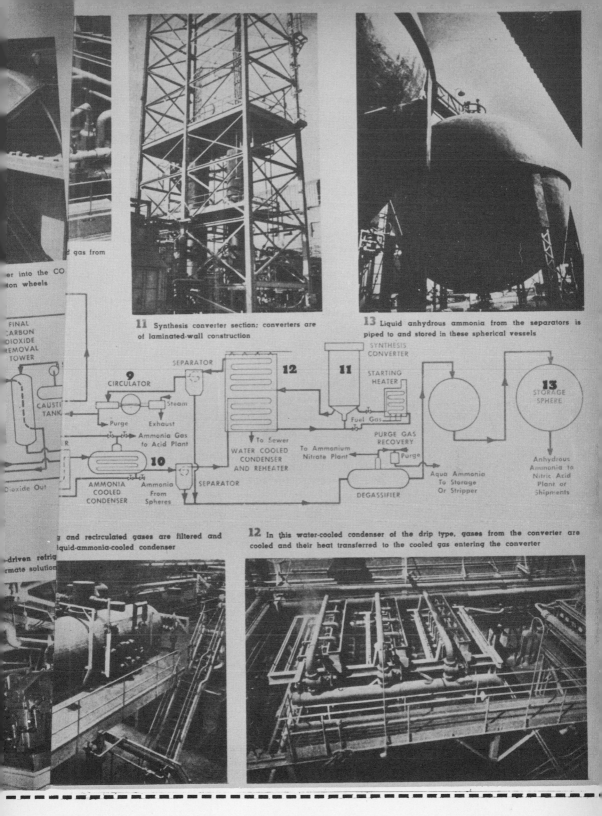

11 Synthesis converter section; converters are of laminated-wall construction

13 Liquid anhydrous ammonia from the separators is piped to and stored in these spherical vessels

FINAL
CARBON
DIOXIDE
REMOVAL
TOWER
CAUSTI
TANK
Dioxide Out
9
CIRCULATOR
Steam
Purge
Exhaust
Ammonia Gas
to Acid Plant
SEPARATOR
12
To Sewer
WATER COOLED
CONDENSER
AND REHEATER
11
SYNTHESIS
CONVERTER
STARTING
HEATER
Fuel Gas
10
AMMONIA
COOLED
CONDENSER
Ammonia
From
Spheres
SEPARATOR
To Ammonium
Nitrate Plant
PURGE GAS
RECOVERY
Purge
DEGASSIFIER
Aqua Ammonia
To Storage
Or Stripper
13
STORAGE
SPHERE
Anhydrous
Ammonia to
Nitric Acid
Plant or
Shipments

g and recirculated gases are filtered and
liquid-ammonia-cooled condenser

-driven refrig
rmate solution

12 In this water-cooled condenser of the drip type, gases from the converter are cooled and their heat transferred to the cooled gas entering the converter

and likely to confuse even the technical minded, they are presented in sequence above and below a simplified diagrammatic chart which traces the flow of materials through the complicated machinery. The chart is keyed with numbers corresponding to those on the pictures, so that the reader can study first one and then the other. Thus aided, even a layman can understand the process.

This is the opening spread of a six-page picture-text combination, published by *The Lamp,* every-other-month house organ of the Standard Oil Company of New Jersey. *The Lamp,* which goes to both employees and stockholders of the company, is an aristocrat among house organs. Its photographs and art work are of the finest quality. It is printed on heavy, glazed paper stock, which reproduces both color and black

VENEZUELA

Oil for the Allies is produced by skilled nationals trained by Creole Petroleum Corporation

MILLIONS of barrels of Venezuelan oil for the Allies are being produced today by trained and capable Venezuelan nationals, who but a few years ago were without mechanical skills and experience. It is their contribution to the war for freedom from the land of Simon Bolivar, liberator of six nations.

Training and education carried on by the oil companies over two decades has brought Venezuelans into the most highly specialized and skilled oil industry jobs in their native land.

They are directing crews as new wells are drilled; they are in charge of transportation of oil by pipeline and tanker; they are working as geologists, technicians, electricians, welders, mechanics, truckmen and caterpillar tractor operators.

Creole Petroleum Corporation, a subsidiary of Standard Oil Company (N. J.), produced about 415,000 barrels of crude oil a day, or more than 50 per cent of the total daily Venezuelan production of about 765,000 barrels during the last quarter of 1944. And the hundreds of Venezuelans employed by Creole had a major part in this production.

Venezuelans also are working at specialized tasks in the refineries at Caripito and La Salina. They are operators and are trained as foremen and for higher supervisory positions.

Crude oils from Venezuela are valuable sources of special petroleum products for war, some being extremely important for

FOUR 50-TON WEIGHTS, placed by floating derrick (left), sink caisson over 150 feet long into bed of Lake Maracaibo through 100 feet of water. Four such caissons, supporting oil derrick over water, form the foundation for underwater drilling. Above is a Venezuelan oil worker; right, derrick above a well in eastern Venezuelan jungle

and white with remarkable clarity. Its editor, a former picture-story writer on a national magazine, has a budget which permits him to send photographers on distant assignments, even to foreign countries, as in the case of the article above on the production of oil in Venezuela. The magazine ardently promotes company development, is less employee-personalized than most house organs.

In wind tunnels like this, tomorrow's airplanes are born. The 24-foot fan of the Allen Memorial Aeronautical Laboratories is powered by an 18000-hp motor. (Photo courtesy Boeing Aircraft Company, Seattle.)

- -

Company magazines are often used to cement good relations with customers. This page from the *Westinghouse Engineer* features a picture taken by Boeing Aircraft (a Westinghouse customer) and Boeing is credited in the caption. The *Westinghouse Engineer* is a slick-paper magazine, published six times a year, presenting excellent photographs and authoritative, well-documented stories on highly technical subjects.

FISH TALK

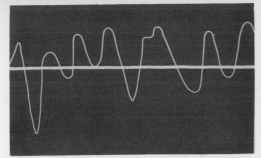

Working with the set-up above, Dr. Christopher Coates of the New York Zoological Society Aquarium has classified fish moods and their corresponding audible manifestations. Trace at right represents the sounds of feeding goldfish

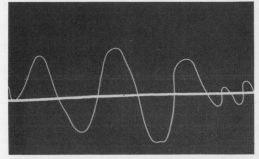

Osculation at left and corresponding oscillation at right, above, characterize an amorous pair of Malayan gouramies. Many fish make sounds by grinding their teeth, while others blow air from swim bladders to make croaking noises

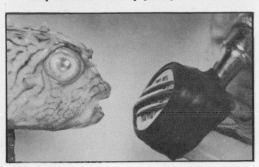

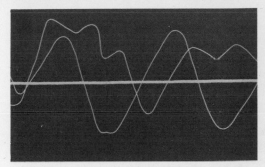

No political implications, just an angry boxfish, above, expressing indignation after having been jabbed with a pencil. Grunts of annoyance form agitated, uneven curves. Happy catfish, below, produces purring sound pictured at the right

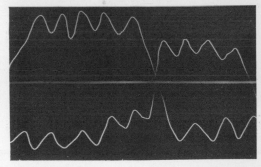

A one-page picture story in the trade journal, *Electronics,* proves that fish can make audible sounds, although it takes an electronic sound track to "hear" them. The article is well put together, with the action in each case placed opposite the sound track it creates, but an obvious weakness, from a reader's point of view, is the complete lack of explanation of the apparatus that does the trick.

Hirohito's Helpers

These workers do not mean to aid the enemy; they are simply thoughtless. But their small acts of negligence, repeated a thousandfold, amount to a serious set-back in our war production. Names listed below are purely fictitious, but they typify some of the offenders who unconsciously give indirect help to Hitler and Hirohito. Added together, their daily shortcomings are more destructive than deliberate sabotage. Only they themselves can correct their own bad habits and put the full strength of industry behind our forces at the front. Although the enemy is on the run, the war isn't over yet. Our fighting men will need everything we can give them until the last shot is fired.

TOM TARDY usually punches in late. He'd much rather be on time, but a few minutes longer in bed put him behind schedule, and before he's through breakfast he sees he can't make it anyway. He loses part of his day's work, and has a bad effect on his fellow workers

WALTER WOLFE likes night life. He doesn't see why he shouldn't spend his wages the way he wants. He's right up to the point where his night prowling interferes with his daytime duties. Nobody can hit the ball at 8 a.m. with too many highballs the night before

PEARL PRATTLE can't seem to keep up with her job. Perhaps if she gave a little more attention to the work at hand, this condition would clear up. All feminine fingers are not equally nimble, but a little extra application will usually keep the production line moving

BILLY BULL believes there's no better way to budge a balky chuck than to hit it a wallop with a wrench. He doesn't appreciate the accuracy that has been built into his equipment and the destruction his heavy-handed methods cause. He'd do better to call the foreman

This is part of a preachment in cartoons published by the trade journal, *American Machinist*. Without much subtlety but with well-aimed force, the article pounds at factory workers who slow up war work, and thus unwittingly aid the enemy by one kind of neglect or another. Throughout the period of war production, factory managers have used similar visual devices in posters and company publications.

Hours Saved
When Planes "Keep Moving"

orth American, at Dallas, has been turning out the AT-6 Texan mbat trainer, the P-51 Mustang fighter, and the B-24 Libera- r bomber on conveyor lines. Here are selected views of opera- ns on the first two, with an idea of some of the savings real- d. Of the 100,000 parts required, Dallas has made **97** percent.

By GERALD ELDRIDGE STEDMAN

SHIPPING INSTRUCTIONS & SERVICE ORDERS

PACKING SHEETS

1 The main-plant loop conveyor, almost a mile long, picks up GFE and other parts from receiving and carries them to sub-conveyor transfer stations, as well as carrying parts from place to place. This conveyor also brings small spare parts back to shipping (shown here) in a variety of containers. On the basket shown here the dial and hand indicate which of 25 transfer stations the load came from. Hand is reset upon reloading to indicate which station receives the load.

2 Dips in the main conveyor bring parts down for unloading at transfer and delivery stations. Where floor area is required for fabrication or assembly, the conveyor runs high, with a framework beneath to catch parts, should they fall, and thus to prevent injury to workers.

In a numbered picture sequence, of which only the first page is shown above, *Wings,* an aviation trade journal, presented the story of conveyor lines which speeded up the production of fighting airplanes at the North American Aviation Company plant in Dallas, Texas. The figure of the gay policeman giving the go-ahead signal is repeated in miniature, holding up a number, to start each caption.

W. F. Thomas conducting a foremen's meeting at the Buick Motor Division plant #5 in Flint. Fifty-two similar groups meet two hours each ▸

BUICK SUPERVISORS STUD[

VETERANS' PROBLEMS

Fitting safety glasses. Bruce A. Trembley, safety supervisor and veteran Donald P. Hollenbaugh.

Eighty-five percent of all war veterans employed by the Buick Motor Division are immediately reabsorbed into a healthy, productive life without difficulty. The remaining 15 percent find their complications eased through the training program.

Operating on the theory that supervision and fellow workers have a responsibility as well as the returning war veteran, Buick Motor Division supervisors are studying veterans' problems two hours each week as part of the Buick executive training program.

A movie of the Buick process in hiring a

veteran is shown foremen, general foreme sistant superintendents and superintendc who are specially trained to handle the vet readjustment.

In the case of veteran placement, all g study the GI Bill of Rights, individual the military's wishes in the matter and Motor Division policy.

Advantages of a sympathetic, helpful tude toward the veteran are stressed. B the same time, these men are reminded th veterans should not be set up as a sep group; that the objective should be th establishment of proper work relationsh that men who have been in the service of country can take their place with fellow wc on a job they are fully capable of han

The Buick Motor Company's plan for re-employing its returned war veterans is the subject of this picture article from *Folks,* one of General Motors' impressive house organs, published monthly by the company's public relations department. Although it is not strictly a picture magazine, *Folks* makes generous use of the picture-story technique in detailing General Motors accomplishments and policies for its employee

s' coordinator George A. Lincoln and William S. Knerr. One of the coordinator's most important functions is to see that the veteran is placed in a job he can handle.

Foreman William E. Cooper instructs war veteran Edward J. Smith in the proper method of covering loaded M-18 "Hellcat" tanks which are produced at the Buick plant in Flint

WAVE Geraldine E. Bendall fills out an application for regular payroll deductions d purchases shortly after being rehired at Buick. Richard W. Ingham assists her

nds for ideas. Gabriel Kovacs didn't wait long after being hired to make a suggestion at won an award. Left to right: Kovacs, F. L. Smith, and George M. Somers.

Leaving the plant after work, veteran Frank Henzarek and his foreman, F. W. Bigelow, discuss the former's placement on a certain type of job for which he is especially fitted.

readership. Like most other house organs, it also devotes considerable space to the activities and accomplishments of employees, whether in shop and office, on the bowling alley or tennis court, or in amateur theatricals. It devotes a page an issue to photographs taken and submitted by employees and their families, and for the best picture of each month awards a $25 war bond.

CHAPTER 9

Writing the Picture Story

In a little book entitled *Writing Is Work,* Mary Roberts Rinehart says:

"Of one thing the reader can be certain: the more easily anything reads, the harder it has been to write. There is no such thing as light-hearted spontaneous creation in the mind, before it is set down on paper."

Ponder those words. In them is wisdom born of wide, successful experience.

"You write with ease to show your breeding,

"But easy writing's curst hard reading."

Writing, as a popular author has said, is a great deal like hitting yourself on the head with a hammer—when you stop, it feels wonderful.

Writing is indeed work, to some extent downright drudgery, and an agonizing kind of drudgery to boot. But for most writers, compensations greatly outweigh the agony. Rarely does even the most case-hardened practitioner lose the thrill that comes from seeing his own words on the printed page.

Picture-story writing has its peculiar aspects and perplexities, but it also has much in common with other forms of writing. Like the others, it has the basic objective of communicating facts and ideas to the reader. All writing worthy of the name is communication, and the more lucidly and immediately it communicates, the better it is.

"Writing," said Laurence Sterne, "is but a different name for conversation." Some writers contend that this is an oversimplification, but Sterne had the right idea. If you can write so that the reader understands you as well as he would understand the conversation of his intimates, you are "getting over" to him and your work is successful—at least to the extent that what you write is worth communicating.

Of necessity, picture-story writing, like most magazine writing, is of the kind called "popular." Do not let the adjective frighten you, even though it may be spoken with derision by your more intellectual friends. Harvey Deuell made excellent sense when he said:

"There is much confusion about what is called 'popular writing,' many speaking of it as if it were synonomous with poor writing. Nothing could be farther from the truth. A popular bit of writing may be a classic, and certainly much of the unpopular esoteric stuff is abominable."

A mass audience should be a spur to qualitative writing, rather than a deterrent. "Mass" means all kinds of people, high and low, rich and poor, Phi Beta Kappas and fifth-graders. Communicating facts and ideas to such a cross section of humanity in a single medium is possible, but many writers with "literary" reputations have never learned how to do it. "Popular" writers have to know how and, in learning, many of them acquire distinction. At the very least, they learn the virtue of clarity.

Anne Hummert, a radio executive who has employed scores of writers, puts it this way:

"It isn't hard to make yourself clear to a Harvard professor. No matter how you stumble or how badly you express yourself, he is fairly certain to understand what you are trying to say. It is the person without education or an elastic mind who must have everything said to him clearly and succinctly. Yet never can the story be so childish that your more sophisticated readers will be offended."

So-called "popular" writing is often first-rate, judged by any standard. Some of it is forever a part of literary history. As has often been said: "A book has one leg on immortality's trophy when the words are for children and the meanings are for men."

In all writing, simplicity and instant clarity are the greatest of virtues and the most difficult to acquire.

Although we have known and dealt with hundreds of writers, we do not know any short cuts to simplicity and clarity. In our experience, they have been achieved only by writers who went laboriously through three processes: thorough preparation; proper organization; rewriting—and still more rewriting.

The first two precede writing, which is discussed later in this chapter. The third follows after your "first-drafting" is finished.

These are the three keys to writing success. Proper use of them will overcome most actual deficiencies in talent. Without adequate attention to them, even the finest talent will fall far short of its potentialities, as many a slovenly "genius" has proved.

Let us consider them one at a time.

PREPARATION

We have noted that at least five sixths of the picture-story writer's time spent on any article is devoted to preparation for the one sixth given to actual writing. In other forms of writing, the percentage will be about the same, although there may be less physical evidence of this ratio.

The hours, days and weeks spent in getting ready to write a story, article or book are known as the "incubation" period. During much of this time, the picture-story writer confers with his editor, his art director, artist or photographer; with or without assistance does a thorough research job on his subject; decides on a focus, or "angle plans"; writes a shooting script; makes arrangements for, and supervises, the making of photographs or drawings.

All these activities add up to considerable preparation for the actual writing job. For example, field work with artist or photographer is certain to develop countless little facts and facets which will be valuable when the typewriter-pounding begins. If the writer knows his business, every conversation with subject or subjects will be an asset in his execution of the finished piece.

In this respect, the picture-story writer is more fortunate than writers dealing only in words. His responsibility for producing a picture story before starting to write it forces upon him a certain measure of preparation. Any "text" writer needs the equivalent of this kind of preliminary dredging, but he is less likely to get it unless he is self-disciplined.

A writer may be doing his hardest work when you least suspect it. We know one who claims that his most fruitful hours are those spent in gazing from a window. This type of "incubation" work is justifiably suspect among editors, but it is a stupid editor indeed who does not acknowledge the value of pretypewriter pondering.

A professional writer on an important assignment is likely to be incubating his story throughout most of his waking hours. Eating, shaving, walking the dog or reading a newspaper, he will conjure up lead paragraphs or "write" descriptions of his central character, or plan the sequence in which he is going to present his ideas. If he is really a writer, he can't help it; and the more of this "daydreaming" he does, the better his final product is likely to be.

Thus, when we stress thorough preparation as prerequisite to good writing, we mean more than research and field work and interviews and notes. We also mean thinking.

ORGANIZATION

Important as it is in any kind of writing, organization of a picture story should be neither complicated nor difficult for a writer who has clearly thought out what he wants to say.

Here again, the picture-story writer has an advantage. Before he can start to write, he has had to decide on a focus and a chronology, or some other continuity device. He has a layout in front of him on which his article has been thoroughly organized visually. He has merely to make his text pattern conform to the visual pattern.

We know that this sounds simpler than it is, but we also know that it is less difficult than organizing a text piece from scratch, whether fiction or nonfiction.

The major problems of organization are solved when the writer has:

1. A definite approach, or "angle."
2. A central focus, personal if possible.
3. A continuity device, or devices, of the kind listed in Chapter 3.
4. A lead (introduction) and a conclusion.
5. A definite plan for tying together lead, middle and conclusion by due attention to the central theme or focus throughout.

In other words, a story is properly organized when the writer has determined on a scheme for telling it logically, simply and clearly. Then, if he has in mind and/or on paper what he is going to say, he is ready to write.

Just how will you phrase or refine your story? This is a vital question, in the answering of which you will need and get editorial help, but the major responsibility will be yours.

REWRITING

One of our colleagues is fond of saying: "There is no such thing as good writing—there is only good *rewriting*."

We know some exceptions that can be cited to prove him wrong, but he is at least 98 per cent right.

We have been told, as you probably have, that Voltaire wrote *Candide* in three days and that even the best copyreader can't cut out a sentence without hurting it. To that, we can only comment that we don't know any modern Voltaires.

We have heard that Heywood Broun used to dash off 1,000 words of acceptable prose in a half hour, and that Clarence Budington Kelland wrote one chapter of *Arizona* while he was "dummy" in a bridge game. Both stories may be true for all we know. Mr. Broun was an exceptional man, and Mr. Kelland to this day is turning out novels at a pace which the average writer can only consider breath-taking. Even so, we suspect that long and concentrated "incubation" was a substitute for rewriting—that Broun and Kelland belong to that small, select company who do their rewriting before they put a word on paper.

If you can do yours that way, you are thrice blessed. We don't know any writers who can. Our experience has tended to substantiate Mrs. Rinehart's contention that the more easily anything reads, the harder it has been to write; we are proud of a writer who can accomplish a good result on the third revision, but we are not shocked by one who needs four or five.

It is, of course, obvious that the more thorough preparation has been, the more carefully a story has been thought out, organized and drafted, the less need there should be for actual rewriting at the typewriter. Some writers prefer to do the bulk of their rewriting before they submit copy to an editor; others like to submit a rough draft and get the editor's opinions before they begin to rewrite. Good results have been achieved from both methods, but needless to say the former procedure is preferred by those responsible for the quality of written copy in a magazine.

In any kind of writing, rewording, rephrasing, revising sentence structure, etc., are important. For most people, there is no other way of producing smooth, polished, logical, simple, easy-to-read prose. In picture-story writing, with its unusual condensation problems, its ever-present necessity to blend text with pictures, rewriting is essential.

There is a story about Woodrow Wilson, possibly apochryphal, which points up the problem of condensation. Mr. Wilson had agreed to deliver a speech, and was asked how long he would need to prepare it.

"That depends," he said. "If you want a two-hour speech, I am ready now. If you want me to talk a half hour, I shall need three or four days to get ready. If you want a 10-minute speech, you had better give me two weeks."

Inasmuch as the picture-story writer seldom has more than a five-minute "speech," in terms of reader time, he must devote a large share of his writing time to compression—to distillation of the essence of his knowledge of his subject.

When he is ready to write, his problem breaks down into several categories:

1. A title, or "head."
2. Subtitle.
3. Lead text.
4. Supplementary text.
5. Picture captions.
6. Conclusion.

These elements are not all part of every picture story. Some articles are published without subtitles, some with pictures and captions only. But in most cases, all six categories must be considered.

1. TITLE

It is best to have at least a working title, or headline, written for an article before the layout is made. A title helps to keep both writer and layout artist from straying from the approved focus. If the writer's later research or written copy happens to turn up a better "selling" title, it can be changed without great trouble. (We use the word "selling" advisedly. Although some writers and editors are shocked to be told so, they are salesmen, every bit as much as—if not more than—the man who calls on hardware stores with order book in hand. For writers have to "sell" readers through words, without the aid of personal contact.)

The function of a title for an article (as well as for an advertisement) is to sell the reader on the product displayed below or above it.

How does a title sell a story? First, by attracting reader attention; second, by persuading the reader that the article is worth reading. In a picture story, the title has help from photographs or drawings, and should be so written as to complement visual elements appearing with it.

To sell well, the title should be as brief as possible. It should contain action and/or color, should conjure up a visual image, appeal strongly to the emotions, or sharply call to the reader's attention a known identity or object in which millions are interested. Ideally, any title should perform more than one of these functions.

Like other kinds of writing, title-writing is best learned by experience, but the experiences of successful editors may give you a few useful hints. One is that there are selling words, basic in their appeal to almost all kinds of readers: love. true, truth, story, inside, expose, reveal, how to, you and your, etc. Among the most important are *you* and *your;* when a story is so written that it can be honestly titled to include either one, it is assured of at least some readership. Like the rest of us, the reader is attracted by anything which promises to touch on his own life, job, family, bank account, skill, attractiveness, physical or psychological condition, to name only a few of the possibilities.

Sometimes, the name of a place or city may be a key selling word in a title: Hollywood, New York, Paris, Reno, Grenwich Village, the Golden Gate are obvious attention-getters.

Names that make news also sell magazine articles—and magazines. Roosevelt, Churchill, Stalin, Hitler, Sinatra, Hope, Crosby, Chiang Kai-shek, Lauren Bacall, Eisenhower, MacArthur, Betty Grable are names that have sold hundreds of millions of copies of magazines in the last decade. They sell because they are loved or hated or admired or despised; because they are controversial; because their very appearance on a cover or a printed page arouses some emotion in the beholder. They are, to use a favorite editorial word, provocative. Good titles, like the most widely read articles, have that quality.

A few examples may serve to point up the importance of titles. Who, for example, would read Hawthorne's book entitled *Old Time Legends, Together With Sketches, Experimental and Ideal* if he could read the same book with the title *The Scarlet Letter?*

Alice in Wonderland, a selling title for many generations, is infinitely more effective than *Alice's Adventures Underground.* The colorful appeal of *Wonderland* makes all the difference.

An American publisher of inexpensive reprints once issued one of De Maupassant's famous stories under its original title, *The Tallow Ball.* It sold 10,000 copies. A reissue, entitled *A French Prostitute's Sacrifice,* sold 54,000. Incidentally, the second title more exactly describes the story than did the first!

2. SUBTITLE

Virtually everything said about titles can also be applied to subtitles, which generally are continuations of the top headline, containing additional words set in smaller type. The subtitle carries on the selling function by exposing a little more of the story and stimulating the reader's already aroused curiosity. Many magazines, to increase pulling power, display subtitles on black, grey or colored panels, or otherwise "dress them up" so that even a casual reader will be impelled to stop and get their message.

3. LEAD TEXT

The "lead" of the average newspaper story is a summary of what is to follow. For this, there is a mechanical reason: when a newspaper is made up in type, the story may be cut to make it fit the forms.

If space is limited, a magazine article may have the same kind of lead. Or it may begin with a climax, or high point of the exposition, and "flash back" to the rest of the story—a common fiction technique. It may also start with a quotation, with dialogue, an anecdote, description, or with a biographical "take out" of the central character.

Before he puts a word on paper, the experienced article writer has decided which type of lead is most suitable for the piece he is doing, just as he has a definite idea of the conclusion he is going to use. He knows that the lead has to live up to the selling job done by the title and subtitle, and extend it. If there is a big name in his story, person or place, he knows that belongs in the lead. Among the other factors he will search for are action, humor, emotional appeal, controversy, excitement, behind-the-scenes flavor, anything that can be brought directly into the lives, hopes and dreams of the reader.

It is important that the lead have pace, that it move the reader quickly and smoothly into the body of the story. A sloppily written lead can be repaired; a dull one has to be thrown away.

In a picture story, it is also important that the lead establish a definite connection with the visual pattern around it. It may or may not refer directly to anything appearing in the pictures, but it must complement and assist the picture story.

4. SUPPLEMENTARY TEXT

The running text in a picture article is usually brief, but its function is important. It carries the load of supplying information not contained in either pictures or captions; it must be packed with facts, but not at the expense of flow or rhythm. Inevitably, it benefits from close editing and much rewriting because, when space is limited, the carefully chosen word, the finely chiseled phrase, the long-pondered sentence must do the work of paragraphs.

Although it should not repeat anything recorded elsewhere in the story, this text must maintain a close alliance with the picture story and continuously build up the central theme or thesis by incident, anecdote, accentuation or additional information. It will inform the reader best if it also entertains.

5. PICTURE CAPTIONS

The role of captions in a picture story is far more important than the uninitiated observer can possibly realize. It bears only faint resemblance to the function of captions under newspaper pictures or those in "illustrated" books—as contrasted with true picture books (such as this one) where pictures and text function integrally.

Captions in picture articles are not mere descriptions of photographs or drawings. They are *part of the story*. This is the lesson about picture-story writing which writers from other media are slowest to learn. Some of them, although adept with other kinds of text, never do learn it. In other words, they never become picture-story writers.

Picture-story captions have a triple function:

1. To provide necessary picture descriptions.
2. To keep the story moving forward.
3. To supply information not contained in pictures or running text.

In mulling over their research before starting to write, experienced picture-story writers invariably set aside tidbits of important or fascinating information which they know can best be used in captions. If it is a personality story, the writer is certain to have facts bearing on the habits, character or idiosyncrasies of the subject which will fit best under pictures emphasizing those facts. In an action story, related in sequence, background facts will always be best presented in connection with one bit of pictorial action or another. Whatever the kind of story, captions should directly force the reader's eye to the picture and then back to the text.

This kind of caption writing is a continuous exercise in supercondensation, for captions are supposed to do their three jobs without loss of punch or sparkle. The correctly dramatic word and the well-turned phrase are as welcome in a caption as elsewhere.

We know of no better training than picture-story caption writing for one who would learn to write "tightly."

6. CONCLUSION

When you hear an editor say "Wrap it up," chances are he is not talking about a brown-paper parcel. He is telling a writer to "wrap up" a story, to conclude it with punch and decisiveness, to leave the reader gasping, laughing, raging—or, at least, pleasantly satisfied.

A good conclusion brings a story to an end smoothly and with finesse. Abrupt endings are as unsatifactory in print as they are in life. A good conclusion restates or reiterates or re-emphasizes the central theme set forth in the title and lead. It highlights the message of the picture story, and if it is properly persuasive the reader will be impelled to devote additional time to the pictures.

A well-written picture story, in all its parts, reveals attention to all the essentials of good writing: knowledge; planning; thinking; organization; rewriting, rewriting, rewriting and rewriting.

Picture interest is heightened by having the meat-market proprietor hold up the large steak for the customer's inspection. Note that first line of caption calls attention to this pictorial focus. The big smiles also help draw reader's attention to same point.

Competing with the steak above the counter for interest here is the lavish display of meats in the showcase. To add information and increase reading time, the art director placed labels on all items not immediately recognizable. A good picture-story writer thinks of such visual aids.

RIB STEAK

LOIN LAMB CHOPS

VEAL CUTLET

HAM

SHOULDER OF PORK

BACON

HAM STEAK

SHOULDER LAMB CHO

This genuine two-and-a-half-pound loin steak proffered. at Rufus Starnes' meat market is a commonplace item in Abilene. It sells at 44 cents a pound. There's also plenty of bacon, but the quota is one pound at a time to a customer. Ham, too, is rationed voluntarily. Hotels always have either ba or ham on hand. Fortunate Abilene, center of rich West Texas livestock a has a municipal abattoir which slaughters 9,000-14,000 cattle each ye

This caption, tied to the picture story by its opening sentence, also carries a big load of information. Transition from picture description to additional facts is made so neatly that reader is likely to be unaware of it.

Because of the crowded shelves in this store, the background of the photograph is cluttered. To keep the important point of this picture—an abundant stock of cigarettes—from being subordinated, art director ordered circles drawn around stock and package.

No hoarding of precious cigarets or chewing gum is necessary in Abilene, as this display of the wealth at W. J. Zickler's newsstand testifies. People just confine themselves to one package a day to preserve their abundance.

And the local newspaper prints, but does not exploit, shortages elsewhere. Yet Abilene, like other cities, has no nylons or cleansing tissues, limited supplies of tires, baby garments, towels, gasoline, spices, electrical equipment.

City Without Food Shortages

Produced by STANLEY GORDON Editor • MAURICE TERRELL Photographer

Millions of us go smokeless and steakless, but Abilene, Texas, has a way of taking care of its own

No block-long queues, no shopping riots, no "Positively No Cigarets" placards deface the wonderful city of Abilene, Texas—a consumers' oasis in wartime America. Evidence of the town's astonishing abundance of such rarities as butter and chocolate bars ap-

pears in the pictures on these pages, which show LOOK's West Coast editor, Stanley Gordon, on a recent tour of Abilene's shops.

The rest of the U. S. may consider Abilene merely lucky. True, the town is located within trucking distance of the fertile Rio Grande Valley and the port of Houston. And its proximity to Camp Barkeley,Army Service Forces Training Center, gives Abilene's 35,000 residents a "critical area" rating, with slightly larger food quotas than other towns of its size.

Abilene, however, points proudly to its anti-black market program as chiefly responsible for its appearance of plenitude. Exhibiting common sense and good citizenship, Abilenians buy no more than they need, share with neighbors, avoid hoarding. Merchants co-operate, divide wholesalers' stocks equitably and refuse to take advantage of competitors by gobbling up supplies of scarce items.

Other cities please note.

(Continued on next page)

The main title is a simple description of the article. It contains no verb, hence is too passive to be ideal, but is attention-compelling because of the very nature of the subject matter. In this case, the name of the city was not considered a "selling" word.

Subtitle extends selling begun in title by: 1. Emphasizing that story deals with reader's common problems; 2. Adding information that Abilene, Tex., "has a way" of solving those problems. This impels more reading to find answer to "How?"

Lead paragraph keeps the reader participating by contrasting the situation in Abilene with that in his own community. It stirs his appetite with "butter" and "chocolate," then calls attention to personalized focus of the picture story.

Supplementary text moves smoothly and naturally from the curiosity - provoking lead into information which satisfies most of the curiosity. Note the choice of words which enabled the writer to load second and third paragraphs with facts.

In this layout, two captions were crammed into space for one in order to give the photographs above and below more display space. Such departure from orthodox practice, occasionally justified by an emergency, complicates the writer's problem; but here he managed not only to describe the pictured situation but also to provide interesting facts of Abilene's hotels, restaurants and food wholesalers.

Butter is stacked high in Abilene's store refrigerators. Hotels and restaurants still serve three generous pats of butter with hot cakes. The town has two creameries, numerous dairies, six wholesale grocers.

Customers may buy as many bananas as they like—at nine cents pound. Bananas are trucked in twice weekly from Mexican plantations. fresh vegetables from Rio Grande Valley. But bags and cartons are sca

As they were intended to, bananas dominate this picture. A large bunch in the left foreground serves as a frame for the central character, the repeated identity who gives this story its vital continuity. The clerk holds a smaller bunch in his hands, and the caption above tells how many a customer may buy, and at what price. Note that it adds information on vegetable supply, paper shortage.

The candy bar in the hand is the focal point of this picture, just as steak was in the first shot, cigarettes were in the second, etc. Repetition of situation, given variety by subject matter, provided visual emphasis.

ndy bars per purchaser is the self-imposed ration. Abilenians do not
e war in terms of personal comfort. Three hundred men from the county
d in battle, 300 others are in enemy prison camps. Citizens are buying
War Bonds to the limit of their capacity. Abilene is prepared to face real
war shortages as they come, yet under its co-operative, city-wide rationing
program, it hopes to continue to carry on as a city without a black market.

The display of candy bars and gum in this final photograph astounded readers, attracted comments from dealers and consumers all over the country. It required little description, but the writer tied the caption to the picture by making his first sentence apply to the candy rationing. The rest of the caption is a conclusion for the story, a summing up of Abilene's attitude, its hope of remaining a city without shortages.

Including title, subtitle, running text and captions, *City Without Food Shortages* contains 592 words. Between its inception and its completion, four weeks elapsed. When it was shipped to the printer, it represented the collaborative effort of eight persons—two writers, two editors, a photographer, an art director, a layout designer and a copyreader. Research and field production required 12 days, actual writing two more. Of 200 photographs taken, five were used. Every piece of text was rewritten at least twice, some captions many times. It is a relatively simple and fairly typical product of magazine picture-story technique.

INDEX

237

Picture Credits